Coming Back Alive

ALSO BY SPIKE WALKER

Working on the Edge
Nights of Ice

The True Story of the

Most Harrowing Search and

Rescue Mission Ever Attempted

on Alaska's High Seas

Coming
Back Alive

SPIKE WALKER

St. Martin's Press 🜄 New York

www.stmartins.com

Title page photo by Conrad Johnsen

Map on page ix by Jeffrey L. Ward

Library of Congress Cataloging-in-Publication Data

Walker, Spike.
    Coming back alive : the true story of the most harrowing search and rescue mission ever attempted on Alaska's high seas / Spike Walker.—1st ed.
        p. cm.
    ISBN 0-312-26971-4
    1. La Conte (Fishing vessel) 2. Shipwrecks—Alaska—Alaska, Gulf of. 3. United States Coast Guard—Search and rescue operations.   I. Title.
    G530.L3 W36 2001
    63.12'3'09783—dc21   2001019678

First Edition: August 2001

10   9   8   7   6   5   4   3   2   1

This book is dedicated to Lynette Bishop.

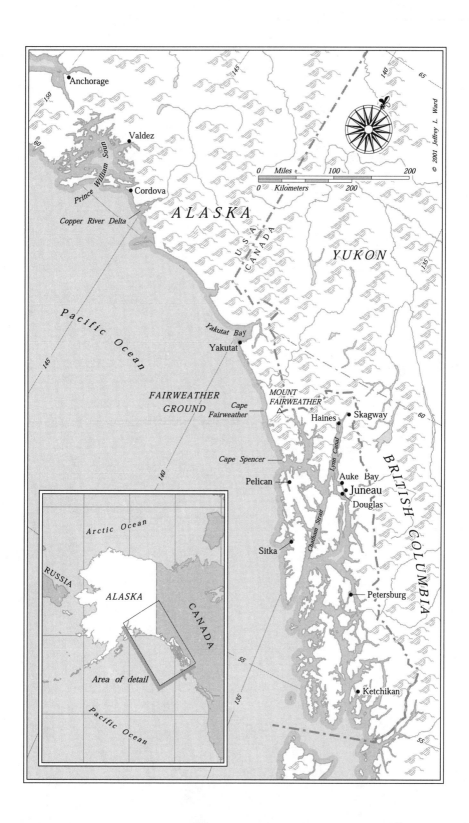

Anchorage

Valdez

Cordova

Prince William Soun

Copper River Delta

ALASKA

U.S.A.
CANADA

YUKON

Pacific Ocean

Yakutat Bay
Yakutat

FAIRWEATHER
GROUND

Cape
Fairweather

MOUNT
FAIRWEATHER
△

Haines

Skagway

Cape Spencer

Lynn Canal

Pelican

Auke Bay
Juneau
Douglas

BRITISH COLUMBIA

Chatham Strait

Sitka

Petersburg

Ketchikan

0   Miles   100   200
0   Kilometers   200

© 2001 Jeffrey L. Ward

Arctic Ocean

RUSSIA

ALASKA

CANADA

Area of detail

Pacific Ocean

Contents

Acknowledgments

I would like to thank the following people for their support and encouragement throughout the research and writing of this book: Ethel "Mom" Bangert, Jan and Denny Dimmitt, Gary and Diane Fountain, Mark and Sally Higgins, Conrad Johnsen and his wife, Margaret "Maggie" Wilhelmi, John Lance, Roger Lucas, Mike Machleod, Jerry and Joyce Marston, Bud Gardner and Jennifer Martin, Ray and Gina Miles, Chris Miller, Sherri Miller, Danny Mjelde, Bobby and Rachael Osborne, Saimi Pesio, Ron and Claudia Robinson, Lonnie Waddle, Lorna Walker, Robbie Walker, Steven Walker, and Don Ward.

A special thanks also goes out to Ms. Sharleen Lucas, a talented young wordsmith, whose editorial skills and creative comments during the early stages of the writing were especially helpful, as well as my editor at St. Martin's Press, Mr. Marc Resnick.

I would be equally remiss if I did not thank the many Alaskans who contributed in one way or another to the creation of this book.

At Air Station Sitka, I would like to thank Capt. Mike Moore, the base commander, who granted me access to his people and facilities and, on occasion, even the chow lines there. And Cmdr. Doug Taylor and his lovely wife, Peggy, for their hospitality and for the keys to both their Jeep and waterfront home, which I used with impunity while they were away on a monthlong sabbatical.

As I gradually came to know the search and rescue (SAR) helicopter pilots and their crews on a personal level, I found that I was often taken aback by the total candor with which many of them shared their worst and most terrifying moments in the air, during what were often distinguished careers. Eventually, it struck me that this was their way of practicing "service above self," the Coast Guard's foundational creed. My heartfelt thanks goes out to them. They are Lt. Bill Adickes and his wife, Carin; Lt. Cmdr. Karl Baldessari; Cmdr. Greg Breithaupt and his wife, Terry; Lt. Cmdr. David "Bull" Durham and his wife, Trish; Cmdr. James Hatfield (ret.) and his wife, Marsha; Lt. Katie Howard; Capt. Ted Le Feuvre; Lt. Dan Madison; Lt. Cmdr. Stu Merrill and his wife, Karen; Lt. Dan Molthen and his wife, Theresa; Capt. David Moore and his wife, Lisa; Capt. Mike Moore and his wife, Ranae; Lt. Jack Newby and his wife, Sheri; Lt. Jim O'Keefe; Lt. Mike Patterson; Lt. Carl Reidlin; Lt. Tom Smilie and his wife, Diana; Lt. Steve Torpey and his wife, Kari; Lt. Bob "Chopper" Yerex and his wife, Tammy; and Cmdr. Russ Zullick and his wife, Debra.

I would also like to thank rescue swimmers Mike Fish and his wife, Amy; Richard "Rich" Sansone; Jason Sheppard; Dustin Skarra; Tom Smylle and his wife, Diana; A. J. Thompson; and Jeff Tunks and his wife, Karyn. My thanks also to flight mechanics Bruce Firth, Harold "Lee" Honnald, Fred Kalt, Randy Kanzig, Wayne Langley, Peter MacDougall, Chris Windnagle, and Sean Witherspoon. Thanks as well to Ron Guinta, Reggie Lavoie, Orion Ryan, and watch captains Lt. Guy Pierce and Lt. Glen Jones.

I would like to thank the following: In Cordova: Debra and Hank Carlson, Per and Neva Nolan, Skip and Marlene Holden, and Phil Thum.

In Juneau: Thelma "Debbie" Aranda, Fred Barkley, Debra Camp; meteorologists Jack Endicott, Bob Kanan, and Russ Page; Lt. Cmdr. Raymond Massie, Roger and Betty Stidolph, and Vaughn Westcott.

In Ketchikan: Ed and Linda Donoghue, Lillian Ference, Maggie Frietag, Carla Gruber, Shirley McCallister, Thomas B. Nordtvedt,

D.D.S., and his wife, Dean, as well as Dave Valentine, Carlie Vanaarn, Jessie Vanaarn, Marie Vanaarn, Pete Vanaarn, and Cleo Weston.

In Kodiak: Bill and Ann Barker; Matt and Heather Corriere; Laurie Doyle; Pastor Frank Gardner; Father Hugh and Margaret Hall; Vern and Debbie Hall; Capt. Jimmy Ng and his wife, Joy; Guy and Merle Powell; Lt. Cmdr. Paul Ratté and his wife, Barbara; Ted Rogers; Cmdr. Tom Walters (ret.) and his wife, Betty; and Cmdr. John Whiddon (ret.) and his wife, Laurie.

In Pelican: Paula Bergner and Ady Linda.

In Petersburg: My friends Norman and Merry Armin; Bart Eaton; Bill and Marilyn George; Dick and Mary Ann Greseth; Denny Heindahl and Bill Olsen of the M/V *Sundance;* Gearhart Hiller; former shipmate Colyn Lyons and his wife, Carlene; Colt Lyons; Bill and Fran Neumann; Richard Spraque, D.D.S., and his wife, Sharon; Lynn Staake; retired bush pilot Bill Stedman and his wife, Carol; John and Bert Winther; Terry and Sandra Wolfe; the Max Worhatches; and the late Sydney Wright and his wife, Vara.

In Sitka: Burgess and Vicki Bauder; Jim and Jill Blades (and Curt, Annie, and Lindy); Clint Blades; Don Brown and wife, Bernice; Walt and Sue Cunningham; Harold and Pat Diamond; Jerry Dugan; Lyle Hilde; Dug and Susan Jenson; Don and Karen Kluting; Peter Mac-Dougal and his wife, Christina, and gentle Jenny, evil Ian, and wild man Ross; Harbormaster Ray Majeski; Mary Anne Maxum; Keith Mork; Ray and Edie Mork; and Howard Ulrich.

In Washington, D.C., United States Coast Guard historians Dr. Robert M. Browning, Jr., and Scott Price.

I would also like to acknowledge Mr. Rand Koler and Mr. Lance Rosen, my razor-sharp Seattle-based agents/attorneys, talented people who know the score and fear nothing.

Finally, and most emphatically, I wish to thank the three survivors of the fishing vessel *La Conte*—namely, my friends Mike DeCapua, Robert Doyle, and William "Gig" Mork—as well as the deceased skipper's soul mate, Tamara Morley; his father, Charles Morley; his mother, Edna Fantozzi; and his brother Jeff Morley. Without the scores of interview sessions that these people so generously granted me, this book would most certainly not have been possible.

Preface

I n the fall of 1998, I moved to Alaska and began the research for this book. From the outset, my intent, as a nonfiction writer, was to present a vivid, unflinching portrait of the legendary exploits of Sitka's elite, handpicked search and rescue helicopter squads, as well as the lives and experiences of the commercial fishermen they encountered along the way.

To come to know the Coast Guard commanders and pilots and their crews over the months I spent, tape recorder in hand, dogging their trails out at the base on the tip of Japonski Island, was a pleasure I will not soon forget. Drawing me into the warm camaraderie of their fellowship, they helped me sweep out the cobwebs of bitterness and suspicion that had crept in, and replace them, I am told, with a bit of the same graciousness that had been so generously granted me.

Then, as the months of interviewing slipped past, and the exceptional nature of the material gleaned from both Coast Guard crewmen and fishermen began to surface, I felt a growing sense of responsibility to try to honor the robust way these passionate people lived and, far too often, died.

In an effort to remain loyal to the spirit of the adventures undertaken, I decided to relate several key events by telling them through the eyes of those who were there, re-creating them just as they happened.

While some of the material herein is quite graphic in nature, it is my fervid hope that by writing about these events, similar predicaments in which young men die may be avoided altogether in the future, and that the soul-shaking grief and sense of utter aloneness felt by those left behind may one day be transcended.

You have to go out, but you don't necessarily

have to come back.

—OLD COAST GUARD SAYING

Book I

Flyboys and Fishermen

Prologue

As he steered his speeding twenty-six-foot gillnet boat *Marlene* out across the Copper River Delta in Alaska's Prince William Sound on a gray, windblown afternoon in 1981, Skip Holden could not have known that within hours he would be engaged in a hellish struggle just to survive, nor could he have imagined how many lives would be so profoundly affected by the outcome.

Bold and enterprising, but never reckless, "Holden," as his friends like to call him, was looking forward to doing what he did best, and that was to net salmon.

Eight years earlier, Skip Holden and his wife, Marlene, had set out from San Leandro, California, to hitchhike to Alaska. They headed north, holding a sign that read ALASKA OR BUST! They arrived in Cordova nearly broke, found work together in a local cannery, and, in a month, managed to save twelve hundred dollars. They bought a twenty-foot boat for exactly that amount. They lived on it, fished off of it, and used a bucket for a toilet.

It was a romantic, albeit bare-bones, beginning in the rugged little fishing village located in a wild, sprawling land bursting with boomtown opportunity and colorful characters. There was a local stripper named

Tequilla, whose writhing style of dancing naked was known to cause almost a riot as lonely, affection-starved fishermen trampled one another for a closer look.

Then there was Machine Gun Betty. She was a large Indian woman who worked as a bartender at a local watering hole. Her way of dealing with a rowdy crowd of drunken fishermen (who refused to leave at quitting time) was to pull out a Thompson submachine gun, level it on her rambunctious patrons, and order them off the premises. "It's closing time! Get the hell out!" she'd say as the bar emptied.

During those eight years of hard work as a commercial fisherman, Skip Holden had seen some sights—such as the time the Fish and Game Department opened the season up in the fjord near Coghill Point, and he and his fishing pals had netted one million sockeye salmon in a single week of red-hot fishing.

Named after Skip's wife, the F/V *Marlene* was known in fishing circles as a Snowball bow-picker. She had a six-foot-high reel mounted in the center of her foredeck. This spool-like contraption was designed to feed the one-thousand-foot-long gillnet off her bow and reel it back aboard via the same route.

Along the way, Skip had learned a few things about the nature of successful fishermen, too. Foremost, he had learned not to try to be like anybody else: The best fishermen fished according to the dictates of their own personalities.

As a rule, Holden worked alone. More of a hunter-type person himself, he liked to motor past the main sandbars (where most of his more conservative fellow gillnetters chose to make their "drifts") and out through the surf. He enjoyed fishing the deep waters of the open ocean. When possible, he liked to intercept the fish well before they reached the main branch of the river, something at which he was quite adept, now having the self-assurance of a seasoned fisherman, one who had paid his dues and acquired a fair amount of fishing savvy along the way.

Armed with little more than a compass and a Fathometer, he roamed as far as ten miles out from the wild and ever-changing sixty-mile-wide delta of sandbars and tidelands known as the Copper River

Flats, fishing the salmon-rich waters as far out as Cape Hinchinbrook.

Some fishermen didn't like the stress of making "sets," laying out their gillnets and fishing out in the open ocean. They generally fished the inside waters. They didn't seem to mind fighting the crowds, or having to pull their gillnets back aboard every few minutes, then run back up the line, lay them out again, and start from scratch. By contrast, Skip Holden liked to fish the deep, outside waters. He liked the sight of free, open spaces and uncluttered horizons. He'd been raised that way. When he was a boy, sailing off the California coast, his father had taught him the art of navigation, as well as how to keep a ship in good repair and how to tie the rope knots that were essential to life at sea. Most important, his father instilled in his son the belief that shallow water is a fisherman's worst enemy.

It was the going out and coming back in over the sandbars at entrance channels, especially those at Softuk, and Strawberry, and Egg Island, that local fishermen feared most. Let an out-rushing tide confront a strong flow of onshore wind, and the waves can really stack up.

Even for Skip Holden, getting trapped out on the open sea in a sudden blow was something to be avoided if at all possible. Let him receive a warning over the local CB fishing channel announcing that the sandbar was closing, and Holden would rush his net aboard and make a mad scramble in over the building breakers before they closed him out. Once inside the punishing surf line, he would wait out the storm in the shelter of one of the tideland coves carved out of tens of miles of sandbars by the thirteen-foot tides that flooded in over the area several times each day.

Miss the closing, get cut off by a sudden storm, and a fisherman would have few options, all of them dangerous. Left unprotected by island or berm, caught tens of miles from Cordova, a fisherman could either jog into the storm and weather (which might last for several days and nights) or make the near-impossible journey around the thirty-mile length of Hinchinbrook Island, running broadside to the storm winds and waves crashing ashore the entire way. Lose an engine, throw a prop, and you would be history.

Regardless, Holden was always hanging it out there, working on the edge. Unlike some wanna-be fishermen, however, Holden had the touch. And during the season, it wasn't unusual for him to intercept as much as four thousand dollars' worth of the migrating fish in a single week.

On that gray day in 1981, Holden had already gone for two days and nights without sleep, standing anchor watch, waiting out the past few days of blustery weather in a featureless, godforsaken reach inside Softuk Bar. It was no big deal, really. Gillnetting the flats had always been a young man's sport. And Holden could go for days without sleep. But when the winds finally did calm down, he thought, That's it. Time to go fishing, and, pulling anchor, he fled out across the bar.

Once at sea, however, Holden soon found himself idling up the high, sloping faces of the unusually large swells lumbering in toward shore. Enormous as they were, the swells weren't breaking, and he drifted over them one by one, the bulging waters passing smoothly underneath him. It was the air around him, however, that spooked him. The enveloping air had turned "eerie calm, like out of breath," as he put it. It was a little like entering into the eye of a hurricane. Skip Holden had never experienced anything quite like it.

Shortly, the sky grew dark, and as the unexpected storm intensified, strong winds burst up the scene. Blowing directly in against the out-rushing tide, the winds soon whipped the sea into a cresting frenzy. In only minutes, thunderous breakers began collapsing across the entire width of the bar, effectively closing off any possible retreat.

Still, Holden was determined to give it a try, and so he maneuvered into the roiling waters of the bar. He had managed to weave his way past several rows of breakers, when, in the gray-black of the dim evening light, he spotted a single white lightbulb mounted atop the mast of another salmon boat. Having learned of Holden's plight, a fellow fisherman had apparently left the safety of his snug anchorage and was now motoring back and forth just inside the breakers, trying to guide Holden into the deeper waters of the main channel, through at least five thousand feet of breaking waves and lathering foam.

Maybe I can make it through this, thought Holden, focusing on the challenge at hand. Now, should I go around this breaker and through that one? he asked himself as he pushed ahead. Is it deeper there? What's my Fathometer reading? Uh-oh—too shallow. I'll try this way.

Finally conceding defeat, Holden fought his way back out through the marching rows of breakers, then began motoring down the sixty-mile delta of sandbars and bordering channels.

When he arrived at the channel leading past Egg Island, he found stiff seventy-mile-per-hour winds driving heavy seas ashore, and the bar closed. Without one of the powerful VHF radios on board with which to call out, he was forced to rely on the comparatively feeble power of his CB radio.

"Hey, Phil, what's happening?" he radioed his good friend Phil Thum. "Is there a way in? Do you see any way in there?"

"No, I don't think you can get in, Holden. It's breaking all the way across the bar here."

The entire time he talked, Holden was jogging along the outside edge of the sandbar at the Egg Island entrance, quickly looking for an opening in the surf. Either I find my way in past Egg Island here, he thought, or I'll be out here all night. It's now or never. He cruised up and down the bar, but was unable to find anything like an opening.

"I really don't see any way in there," Holden radioed Thum finally.

"There is no way in," cut in the anonymous voice of another fisherman.

And suddenly, all cross-chatter on his CB radio ceased, followed by a dead silence. Holden caught the full measure of what this meant. Everyone listening knew that there was no way back, and that in the building seas, the trip out and around Hinchinbrook Island would be pure suicide. His only hope would be to try to jog into the storm, however long it might last, however severe it might be.

Well, this will be good for a laugh with my buddies back at the Reluctant Fisherman saloon in Cordova, he thought. Old Holden thought he could beat Mother Nature, and he got his butt kicked.

"Boy, I'm sure glad I'm safe and sound and anchored up in here," bragged another fisherman over the CB, laying it on thick.

"I sure wouldn't want to be out there in this kind of weather," remarked another in a tone of sincere empathy.

Sometimes, Holden knew, a fisherman could find a place where he could kind of surf in where the waves weren't actually breaking. But the winds were gusting past eighty miles an hour now, and as the dark, peculiar cloud cover pressed down on him, Holden continued to motor back and forth along the outside edge of the breaking surf, praying all the while for a freak opening through which he and his boat might pass.

It was then that the steering on his boat went out.

"Damn!" he said aloud.

Suddenly caught dead in the water, Holden knew that he was in serious trouble. The winds seemed determined to blow him broadside into the Hawaiian-sized breakers now folding over and exploding with boat-crushing furor all along the mouth of the bar.

He refused to let the instinct to panic have its way. Somehow, in the breaking seas and wild, punishing winds, Holden searched for a way to stabilize his boat. Like any seasoned fisherman, he knew the score: Lose the boat, lose your life.

Then, cleverly, he hit upon the solution. He would play out three-quarters of his one-thousand-foot-long gillnet and, if the tide was right, catch a ride on the tidal currents as they flowed offshore and away from the breakers, all the while using the net (with the departing waters pushing against it) as a kind of sea anchor.

He fed the 750-foot trail of webbing and buoys off his bow roller and watched as the offshore flow caught it. He was in luck. The tide was going out. The net, buoys, and ship were being swept out to sea and away from the pounding surf. The vessel's bow swung to point into the accelerating storm winds, exactly as he had hoped.

Holden tied the net off on the ship's bow cleats to prevent the six-foot-high, four-foot-wide aluminum reel from being torn from its steel deck mounts and jerked overboard.

As the darkness closed in, Holden found it difficult to see anything clearly. His eyes strained toward something in the distance. He stood squinting in the dim light, peering through the haze of rain and blowing spray. He couldn't be certain. The misty vision was either one of breakers demolishing themselves on nearby rocks or the flash of the buoy marker over on Wessels Reef.

"Holden, how are you doing out there?" radioed Phil Thum, who was anchored off in a wind-raked channel amid the barren sands of Egg Island. "Do you want me to call the Coast Guard?"

"Well, Phil, I'm still alive here," replied Holden. "If a Coast Guard rescue basket were to somehow land on my deck, I'd climb right in. But there's just no way a helicopter could make it out here. It's too damned windy."

As the night progressed, the storm intensified and the wind pushed the waves higher. In the gathering darkness, the winds were soon hissing across the water at ninety miles per hour, with stronger gusts ranging out of wave valleys large enough to hold a football field, complete with goalposts.

Getting trapped on the outside in such a blow in a relatively tiny boat (26 feet compared to one of the weather-busting king-crab boats, some of which are 150 feet long and 40 feet wide) was one of the worst experiences a Prince William Sound salmon fisherman could have.

Holden was hoping that the driving wind and torrential rains would soon blow themselves out. What he could not have known was that one of the most formidable storms in the history of storm-ravaged Prince William Sound had pushed into the area, catching him flat-footed and leaving him cut off, with nowhere to run. In addition to the wicked winds, more rain would fall on the area of the Copper River Flats over the next three days in the shortest amount of time ever recorded, some fourteen inches in all.

Skip Holden opened the door leading into the tiny space of his wheelhouse and quickly stepped inside. He was still dripping wet when the F/V *Marlene*'s main engine coughed heavily. Holden bent over, removed one section of the floorboard, and peered down into the small engine compartment. It was not an encouraging sight. The bilge area was full of water, which was now lapping at the sides of the gas engine.

Then Holden recalled how he'd been running along with his back door left open slightly to flush out all engine fumes from inside his cabin. Seawater, he surmised, had silently and surreptitiously been seeping in through the opening since the storm had first kicked up. The engine's carburetor and wiring were getting drenched. I need to get busy now and bail some water out of here, he told himself. I've got to shut down this engine and very methodically remove the seawater from the bilge. One thing at a time.

Holden slammed the back door and tied it shut, securing the handle with a length of rope. With the engine turned off, he knew that the bilge would soon run the battery down to the point where it could no longer turn the engine over. Then all hope of somehow getting the carburetor dried out and the engine started would be lost. Holden tore away the remaining floorboards, leapt down into the chest-deep engine compartment, and immediately went to work bailing out the water. When, more than a hour later, he looked up again from his sweaty efforts, the compartment was relatively free of seawater, while outside, the dull gray evening had given way to a coal black void of blasting winds and pummeling rain.

Normally, when he was fishing and drifting along on a given set, Holden could feel the currents gently tugging at his net. On this night, however, the gillnet playing off his bow roller (and now stretching several hundred yards beyond it) remained as tight as a bowstring as the offshore currents tugging at his net and buoys came into direct conflict with the force created by fierce onshore winds driving hard against every exposed inch of the *Marlene*'s superstructure. The wind shrieked constantly over the wheelhouse, and the torrential rains and surf thrumming against the fiberglass hull of the *Marlene* echoed inside with the irregular thump of beating drums.

Well, what do you think we should do here, Skip?" radioed Phil Thum finally. "Do you want me to call out a Mayday and get the Coast Guard people on their way?"

Thum knew that such a decision was not to be taken lightly. A commercial fisherman could not justify sending out a Mayday unless someone's life was in imminent peril.

"I don't know what to do," replied Holden finally.

The pocket in which Skip Holden was cornered, in between the sandbars and channel entrances at Softuk and Strawberry, was famous, Thum knew, for turning boats into kindling. Under the current conditions, the place had become a kind of death trap, a small-boat killing field. Thum was certain that his friend was about to lose his life there.

Undeterred by fear or the gravity of the decision, Phil Thum lifted the handheld mike from his powerful VHF radio set. "Mayday! Mayday!" he called out for the entire fleet to hear. "This is the fishing vessel *Keeper*! The fishing vessel *Keeper*! We have a fisherman in trouble, and we are in need of assistance."

"This is United States Coast Guard, Comsat Kodiak! Comsat Kodiak!" came the quick reply. "We receive your message. Please give us the name of the skipper and boat in trouble and its exact position. Over."

Thum identified himself and gave Holden's current position. "I am relaying this message from a CB radio broadcasting for a man named Skip Holden," Thum explained. "He is on board the F/V *Marlene*, and he's been caught outside near the Egg Island entrance. He doesn't have a VHF, so I'll be talking to him and relaying that information on to you, and I'll relay what you say to me back to him."

Not until every question had been asked and answered did the Coast Guard finally render their decision.

"Please relay to Skip Holden that we're on our way," radioed the petty officer.

"Roger. I'll be standing by on channel twenty-three," Thum confirmed.

"Holden, the Coast Guard is on their way," Thum announced, excitedly passing on the message.

"Good," acknowledged Holden.

As soon as Holden heard the news, he turned and began donning his survival suit. I've got to keep my eyes peeled, he told himself. If those chopper boys are really going to come out here in this crap, I want to be ready and help all I can.

Holden knew it was easily the most impossible predicament that he'd ever faced. Inside the rocking, battering space of the ship's cabin, Holden tried to prepare himself for the end. In the scheme of things, he knew, he was just an ant-sized creature caught in an exceptionally tough spot. Yet he refused to allow himself to slip into the emotional quicksand fear produced. Even as the storm outside seemed about to tear his boat to pieces and bury him on the spot, Holden made a conscious choice to stay focused, concentrating on performing each individual task he faced as quickly and efficiently as he could.

If the gillnet jumped out of the bow rollers and slid amidships along the pivoting boat, however, Holden was certain that the *Marlene* would instantly flip over and all would be lost. He made repeated trips out the wheelhouse door to see if the net, reel, and cleats securing it were in need of repair. Each time, as he worked his way forward, thigh-deep water came crashing in over the sides. The rampaging sea threatened to knock his legs from under him and sweep him down the open deck and over the side.

It would be several hours before a four-engined U.S. Coast Guard C-130 search and rescue (SAR) airplane reached the scene.

How are you doing down there?" radioed Lt. Jim Hatfield, the copilot and officer in charge of the C-130 now circling at some 18,000 feet overhead.

Although Holden had been unable (other than relaying his messages through Phil Thum) to even come close, with his tiny CB radio, to reaching Air Station Kodiak some three hundred miles away, he could now hear Lieutenant Hatfield's voice clearly.

"The boat's hanging on," said Holden, "but I don't think there's any way you're going to be able to hoist me off of her. It'd be like trying to thread a needle from up there."

"Let us worry about that," replied Hatfield. Then he informed Holden that an H-3 "Pelican" Sikorsky helicopter had landed in Cordova (following the terrific beating of a three-hour flight over from Kodiak Island) and was preparing for the rescue attempt.

"Don't be surprised if you get a static electric shock when the basket first gets to you," Hatfield said. "But don't worry about it; it won't hurt you. He'll be shooting a cradle [a body strap] down that line to you."

Hatfield's plan was to guide the H-3 chopper close enough to pluck Holden off the *Marlene*'s front deck, air-lifting him into the stormy heavens like a sack of potatoes.

"Right now, I need you to take your antenna down, because we don't want it to get tangled up in the rescue basket."

"Roger," said Holden coolly.

Up until that time, Holden felt sure that he'd kept a tight rein on his emotions. But he was soon forced to acknowledge that he had felt a bit more shaken than he'd been letting on, because when he hurried outside and grabbed hold of the two-inch-thick base of the twenty-foot-high CB antenna, it broke off in his hand, snapping in two, as if it were no more substantial than a bone-dry strand of uncooked spaghetti. Suddenly, all communications with the outside world came to a close, as far as he could tell. He would continue to send out messages on the CB radio, but he would have no way of knowing if anyone could actually hear them.

It was approximately 1:00 A.M. when Holden spied the blinking navigation light of a helicopter far off his stern. He rushed to illuminate his cabin and make sure that his small mast light was turned on and shining brightly. Lit up like I am, thought Holden, I must look like a little torch out here on the water.

Then he set off a flare, launching it out the side window of his wheelhouse. He was sure the helicopter pilot had spotted him. Okay, thought Holden. Now I've got to get ready here for what's going to happen.

Leaving the security of his radio and the protection of his bathroom-sized wheelhouse, he crouched down like a wrestler against the wind and currents, waded out onto the front deck, and stood there waiting for the helicopter to arrive.

When Holden caught sight of them again, they were gunning their engines and coming straight for him, closing along an invisible line stretching directly downwind of the boat. Holden could see that the pilot was making an attempt to pull up even with him. What worried Holden, however, was the straining sound of the helicopter's engines and gears. They were producing an unbelievably loud whining, a kind of metallic screaming.

Just then, Holden looked to his left and spied a large sea otter floating alongside his boat. The otter was lying on its back and wore what appeared to be a broad grin across its face. Isn't that weird, thought Holden. The sea otter seemed to be saying, Look, the next step will probably be to come in and join me, and when you do, it's not going to be a big deal. Holden was beginning to understand that it might just come to that. If I somehow wind up in the water in my suit, he calculated, I'm going to act just like that sea otter. I'm just going to dig it and have a nice big smile and a good time.

Holden was also aware that he was caught in a steady drift that was carrying him ever farther out into the vast wind-raked reaches of the Gulf of Alaska. Each time his small boat teetered up and over the top of one of the long, sweeping faces of the storm waves, he thought he could make out, through the demolishing forces of wind and spray, the indistinct speck of a buoy marker's light blinking off in the distance.

The downpour and the blowing spray tumbling across the face of the sea had joined forces and were now creating near whiteout conditions. Out of the vacuum of sea spray, rain, and wind engulfing him came ungainly waves twenty-five feet high. Now and then, in the reflective glow coming from his wheelhouse, Holden could make out the mountains of seawater approaching. He could feel each wave lifting him, sweeping him up and up and up, and then the free fall as the wave discarded him and moved on. And he thought, I've fished Kayak Island and Cape St. Elias in a big swell, but this is something that I've never seen before. At times, the winds blew so hard that the sea itself seemed to contort under the pressure.

Abruptly, the chopper pilot turned on his floodlights, and for a few seconds, it looked like broad daylight. Several times, as the helicopter maneuvered overhead in the intensifying storm, Holden found that he could no longer determine for sure whether he was hearing the roar of the jet engines or the sound of the wind shrieking past. He was certain that if someone were standing right next to him and he yelled into that person's ear, the sound of his voice would never be heard.

Holden felt a tremendous surge, and the *Marlene* was swept to the top of a wave. From its crest, he could see the helicopter clearly in the wave valley stretching out before him. Just 150 feet away, Holden took in the startling vision of the chopper's main rotor blades spinning at eye level with him. And yet the chopper's fifteen-foot-tall body hung down into the trough below. Man, he's way too close to the ocean, thought Holden. His blades are going to hit that wave! Seconds later, however, the chopper's volatile course carried it past directly overhead.

Though Holden felt relieved, something was still bothering him. Then, as he watched the chopper maneuver, it struck him. The pilot was flying as though he couldn't actually *see* the waves; it was as if somebody else were describing the water below to him. One second, the waves would be practically licking at the bottom of the helicopter, and in the next, the helo would be one hundred feet above them. The helicopter staggered along like a drunken sailor—inebriated but still on his feet. And as it drew nearer, Holden noticed the sharp, clipped flash of a tiny blue-white strobe light mounted on the aircraft's underbelly.

The F/V *Marlene* was yawing back and forth when a sneaker wave struck her from the starboard side, flooding her main deck and knocking her sideways through the frenzied surf. She was still pitching violently, pivoting from one side to the other when the helicopter swung in overhead again.

Holden was more than a little taken aback when a shot bag with a line attached to it plopped down next to him, smack in the middle of his deck. The valiant Coast Guard crewmen aboard the wind-tossed helicopter overhead had managed to zero in on a space just eight feet wide, hitting the mark as if it were the most common, everyday thing to do. Holden was amazed. These guys are phenomenal! he thought. They're out here risking their lives for me. I've just got to do the best I can for them.

Yet, with no way of communicating, Holden couldn't have known that the line trailing the shot bag was a tending line. In less extreme weather conditions, Coast Guard helicopter crews ordinarily used it as a way of feeding the basket down to the party awaiting rescue on the deck below. Holden grabbed the line trailing down out of the sky, thinking, If they can't get the rescue basket down to me, maybe they can just reel me up. If I feel something solid on the end of this line, he reasoned further, I'm just going to wrap it around my hand, swing from the end of the line, and just go for it. I'll pull on this line until I feel some tension, and when I feel something really secure on the other end, I'll hook it around my body and they'll just winch me up. What worried Holden most was the quality of the cord line that he held. It was made of loosely woven polyester fiber. Just three-eighths of an inch thick, it looked little more substantial than a dog leash.

At that moment, an overpowering gust of wind swept the helicopter away, carrying it tail-first, well downwind of Holden. The line in Skip Holden's hand went slack. What do they want me to do with this now? he wondered. Oh, they *had* to let go of the line, he then realized as he coiled it aboard.

When the helo drew near to Holden once again, he spotted the rescue basket. It was swinging violently about in the wind, below the open side door, underneath the aircraft's white belly. The helicopter managed to pull almost even with his bow, when, once again, he heard the high-pitched, almost supersonic whine of the aircraft's engines. With it came the grinding sound of metal crunching, like a washing machine falling apart. It didn't sound right. Holden was certain that they were in serious trouble.

Then it appeared as though some powerful hand had reached out and grabbed the helicopter and catapulted it back into space. One second, it was holding its own; the next, it went shooting back off the *Marlene*'s stern as if shot out of a cannon. It appeared to be traveling backward at about the same speed as the wind, as helpless in the one-hundred-mile-per-hour blasts as an errant mosquito. Holden hung on to the gillnet reel with both hands, his legs spread-eagle, as thigh-deep water crashed aboard and drained out of the boat's side scuppers.

Then, well downwind of the *Marlene*'s stern, the rescue helicopter staggered several hundred feet into the air and paused there—a minuscule dot of tentative light hovering against a vast backdrop of all-enveloping darkness. All Holden could see was the tiny pulse of her navigation lights blinking and the hazy swath of a spotlight shining down on the ocean. They must be having some kind of trouble, he reasoned. Or perhaps they're having a powwow of some kind.

He was still studying the lights of the chopper, now suspended in the air more than half a mile away, when, as if in a slow motion, the helicopter dipped sharply to one side and toppled from the sky. With its nose down and its tail trailing up and behind, the helo plunged toward the water. A moment later, the rotor blades on one side plowed into the ocean's surface. "Oh no! No! No! No!" screamed Holden as the aircraft crashed into the sea. "Oh my God, I can't believe this!"

Time seemed to stand still. For one long moment, he could see the glow of the navigation lights blinking beneath the water. Then the night just seemed to swallow them. Holden's mind raced. What if there are survivors inside that helicopter? he asked himself. They must still be alive back there. And now they're waiting for *me* to rescue *them*. But how can I pull this off? I don't have a searchlight. I don't have a radio. My steering is bonkers. Maybe I can get my engine warmed up and see if I can't somehow back down on them and pick up whoever has survived. But if I get too near the helicopter in these winds and seas, it'll put a hole in my boat and I'll go down, too. Then we'll all be lost!

Still, I've got to try, reasoned Holden finally. I'll just fire up my engine and see what I've got here. Then I'll untie my gillnet from the cleats and reel and play out some more net. If I can play it out far enough and drift in close enough, perhaps some of them can swim over to it and grab ahold.

First things first, Holden, he told himself. Let's start the engine. He turned the key and was pleased to find that his battery was still strong. But although his engine cranked over and over, it ultimately refused to start. The wiring on my engine is soaked, he was forced to acknowledge. Just totally soaked.

Each time he'd gone out the back door to await a rescue basket, more of the torrential rains and sea spray had washed down onto his motor. He deeply regretted now not having bought the diesel engine that he'd contemplated installing the winter before.

Holden was certain that the crewmen were back there in the water, freezing their tails off, if they were alive at all. Frantically, again and again, he cranked over his sea-soaked engine, but with no luck. Finding himself entirely without power now, Holden asked himself, Is there any way in the world I can still rescue those guys?

"*Mayday! Mayday!*" called Skip Holden over his silent radio. "This is the fishing vessel *Marlene!* The fishing vessel *Marlene!* Does anybody hear me?" Though he heard no response, he continued to send out the call. "The Coast Guard helicopter that came out here to get me has crashed! The helicopter's there, but I can't get my engine started!"

With his antenna gone, his battery power running down, and the regenerating powers of the F/V *Marlene*'s main engine flooded out, Skip Holden's radio transmissions had been reduced almost to nothing.

Though Jim Hatfield could no longer hear anything, at that very moment Phil Thum was hanging on every syllable of the bitter news spilling out of his static-filled CB radio. His friend's voice was racked with emotion.

"Oh God, the helicopter crashed!" added Holden. "It got too low and it crashed! The chopper's down! I've got to try and get over to them!"

Thum wasted no time in relaying the message to Lt. Jim Hatfield and his crew in the C-130 circling above.

"Sir, I just received a CB radio transmission from Skip Holden, the skipper aboard the F/V *Marlene*. And he reports that your chopper has just crashed into the water."

The C-130 pilot wept over the radio.

When Skip Holden came back over the radio once again, he, too, was crying. "Don't send anybody else! No more! No more!" Then all radio transmissions from Holden went dead. It was the last anyone heard from him that night.

With the helicopter down, the long nightmarish hours that followed were filled with incessant waves of guilt. Without his engine, Holden knew, he had no hope of saving the crew of the downed Coast Guard helicopter. They would have to make do for themselves, or be lost. For Skip Holden, it was the sickest feeling in the world to know that there was nothing more he could do.

Perhaps the chopper has sunk to the bottom of the ocean with the Coast Guard crew trapped inside, he thought. Or maybe they were able to deploy their life raft and save themselves. He prayed that the latter had happened.

Battered and fatigued, but still in the battle, Skip Holden stood out on deck in the first gray light of day and took stock of the prodigious combers that continued to sweep through the area. The wind still howled across the deck and around his wheelhouse, but it was gusting to around fifty miles per hour, rather than the primitive forces of the previous night, which clearly had exceeded one hundred miles per hour.

At last, he felt like he had a chance to do something about his predicament. He finished bailing the latest influx of seawater from his bilge, hauled the remaining bucketfuls of water up out of the hold, and flung them out the door. Then he attempted to repair the CB antenna, but again without luck. Finally, he grabbed a can of starter fluid, sprayed it into the carburetor, and turned the engine over. This time, it rumbled to life.

Throughout the night, Holden's gillnet had been his lifeline. Now, with the engine started and a lonely gray light marking the dawn, he decided to pull in his gillnet and go search for the crew of the Coast Guard helicopter. When he began reeling the net in, however, he found it choked with silver salmon.

If the crewmen were still somehow clinging to life, he needed to move quickly. Tossing several hundred pounds of the fish into the bottom of his hold for ballast, he took a deck hatchet and chopped at the net. The thousand-foot line parted with a sudden explosion, freeing up the boat and releasing the net, buoys, and mother lode of salmon back to the currents.

Holden raced back to the wheelhouse and immediately pointed the *Marlene* toward Cordova. Though he tried to take it slowly, idling carefully along, he found himself from time to time literally surfing down the faces of the towering spires of gray-green ocean passing by underneath him. Any slower and the wheelhouse of the tiny *Marlene* could have been decapitated by the storm waves; any faster and the vessel would have ended up pitchpoling end over end, and he'd have been lost.

Holden had been inching his way along toward the Softuk Bar for close to an hour, keeping his eyes focused on his compass, when, entirely by accident, he stumbled upon the Coast Guard helicopter floating upside down. Except for a set of tires jutting skyward from her amphibious white underbelly, the hull of the inverted H-3 helicopter might have been mistaken for an overturned boat. The two black tires sticking up on a single strut, he would learn later, were part of the nose landing gear, which extended automatically when the aircraft's electrical power was lost.

In the light of day, with his bilge emptied and his engine finally running, Holden had chanced to run upon them. He was ecstatic. Now I can rescue these guys, he thought. Even if I just get one, it'll be worth it. Holden could hardly believe it. Had he varied so much as a single degree on his course either way, he'd have missed them completely.

A greasy island of fuel and oil lingered around the inverted wreckage, and it somehow appeared to be keeping the foamy portion of the waves from breaking quite so forcefully in the immediate area. He made a large loop out and around the helicopter, "surfing" much of the time, working his way downwind and slowly back again. It was then, as he drew close, that he spotted one of the crew members. He appeared to be tethered by a single hand to the wheel well of the chopper. He was lying facedown in the water in a dead man's float.

"You better be alive!" screamed Holden over and over as he approached. "You better be alive!"

He knew how he was going to rescue the man, too. He was going to motor upwind and toss out a buoy ball with a line attached to it. He'd feed it out and float it back downwind to the waiting crewman. But when he pulled to within twenty feet of the body, he could see that the man was dead. His body was motionless, his arms and legs both outstretched.

Every time a swell went by, the big white hull of the overturned helicopter would sink, disappearing into the depths, a hundred feet or more below, dragging the man's body along with it. To Holden, the helo seemed to remain submerged "forever," before floating back to the surface once again. Realizing finally that there was nothing more he could do, Holden began motoring in around Cape Hinchinbrook. Three hours of running time later, he ran into fellow fisherman Andy Halverson. Halverson thought he was seeing a ghost. "He thought that I was dead," recalls Holden. "He'd heard it on the radio. He'd heard that the F/V *Marlene* was lost and that the four USCG guys were lost, as well."

U.S. Coast Guard helicopter pilot Lt. Pat Rivas (pronounced ree-vas) and copilot Lt. Joe Spoja, as well as flight mechanic Scott Frinfrock and navigator John Snyder, had been out on an ordinary training exercise over on Kodiak Island when Phil Thum's Mayday call first came in.

Several hard-won hours of flight later, they found themselves caught in an unending torrent of record-breaking rainfall, battling fierce ninety-mile-per-hour winds in Prince William Sound. They were flying blind in near whiteout conditions when their Loran C navigational computer shut down, their radar quit, and the onboard HF radio went out. With so much critical equipment malfunctioning, and without the light of day to aid them, it would be tough going.

"Do you know where you are?" asked the C-130 pilot, Lt. Dale Harrington. "Could you give us a position?"

"Okay," replied Pat Rivas. "I think that I'm on a two-hundred-and-twenty-degree bearing from Cordova, about twenty-two miles out. That's the best I can do for you."

A little later, copilot Lt. Jim Hatfield checked back with them. "Hey, boys," he radioed. "Are you all right?"

"We're all right," answered Lt. Joe Spoja. "But we're busy. Please stand by."

Lt. Jim Hatfield remembers it this way. "They made several attempts to get the basket down, with little or no luck because it's such a small boat, a small target, and the seas were terrific and they could not see what they were doing and the boat was swinging around. Pat Rivas was obviously getting concerned that his fatigue would become a factor in this. He mentioned that he was going to be going to Cordova to land . . . that they were getting tired and kicked around quite a bit."

Lt. Dale Harrington recalls that "there was some discussion going on, concerns about fatigue, and Pat felt that he had given it his best shot, obviously, and his comment that I recall was, 'I have tried everything that I know how to do, and under these conditions, the seas, the smallness of the boat, it bobbing around in the wind, and with no hoist reference, I've done everything that I can. Maybe somebody else can come out here and perform this hoist, but I can't. It's beyond my capability. I just can't do it."

It was the last transmission anyone received from the pilot of the doomed chopper.

Faced with dismal weather conditions and massive instrument failure, the crew of helo 1471 had been attempting the rescue under very demanding conditions for an extraordinarily long time; hoists under favorable conditions are often completed in as little as ten minutes. Proceeding with the mission under highly stressful conditions, with no water references except for the occasional glimpses of the fishing vessel *Marlene*, they spent their final hour battling on-scene, trying to remain over the boat and out of the water. And this came directly on the heels of an exhausting three-hour flight from their base on Kodiak Island, which was preceded by another hour or more of flying assigned maneuvers before even being called out on what would be their final mission.

Ultimately, Rivas was forced to acknowledge that he would not be able to complete the hoist. But the decision was made that, before recovering to Cordova for fuel, food, and rest, and to await daylight, they would try and deliver a handheld radio down to Skip Holden. It was then, as they were preparing to do so, a Coast Guard Accident Analysis Board would later surmise, that "they probably relaxed a little. And a slight relaxing was all that was necessary to invite disaster."

The helicopter, the board found, had probably backed down, tail-first, into a passing wave crest. Spinning within precise tolerances at blinding speeds, the tall rotor blades exploded upon impact with the seawater, instantly shearing the four-inch-thick, fifteen-foot-long steel tail-rudder shaft.

The initial impact with the water bent the tail section up. A micro-second later, the chopper's main rotor blades severed it from its own body. This catastrophic mechanical failure sent the H-3 helicopter into a ragged teeter. Staggering through the air like a gyroscope in its last energetic throes, the helo struggled to right itself. Ultimately, however, the unbridled torque toppled the helicopter from the sky as if it had been shoved over a cliff.

When the main rotor blades plowed into the sea itself, they disintegrated upon impact, shattering like icicles fragmenting. Amid the scattering of G-forces and flying plane parts, the twenty-five-foot-long blades were instantly reduced to jagged stubs just twenty-eight inches long. With the weight of her main engines and gearbox both mounted atop the aircraft's back, the straying helicopter immediately flipped over.

The crash and the struggle to survive it must have been nothing short of a nightmare. In the panic of the moment, as the jolting black ice water roared into the inverted space of the helicopter's cabin, the four gasping Coast Guardsmen fought to free themselves and get out.

Those who gained the surface faced what must have been a kind of elemental madness. The spray stung their faces, and as they struggled to see in the wet, suffocating darkness, and to be heard over the roar of the wind filling their ears, twenty-five-foot storm waves began crashing in over them.

Though his body was never found, copilot Lt. Joseph Spoja, thirty-one, exited the plane without a survival suit. The exact specifics of most of his experience will forever remain a mystery, but left to tread the wild, flesh-numbing, forty-four-degree waters of the Gulf of Alaska that night, he could not have survived for long without the thermal protection of either a survival suit, or a wet suit, and none were found to be missing.

It was Lieutenant Spoja's first night on duty at the base in Kodiak. The father of three young children, his wife pregnant with the fourth, Spoja hadn't even finished unloading his furniture and belongings back in Kodiak when he was called out on the mission.

Only recently married, twenty-one-year-old radio man John Snyder probably succumbed soon after the crash as a result of partial incapacitation from head injuries and because his flotation collar had not been inflated. Clad in a wet suit as he was, Snyder might have lived for several hours, eventually expiring due to his injuries and his inability to keep his head out of the water.

Although no one was killed outright by the impact of the crash itself, the helicopter's pilot, the ever-popular and athletic Lt. Earnie "Pat" Rivas, age thirty-three, was tossed forward so violently that he struck the instrument panel with his head, shattering the sixth cervical vertebra in his neck. Still, he did manage to exit the inverted aircraft.

With his neck fractured and blood draining from a cut on his forehead, Rivas was no doubt certain in the knowledge that since he was without a survival suit, hypothermia would soon disable and kill him. Yet somehow he maintained enough clarity of mind in his injured state to unlace and remove both of his heavy, steel-toed flight boots, probably in an effort to facilitate swimming.

Somebody had to go back inside the inverted helicopter to locate and retrieve the life raft strapped inside. Perhaps Scotty Frinfrock had also helped. Dragged to the surface, the powerful CO_2 canisters inflated the raft with a burst, and the pressing storm winds immediately launched it across the water. But when the sea-painter line (which serves as both the canister activator and the line tethering the raft to the individual holding it) came tight, unbelievably, the knot on the raft-end parted, and the windblown raft began to streak away. The speed of its departure was checked only by the fact that the raft was ballasted with pockets of cloth that fill up with water, built into the bottom of the raft.

After all the equipment failure, and the surreal experience of the crash itself, and with two small children and his lovely wife Linnea at home awaiting his safe return back in Kodiak, the vision of the departing life raft must have broken Pat Rivas' heart. Shattered vertebra or not, he was in exceptional physical condition and, as those close to him will tell you, bulldog-determined to wrestle the best that could be had from any given situation. Having already disposed of his flight boots, and dressed in little more than his standard pilot's thin blue cotton jumpsuit, with his water-wings inflated (two sets of air bags connected by straps slung under both armpits), Pat Rivas probably decided to give chase. He must have known that the life raft was their only real chance.

Seated by the helicopter's side door, twenty-five-year-old hoist operator (flight mechanic) Scott Frinfrock was, in all likelihood, the first to escape, and the last to die. While his crewmates swam off, were washed away, or were fast dying of a combination of hypothermia and injuries, he carried out a furious campaign to remain with the aircraft and to survive the ordeal. Despite the icy sweep of angry wave-water twenty-feet deep pounding over him, Frinfrock not only refused to give up; he waged open war.

Wearing a one-piece wet suit, booties, and a survival vest, Frinfrock battled the impossible. When the F/V *Daryl J* came upon the inverted helo several days later near Naked Island up in Prince William Sound, divers flown to the scene soon discovered that someone had removed the strobe light and the ancient AR/URT-33A Emergency Locator Transmitter (ELT) from inside the overturned helicopter and had tied them to a fitting near the aircraft's side door. The MK13 flares had also been removed and were missing, as was a signaling mirror.

Five of seven cartridges in Frinfrock's own pen-gun flare kit were either spent or missing. Scotty might have made it, too, had his ELT worked properly, but its off/on switch had somehow been broken off, leaving him no way to activate it.

When they found his body washed up on the rocky shore the next day, he was wearing an orange wet suit, an uninflated neck pillow, and no headgear or gloves. Coast Guard searchers also found a thirty-foot-long section of yellow trail line attached to him. In one final, last-ditch effort, Scotty Frinfrock had apparently tried to tether himself to the hulk of the overturned helicopter. He may have continued the struggle for as long as six hours before the force of the pummeling seas finally broke the line that held him, sweeping him away.

And so, with the life raft gone, the relentless onslaught of storm waves thundering down upon them, and no electronic means of signaling others of the location of their downed helicopter, the fate of the heroic crew of helo 1471 was sealed. Lost and adrift at night, scattered across the vast wilderness waters of the Gulf of Alaska, these men stood no chance of being rescued.

At first light, a massive manhunt was launched. Search and rescue airplanes, boats, and helicopters from the Coast Guard and air force bases in Anchorage, Juneau, Kodiak, and Sitka relentlessly combed the area for any signs of life.

Searchers soon found the life raft, fully inflated and in perfect repair (without the tethering line), washed up on rugged Montague Island. Nearby, they came upon the body of one of the crewmen lying face-down, partially buried in the surf and sand. The man was wearing little more than a pilot's thin, blue cotton jumpsuit and a set of water-wings under each arm. Then the shaken Coast Guard searchers noticed something odd; both of the man's flight boots were missing.

CHAPTER 1

The search and rescue flyboys stationed out on the weather-flogged tip of Japonski Island in Sitka Sound were well aware of the historic night Pat Rivas and his crew were killed. But over the years, as successive crews had come and completed their tours and then departed again, recent memories of new adventures had understandably replaced the old, and the specific details of that infamous mission had gradually become muddled in translation; some parts lost altogether.

These days, at Air Station Sitka, the story was passed down in a kind of loose, anecdotal form; scuttlebutt, really, bits and pieces recollected by longtime "sourdough" pilots who'd been kicked upstairs, or retired nearby, much the way World War II fathers, just home from the front, had once handed out machine-gun shell casings to their wide-eyed sons.

Even after nearly twenty years, approaching the subject of the crash of the 1471 is still a kind of walking-on-eggshells thing. And to ask a pilot who was currently faced with the the day-to-day challenge of staying alive while flying in southeast Alaska about it was a little like talking about the history of fatal crashes with a race car driver about to compete in the Indy 500. The heroics that Pat Rivas and the boys displayed that night, as well as the incredible run of plain old bad luck, is treated with both reverence and discretion, the plain truth being that it is really nobody's damned business.

There are, however, those heroic tales that just won't go away, the ones that have grown to almost mythological proportions; the true stories of those who'd somehow managed to fly into hell and return with survivors, crew, and helicopter still intact.

For instance, there was the time Capt. Jimmy Ng (pronounced "Ing")—a highly decorated former Sitka-based helicopter pilot (and now the commanding officer of the Integrated Support Command at Air Station Kodiak, the largest Coast Guard base in America)—encountered one of the most deadly anomalies of nature any chopper pilot has ever faced. While flying a rescue mission over on the Alaskan mainland, he came upon a 2,500-foot-high, 20-mile-long swath of powdered snow that was being blown down out of the mountain passes and out to sea at no less than 118 miles per hour.

Unable to ignore the pleas for help coming from the crew of a commercial fishing boat trapped inside the strange aberration, Ng deliberately plunged ahead. With his helo icing heavily in the −10-degree-below-zero winds, he was slammed around by the typhoon-force winds, like a racket ball in play, and yet somehow managed, in the blinding blizzard, to find the last few feet of the frozen vessel still sticking above water, and to hoist the four otherwise doomed fishermen aboard it to safety.

Although he was only a young lieutenant when chopper #1471 crashed, Ng also just happened to be the same young man who, even at that age, had the red-blooded temerity to think for himself, politely side-stepping the suggested search area, "because it made no sense." Instead, evaluating the situation for himself, Ng calculated that the shore of Montague Island was the most likely place to look for survivors. A short time later, he landed his H-3 Pelican on the beach next to what appeared to be the blue-clad body of a pilot. He set his chopper down so close that when one of his crewmen turned the body over, Ng could decipher the name tag on the man's jumpsuit pocket. It read

"Lt. Pat Rivas." Ng felt as if a sword had run him through. Pat Rivas just happened to be Ng's best friend.

Nor can the legendary exploits of former Sitka helicopter pilot Cmdr. Tom Walters in any way be omitted. Long retired from the Coast Guard, these days he continues to work as an active pilot flying choppers commercially out of Kodiak. During the years he spent in the Coast Guard, he earned a reputation among those who flew with him of being "intimidating. And absolutely fearless." And in so doing, he rewrote the history books, often performing with seeming impunity that which had never been attempted before.

Flying one wicked night along the coast at the base of the Aleutian Mountains, Walters found himself caught short while trying to rescue two castaway fishermen, who were being washed by mean sets of thirty-foot waves toward certain death on the five-hundred-foot face of the nearby cliffs. It was then that Walters abruptly announced that he was going to try to land on the top of one of the storm waves at precisely the moment when the two crewmen drifted over its crest.

There was no precedent for this, yet this he did. With the red glow of his fuel warning light pulsing in his face, he touched down just long enough for the astonished members of his own "heart-attack crew" in back to lean out the side door, reach down into the water, and drag the severely hypothermic fin-chasers aboard.

Now another problem arose: Walters had remained on-scene too long. Running on empty, with too little fuel to return to base, Tom Walters diverted into the nearest bay and searched the drenching black space for an island flat enough and large enough to hold him. And that's where searchers found them the next morning, tanks empty, but alive.

Today, friends and pilots scattered all across America will tell you that Tom Walters is a stand-up guy as well as an extremely capable pilot, who has lived, more or less, by the proud and extremely honorable old-school Coast Guard motto, "You have to go out, but you don't (necessarily) have to come back."

Historians credit this saying to a lifeboat oarsman during the early 1900s. In a letter to the editor published in the March 1954 issue of *Coast Guard Magazine,* a Clarence Brady wrote in to explain that the first person to make this remark was a man named Patrick Etheridge. Brady knew him when both were assigned to the Life Saving Station at Cape Hatteras, North Carolina.

Brady's letter explains it this way:

> A ship was stranded off Cape Hatteras on the Diamond Shoals, and one of the life-saving crew reported the fact that this ship had run ashore on the dangerous shoals.
>
> The old skipper [Etheridge] gave the command to man the lifeboat, and one of the men shouted out that "We might make it OUT to the wreck, but we will never make it BACK." The old skipper looked around and said, "The Blue Book says we've got to go out, but it doesn't say a damned thing about having to come back!"

The gallant dory captain was not exaggerating. The 1899 edition of the Life Saving Service Regulations (the Blue Book), in force at the time (the precursor to today's Coast Guard Boone & Jackets Manual), in Article 6, entitled "Action at Wrecks" (section 252, page 58), makes it clear that while attempting a rescue at sea, those so engaged may not cease their efforts ". . . until, by actual trial, the impossibility of affecting that rescue is clearly demonstrated. . . ." It goes on to say that any after-the-fact statements made by those in charge ". . . that he did not try to use the boat because the sea or surf was too heavy, will not be accepted unless attempts . . . to launch it were actually made and failed."

This regulation, emphatic and uncompromising in its tone, remained in force long after the Life Saving Service became the U.S. Coast Guard in 1915. In fact, in 1934, when the new U.S. Coast Guard regulations were published, this section in particular was copied word for word and was published just as it appeared in the 1899 edition.

"That attitude," one retired Coast Guard pilot recently told me, "has changed a lot. These days, you damned well better come back. And bring that search and rescue resource, and all those people along with you."

On a clear day in southeast Alaska, the cockpit view of a Coast Guard aviator as his or her helicopter glides along is unparalleled. Perched in the front right-hand seat, a pilot flying out of Sitka can experience the rain forest, islands, tidelands, and inland sea (known as the Alexander Archipelago) that comprise southeast Alaska at a speed and altitude entirely subject to his or her own whim.

The H-60 helicopter they fly has a blunt nose and a long, muscular body. In overall form, it bears a striking resemblance to a hammerhead shark, complete with canted tail fin. These aircraft, referred to as Jayhawks by the Coast Guard, and Blackhawks by the U.S. Army, are built by Sikorsky Corporation in the state of Connecticut.

In the air, the H-60 is a high-tech marvel of power and potential. It can cruise along at better than 150 miles per hour, and can accelerate to all-out sprint speeds of over 195 miles per hour. It has a de-icing system that heats not only the windows, but also the helicopter's rotor blades and intake manifolds. It has midair refueling capabilities, and a hoist that allows its operator to raise six-hundred-pound loads at will.

Her twin General Electric turbine engines cost about $1 million apiece. Together, the two 1,980-horsepower engines propel the fifty-three-foot-wide main rotor blades at three hundred revolutions per minute, creating nearly 22,000 pounds of lift, and enable the H-60 to pick up and fly off with a whopping 6,000-pound load. Under ideal conditions, pilots can command her onboard computers to hover and land the aircraft all by herself. By comparison, the H-3 Pelican (the H-60's predecessor) that Jimmy Ng and Tom Walters piloted flew like a bread truck with wings.

At $18 million a helicopter, however, the H-60 is expensive. For about the same price, one might purchase 400 new Lincoln Continental automobiles.

Handpicked out of the ranks of fellow Coast Guardsmen from all across America, the pilots who fly these helicopters and patrol this hostile portion of Alaska are the chosen few. They are lean, clean, fit, and disciplined. Overwhelmingly male in gender (fifteen of the sixteen helo pilots stationed in Sitka are male), they keep their hair trimmed "high and tight," as they call it. They are intelligent, educated, thoroughly screened, highly trained, well paid, and often remarkably gifted. They are, it is said, America's finest. And they love what they do, piloting the finest gleaming orange, black, and white state-of-the-art toys ever produced, as they patrol the last great frontier.

A Coast Guard helicopter pilot stationed in Alaska will pull down close to $70,000 a year, more or less, plus medical and dental benefits (within limits). Pilots are allowed thirty days of vacation a year. And while the U.S. Government carries a basic $200,000 life insurance on them, those who fly often carry policies that would pay out an additional two to three times that amount to their families, should they be killed in action. After twenty years of service, most will live to enjoy retirement checks in the amount of two-thirds of their base pay for the rest of their lives. Many will immediately be scooped up by one of the commercial airline companies.

I wondered at how, with so many assets, they went about keeping their pride in check, and the goal of helping others solidly in their sights. One pilot told me that the flying conditions in the outback of Alaska were, on occasion, so challenging that "from time to time they make even the best of us eat humble pie."

Capt. Jimmy Ng explains it this way: "From the get-go a pilot is taught that aviation is so dangerous that you cannot do it by yourself. And so if a crew goes out and they almost fly into the water, ninety-nine times out of a hundred, that crew is going to come back and fess up, and they are going to tell everybody. And the reason they're going to tell everybody is because they don't want their buddies to make the same mistake. That's part of 'service above self.' "

Pilots also aid one another in remaining right-sized by practicing a self-deprecating type of humor within their ranks. When one newspaper reporter mistakenly wrote that the popular and good-natured Lt. Dan Molthen, a much decorated helicopter pilot who had twice been awarded the Distinguished Flying Cross (one of the highest accolades a pilot can be awarded), had vomited into his own lap during a rescue mission, the boys at Air Station Sitka never let up.

"Hey, Russ," shouted one tongue-in-cheek pilot to another in the ops center, loudly enough to draw everyone's attention. "Did you hear about Madison? He had a really tough flight last night. Snow, wind, vertigo, the works. And I'll bet you already guessed what happened to him. Yeah, he Molthenned."

Under normal conditions, each H-60 helicopter has a crew of four, which includes a pilot, a copilot, a flight mechanic, and a rescue swimmer. Essentially, the pilot flies the helicopter while the copilot plots their course, entering the navigation way-point positions into the onboard computer.

Unless they have something important to share while en route to the scene, the flight mechanic and rescue swimmer generally contribute by keeping quiet. The pilots up front, they know, are working hard; they are the navigators and fuel managers, and until the hoisting actually begins, communication with them is kept to a minimum.

In the severe weather, the flight mech (who operates the hoist) is crouched in the doorway, his heart racing a mile a minute as he faces a never-ending series of fight-or-flight predicaments. During missions launched in the subzero temperatures of winter, his hands may literally freeze from the 120-mile-per-hour downdraft of the chopper's blades; in summer, his body will sweat profusely inside the sweltering confines of his dry suit.

Regardless, with one hundred feet or more of slack cable playing out far below him, he tries to guide the pilot and aircraft in over those waiting to be saved while simultaneously lowering the rescue basket without bludgeoning those in the water to death with the difficult-to-control basket.

In a bad storm, a flight mech's task is somewhat like trying to drop a clothespin dangling from the end of a one-hundred-foot length of string into a milk bottle from the seat of a moving Ferris wheel.

It is the rescue swimmer, however, who, when lowered into the water, faces the modern-day Coast Guard crewman's most dangerous and unpredictable task.

When not out flying, which is about 90 percent of the time, both rescue swimmers and hoist operators serve as helicopter mechanics on the ground. Using one of the most advanced computerized diagnostic systems in the world, they do maintenance work on helicopters inside the base's giant hangar.

As chief engineering officer at the base in Sitka, Lt. Stu Merrill decides what must be done, and he schedules people to do the work. "I have the best job in the Coast Guard," he says. "And the reason it's the best job is because I work with fifty of the hardest-working, most talented people I've ever met in my life."

His right-hand man is Reggie Lavoie, who has been working at the Sitka base since 1977, when it first opened. Lavoie is looked upon as the perfect example of the farm-boy work ethic. "He starts when the sun comes up," says Merrill, "and he won't quit until the work is done."

Merrill and Lavoie are also quite aware of the fact that the one undeniable drawback to the high-tech H-60 is the amount of maintenance and money needed to sustain her. Roughly fifteen man-hours of mechanical labor are required to support each and every hour of actual flying time.

It is a rare occasion when all three choppers are mission-ready at the same time. The three helos at Air Station Sitka fly roughly 2,100 flight-hours per year, or 700 flight-hours per aircraft. This means that their mechanics must work 31,000 hours, more or less, each year to keep just two of the base's three "birds" on-line at all times.

If Lavoie and Merrill receive a request for an additional one hundred hours of flyovers by the fisheries enforcement, or National Park Service people, they and their crews are faced with an additional 1,500 man-hours of maintenance work—the equivalent of one mechanic working for nearly a year, just to support those few extra hours of flying time.

E ach morning, pilots meet up in the ops center to be briefed on the day's flight assignments. It sits on the second floor of the two-story, flat-roofed office building that is attached to their hangar and extends out past it on both ends. The room at the head of the stairs is filled with expensive-looking communications equipment and large, square map tables. It looks out over one end of the hangar building, the helicopter pad just beyond it, and the broad, spacious, island-dotted waters of Sitka Sound, which splash up against the entire length of the airport runway.

Night and day, at least one set of pilots and their crew remain at the ready, staying overnight in the ward shack, a compact little bunkhouse built on the rocky knoll across the way. When hungry, search and rescue flight crews make the short hike to the "gazebo" nearby. This octagonal kitchen sits beside the water on the Sitka side of the narrow island. When not on duty, pilots and their crews may often be found exercising at the on-base gym. During off weekends, they may be found next door at the Eagle's Nest, leaning over a cool, tall, wet one.

Today, drinking to excess is frowned upon. A pilot who has drunk so much as a single beer on any given day is not considered mission-ready for the next twenty-four hours. In fact, in today's modern Coast Guard, a hard-partying young enlisted man with an understandable penchant for malt liquor and impromptu sessions of stand-up love-making, who may accept a fight-for-fun challenge from some local fisherman on the end of a three-day drunk, will quickly find himself expelled from that branch of the military. One alcohol-related infraction is the limit; two will get you booted from the service. Guaranteed.

CHAPTER 2

Nearly all the tiny, weatherbeaten villages that dot the Alexander Archipelago, which comprises southeast Alaska, are positioned by the sea at the head of a bay, or near the mouth of one of the pristine rivers that flow out of the lush green rain forest here. And Sitka, though her eight thousand residents give her bragging rights as the sixth-largest town in the entire state, is no different. She sits huddled along the shoreline, inside the protective width of Japonski Island and the wave-snuffing reefs and tree-covered islands that are dispersed across Sitka Sound itself. As further protection against the wild fluctuations of the Alaskan tides, the canneries and fuel docks and cargo sheds that stand shoulder to shoulder along the waterfront are balanced upon wooden pilings so tall they appear to be mounted on stilts.

A robust walk along the water's edge in either direction from Sitka's downtown area leads one past a sprawling maze of interwoven marinas and boat docks. A thousand or so yards inland, the town rises up on terraced lots carved out of the surrounding wilderness, her back pressing up against the steep, forest green slopes of undeveloped wilderness that dominate bear-infested Baranof Island.

At night, especially in winter, the cold, rarefied air and strange atmospherics of the place serve to create an illusion that seems to draw the pointed, snowcapped peaks such as 4,200-foot-high Bear Mountain much closer; so near, in fact, that the threat of an avalanche to the town itself appears quite real.

Sitka, once called "Sheet'ka" by the Tlingit Indians, means "where the mountains cascade into the sea." Around 1800, Russian imperialists led by Alexander Baranof sailed into Sitka Sound and abruptly claimed it for themselves. Then, using hundreds of Aleut slaves brought in from the Aleutian Islands to hunt from kayaks, Baranof's forces set out to kill every living sea otter.

For several thousand years, by most estimates, the local tribe of Tlingit Indians had ruled the land and waterways of Sitka Sound and beyond. Rival tribes, such as the Haida, looked upon them as a fierce but tactical lot. Politely acquiescing at first to the strange but well-armed newcomers, the puzzled Tlingits soon grew sick of the intrusive and unpalatable combination of Russian arrogance, greed, and piety. They waited until Alexander Baranof was away on business over on Kodiak Island to attack; then they burned the new fort to the ground and drove its inhabitants into the sea.

Several years later, the Russians returned, led once again by Alexander Baranof and backed by three fighting ships and several score of cannons. The Russians pounded the Tlingits for six days, shelling men, women, and children, killing the young and the old alike before finally routing what remained of the brokenhearted people.

This time around, Alexander Baranof came determined to stay. He named the spot New Archangel, a site that would serve as the Russian-American capital for decades to come. While his hunters once again resumed the hugely profitable slaughter of sea otters, Baranof put his carpenters to work. They constructed a fort, a huge bunkhouse for his men, extensive storage facilities, and even a library and a small school. Sitka's new identity would also soon include one of the most advanced shipyards to be found anywhere in the world.

Baranof's own modest but comfortable home was built on a point of rock close to the sea where he could overlook what he must have considered to be his own wild kingdom. Today, from that same promontory (known as Castle Hill), one of the original cannons remains, aimed harmlessly out to sea. Looking closer at the jet-black surface of this ancient cannon, one can see letters painted in nail polish inside the form of a heart; an innocuous bit of young lovers' graffiti applied, perhaps, as a small rebellion against the bloodletting of the past.

Across the way lie the floating docks where, during the long, industrious days of summer, local fishermen come in their boats to repair their worn purse seines and gillnets, or string new ones. Farther up the shoreline, a solitary pier stretches out into the deep waters of the main channel. Often the Coast Guard buoy tender *Woodrush* is moored to it, taking on food stuffs and replacement parts in preparation for her next sea patrol.

Back on the Sitka side of the channel, the downtown area is lined with trinket shops, banks, apartments, and old, square-fronted hotels, as well as the watering holes frequented by local fishermen. There is Earnie's Bar, The Bilge, in the basement of the Sitka Hotel, and the museumlike Totem Bar, whose interior walls are covered with hundreds of framed photographs of wrecked fishing boats that have run aground.

Most of the businesses in the downtown are positioned along two narrow one-way lanes of twisting pavement that lead cars and people around the old Russian Orthodox church. Its clean blue belfry and chapel tower rise up smack in the middle of downtown, oblivious to the ever-encroaching nature of modern man.

Near the breakwater and boat docks, hand-carved totem poles rise from a flat chunk of grass-covered ground known as Totem Park. The radiant green grass flows from the bank at the water's edge, fills the rectangle of the park itself, leap-frogs a street, and then begins again, ending in an invitingly landscaped sweep of lawn and rose gardens at the front steps of the Pioneers' Home. This large, four-story building was established by the State of Alaska in 1913 as a place where indigent prospectors and homesteaders might come when, in their later years, they could no longer care for themselves in the wilds.

Just a stone's throw to the south, a massive suspended bridge extends for over 1,200 feet out across the channel that leads into Sitka

Harbor. Christened in 1977, the O'Connel Bridge allows locals free and open access to the airport and Coast Guard base over on Japonski Island, while doing away forever with the need to ferry commuters back and forth across the channel.

At one time, any able-bodied man who did not mind extremely hard work could find "three hots and a cot" and a good-paying job in any one of nearly one hundred bustling logging camps scattered across southeast Alaska. These camps opened in April and ran until late in October, when the winter snows once again shut them down. Flying into the primitive backwoods, these loggers would live in bunkhouses, gorge themselves on literally mounds of cookhouse grub, and work ten to twelve hours a day, often seven days a week, to cut and haul prime spruce, cedar, and hemlock trees, forming floating log-booms from their wooden torsos in the nearest bay.

Fresh out of college when I first came to Sitka in 1977, I quickly found work at just such a camp. It was situated on the remote shores of Rowan Bay over on Kuiu Island, about an hour's ride by bushplane from here. It proved to be a good, honest life ruled by long, sweat-soaked days, hearty appetites, enough quirky characters, and bunk-house bull sessions featuring classic storytelling one-upmanship to fill several notebooks with Alaskan myth, lore, and legend. At the time, there were perhaps sixty camps still operating in the area. Today, un-derstandably, only a handful remain.

The logging boom is over, now. These days locals find work in the commercial fishing industry, seining or trolling or long-lining for a va-riety of salmon, halibut, and bottom fish, or they may leave the famil-iarity of home for a few months to fill any number of seasonal positions. They may fight forest fires in Alaska's vast interior for the DNR (De-partment of Natural Resources), or thin trees in one of the replanted clearcuts, or process salmon in a cannery, or improve the salmon's chances by spending the long summer days wading in thigh-deep water working in one of the stream enhancement projects.

Others will hire on with one of several hotels in Sitka, or with any of many hotels in Juneau, and even Anchorage, or perhaps at one of many lodges in the wild that cater to the dizzying flood of tourists, sport fishermen, and nature lovers that pours into Alaska during the beautiful, but often frenetic, days of summer. The most coveted jobs, however, remain those with state or federal agencies that provide steady paychecks, tenure, and full-benefit packages the year round, such as those with the state's social services, the school systems, the postal service, or a civilian job with the U.S. Coast Guard, or, more likely, a post within the growing bureaucracy of the U.S. Forest Service.

CHAPTER 3

While attempting to describe both the history and geography of the area, I fear that I have skirted the heart of the matter. For it is the living treasure trove of people who inhabit Sitka that makes the place seem so agreeable. I find them to be overwhelmingly congenial, strongly opinionated, and always interesting. Many of those I met were also quite gregarious—as unique and colorful as the land itself.

Merely by chance, for example, I met Burgess Bauder, a local veterinarian with a dynamic personality who, though ever-popular with fellow students, left a Ph.D. program at Texas A&M in Amarillo, at least in part because he was, by his own admission, a "loose cannon; I just didn't fit in." His long blond hair, otterlike mustache, and adamant refusal to wear a white shirt and tie, as well as his openly creative mind, were infractions deemed sufficiently grievous, at the time, to draw the venomous ire of the conservative school administration.

Burgess now lives in a small cabin near Sitka's waterfront with his wife, Vicki Vosberg (also a veterinarian), and runs his own pet clinic almost pro bono. He is often captivated by the illusion of the brilliant red orb of summer sun settling, as it seems to do, into the cauldron of

Mt. Edgecumbe. When not working in his clinic, or as a commercial deep-sea diver, he builds beautiful, even elegant, Coast Guard–certified lighthouses on the side.

"There are people who live here for twenty years," says Bauder, "and still moan about the weather and the isolation. They will never, in their hearts, ever actually be Alaskans. And then there are people who get off the ferry, and, from the day they arrive, just love it here. When it's black and rainy and stormy out, they are absolutely invigorated by it. The secret of Alaska is to love the land just the way you find it." For people like Burgess Bauder, and those who enjoy living on the edge of the out-of-bounds, there is nothing better.

And there was the man and wife I met who used to work at the local radio station. They lived in a cabin on the top of a small cliff near the water's edge just outside of town, cooked their meals on a wood-burning stove, and moved about in the long winter darkness by the light of a kerosene lamp. In an effort to preserve the sanctity of the place, the homestead was left deliberately roadless. With no driveway, and brown bears wandering undisturbed through their front yard, each commute to town, as well as every can of food and roll of toilet paper (and every board and nail and piece of plumbing used to construct the place, for that matter), had to be carried in over the only access route, a one-thousand-foot-long moss-covered trail that, even today, winds its way down through a pungent wonderland of untouched rain forest.

And how could I forget Bauder's friend Dr. John Zarley, who excels in the field of internal medicine, and who, with his own artistic hands, and with no prior experience in the construction trade, designed and built two singularly uncommon timber-framed homes in Sitka. Using almost obscenely heavy timbers available locally in abundance, he shunned the use of nails and spikes and brought the specifically shaped chunks of wood together at precisely fitting junctures, using nothing more than wooden pegs. "And the man had never so much as run a band saw before," adds Bauder.

Zarley also wrote a stage play, and, during his youth, worked for several years as a deckhand on a tugboat plying the lower one thousand miles or so of the Yukon River in Alaska's interior—before completing medical school, that is.

Then there is John Williams, a former research physicist, "an absolutely fascinating man," says Bauder. While working for an aircraft company down in San Diego, Williams reportedly built a forty-two-foot-long sailboat in his backyard. He christened it *Faraway*. Then one day he quit his job and, with his wife and equally robust mother, sailed the vessel around the world. In due time, he voyaged from the South China Sea, up along the coasts of Japan and Russia, and along the entire, one-thousand-mile length of the Aleutian Islands—in November.

Though he had literally sailed the world over, when he tacked into Sitka Sound on the final leg of his journey, something touched him; so he bought a portion of land on a nearby island and moved onto it. These days, he beach-logs to supplement his income. He winches red cedar out of the sand or off the rocks wherever he finds it, and drags the logs out to sea with a boat, persevering in the dead of winter off some of the most rugged and weather-assaulted shorelines in southeast Alaska.

Open access to Burgess Bauder's circle of friends also led me to Sitka's Harold and Pat Diamond. As youngsters, back when Alaska was still a territory, the Diamonds fished "all over southeastern, from Ketchikan clear to the Fairweather Ground," says Harold Diamond. "Alaska has always been a neat place to live."

Now retired, they recall that the best job they ever had was while working as the caretakers of a cannery out at Sitkoh Bay. Situated at the end of Peril Straits, a winding, often perilous sixty-five-mile boat ride from town, the Diamonds lived there for several years in the early 1980s, watching over the old cannery's facilities, the bunkhouses, and the cabins for the Native corporation that owned them. Each summer, they would can an abundance of fresh-caught salmon, and during the fall, they would make jerky and sausage from the Sitka deer they hunted. Every six months or so, they made one of their seven-hour boat rides to town to purchase ammunition and the basic food staples such as flour, sugar, lard, and vegetables.

With his shepherd dog, Diamond, standing his ground and aggressively giving chase to any brown bears that wandered near their encampment, Harold Diamond awoke each morning faced with what he likes to joke about today as the same excruciating quandary of difficult decisions: Should he fish for steelhead from the world-class steelhead stream nearby, or go deer hunting, or run the family trapline, making sets for martin and mink? Or perhaps work on a pet project?

Sometimes, in winter, a cold snap would grip the area. And then Harold and Pat would strap on their ice skates and set out together, gliding across the frozen surface of the bay as freely and impulsively as youngsters.

Now and then, during the long winter nights, the captivating colors and forms of the aurora borealis would appear on the horizon, dancing across the heavens above the mountains over toward Juneau. "At times they'd cover the whole sky," recalls Harold Diamond. Once, after a day out fishing, he and Pat were treated to the most beautiful display of northern lights that they had ever beheld. As nature's own psychedelic show continued overhead, the Diamonds decided to toss down some blankets on the deck of their salmon boat. "We just lay there on our backs and watched those darned things for hours. It was awesome. Just gorgeous. We couldn't believe it."

The colorful and mysterious electromagnetic bands looked like ribbons of flowing silk. "Every color that you could imagine," recalls Pat Diamond fondly. "They were just dancing across the sky in pinks and greens, and violets and pale yellows. Sometimes, it'd get moving so fast up there, you could hear it crackle."

CHAPTER 4

Growing up close to the water is a way of life for most "southeast-erners." Let the crowd at Sitka's Fourth of July parade catch sight of the U.S. Coast Guard contingent marching down Main Street, and enthusiastic cheers erupt. Most everyone knows someone whose life has been spared when the Coast Guard intervened.

"And nobody," adds Burgess Bauder, "who does anything around the water up here will bad-mouth the Coast Guard. There's a whole bunch of testosterone associated with what those guys do. And they do a great job. They risk their lives to save the lives of people who have often made some really dumb decisions. Those guys are genuinely, certifiably heroic."

Flying a helicopter virtually anywhere in southeast Alaska brings with it the deadly, and almost continuous, threat of navigational error. A pilot usually advances with the body of his aircraft pointing into the prevailing wind. Cocked to one side at an angle occasionally as severe as forty degrees, the helicopter will nevertheless advance along at a steady pace in the intended direction. This is called "crabbing." The critical dilemma the pilot faces is that when the aircraft is so engaged, the radar points off to the side, leaving those inside the helicopter essentially blind in bad weather.

No matter where pilots fly in southeast Alaska, they are always fighting head winds of some kind. At such times, new pilots often feel frustrated; it seems that they can never make the plane fly fast enough or straight enough. It is something that seasoned pilots eventually come to accept.

Helicopter pilots typically fly within sight of shore at about a three-hundred-foot level. That's the magic altitude. The majority of the maneuvers they perform, including the hover-downs to the water, are generally predicated off the three-hundred-foot mark.

Above all, a pilot cannot permit him- or herself to become distracted. Screw up in bad weather, allow something to draw your attention to a problem you may be having with one of your engines, as the chopper pilot did in 1985 over on Kodiak Island, and you could end up exploding into a ball of flames, killing everyone aboard on some lonely, barren hillside, just as he did.

In Alaska, virtually no one, except search and rescue pilots, flies after dark. During the fierce winter storms that routinely pound southeast Alaska and dump upward of two hundred inches of rain, and tens of feet of snow a year in some places, entire weeks may pass without a single civilian aircraft flying into or out of some of the remote villages that dot this vast land.

In cases of emergency, it is the search and rescue helicopter squads in Sitka who are called upon to respond. Flying blindly through mountain passes at night is not at all unusual. At such times, it's like trying to navigate through the mountains while trapped inside the prisonlike confines of an aircraft with no windows, no radar, and only one's ability to use a map, a stopwatch, and instruments to see one through.

Even with the advent of the high-tech global positioning system (GPS), a pilot's worst fear remains that of running into a mountainside. Only in recent years has the GPS been used in conjuction with the radar picture, allowing pilots to fly with minimal dependence upon visual input as long as they maintain adequate clearance and stay the course. Whether it is a mission to Skagway, Lynn Canal, Haines, Juneau, Hoonah, Gustavas, Yakutat, Chatham Strait, Angoon, Kake, Meyers Chuck, Pelican, Port Alexander, Point Baker, Rowan Bay, Security Bay, Petersburg, Wrangell, or Ketchikan, the trick is to remain on the beaten path as long as you can. The real adventure begins when you are forced to veer off and venture out into the wilderness alone.

In bad weather, the winding, cliff-lined route through North Inian Pass that leads into the unlighted dirt runway outside the ancient Tlingit village of Hoonah is exacting enough to turn a young pilot's hair prematurely gray. "When you commit to go in there," says one longtime pilot, "you've just *got* to have that place etched in your mind."

In freezing weather, when ice begins forming outside, the little red ice-detector warning light will begin to pulse. Then the deicing heater will switch on. Soon, the ice will begin breaking apart and sliding across the windshield in irregular islands, offering up a disorienting visual display.

Other times, pilots will face the thick, frosty layers of fog rolling in off the massive glaciers near Petersburg and Wrangell, or up in Glacier Bay or Lituya Bay. Though the sophisticated radar capabilities of the H-60 are far superior to those of the old H-3, those fine white crystals can render even that system useless in just minutes.

Calls to aid a stroke or heart-attack victim, or perhaps someone who has sustained a serious injury in an automobile or snowmobile accident, or while fishing or logging, are all understandable. But other missions often leave pilots questioning the judgment of those who summoned them. At such times, a Coast Guard pilot will invariably find himself saying, "This better be for real."

As storm warnings were being broadcast over the radio, alerting all mariners, one pilot who was forced to fly through horrific weather to pick up a man injured in a bar fight in one of the villages found himself thinking, Why did this drunken jerk get us into this position? Why do we have to go out on a night like this and risk all our tails just to save this guy's sorry ass?

On a clear, moonlit night, a pilot wearing five-thousand-dollar night-vision goggles (NVGs) can see almost as well as one flying through broad daylight. On dark nights, when no moon is showing, he can still spot the flame of someone lighting a cigarette match as far as ten miles away. Once, having searched long and hard for an overturned boat on a wet and miserable night in a remote bay over on Kodiak Island, Capt. Jimmy Ng spotted something. It turned out to be the tiny sparklerlike flicker of a Bic lighter that wouldn't ignite. Though one youngster died from hypothermia after being trapped beneath the boat, two severely hypothermic men, one of whom was the boy's father (both men had tried repeatedly to swim under the boat and save the boy), still managed to convey their position, saving both of their lives.

About once a month, a seasoned pilot will fly into a situation where his awe of, and his affection for, Alaska is overwhelmed by some discomforting factors that begin to gnaw at his psyche. Flying along at better than one hundred miles per hour in high winds and torrential rains in "zero-zero" weather (with no ceiling and no visibility), crabbing sideways as he goes, all the while fighting against the dead-man's state of total vertigo, is enough to make a pilot want to crawl up into the fetal position and pull a blanket over his head.

Seasoned pilots flying out of Sitka know only too well what it's like to travel along in total darkness through a blinding snowstorm up the ninety-mile-long fjord of Lynn Canal to Haines or Skagway to make a pickup or delivery with nothing but fluorescent green ridges on a tiny radar screen pointing the way. Caught in the whiteout conditions of a blizzard, the view from the pilot's seat is obliterated. The result is sensory deprivation. Then the trip becomes a carnival ride, with the lives of everyone on board resting on the pilot's experience, savvy, and ability to adapt. At such times, copilots, rescue swimmers, and flight mechanics alike get to experience one another's threshholds for fear, their own included. Everything that they are, and everything that they have learned, or failed to learn, through the years will dictate how they respond.

Shortly after one well-known Sitka pilot first arrived in Alaska, he came very close to running into some real estate under those exact conditions. He was flying down Lynn Canal at the time, returning home to Sitka in the dark after plucking several injured, but grateful, survivors off the glacial crash site of their downed bush plane, and was about halfway through a ninety-degree course correction when his navigator, who was seated behind him, suddenly inquired, "Hey, is there a reason we're flying at only sixteen feet?"

CHAPTER 5

O ne would be hard-pressed to come up with an active pilot who has faced more of these hazardous conditions, and who feels more passionately about his family, his job, and the Alaskan wilderness he watches over, than Sitka-based helicopter pilot Lt. Russ Zullick.

Zullick was raised near Allentown, Pennsylvania. As a youth, he hunted and fished with his father, a former Coast Guardsman himself, who also happened to be a direct descendant of the Iroquois tribe. He grew up thumbing through magazines like *Outdoor Life, Field & Stream,* and *Sports Afield,* and he noticed that many of the most exciting adventure stories he came upon took place in Alaska. In his youthful heart, all roads seemed to point north. When Zullick graduated from high school, he joined the Coast Guard and soon found himself stationed on board the USCG cutter *Ironwood,* patrolling the waters west of Adak in the Aleutian Islands.

From the outset, Zullick fell in love with the "Big Bear State." Quickly working his way up through the ranks, he served for a time as a chopper mechanic. Eventually, he became an officer. Now, as a pilot, he looks forward each day to what he calls "flying the mission." Not one to sit idle, he also runs a taxidermy business on the side; and during the summer months, he takes sportfishermen out on his family-owned-and-operated charter boat.

Zullick had been stung early in his flying career in Alaska. He was just a mechanic stationed out on Kodiak Island, back in 1981, when the 1471 went down. His roommate, he recalls, was a "tough kid" whose best friend was John Snyder, the radioman who died in the crash. Zullick would always remember how the youngster "just sat and cried for two days straight."

"These days," says Zullick, "we don't pass blame; we don't say 'These guys were stupid.' We just say, 'This is what happened. Don't let it happen to you.' "

Even for experienced pilots such as Zullick, who has six thousand hours of time piloting a helicopter, flying out of Sitka can still be intimidating. "I kid you not," he says, "we fly routine missions out of Sitka here in weather they wouldn't even open their hangar doors to in San Diego, or Elizabeth City [North Carolina]. They couldn't even *fathom* flying in the kind of weather that we encounter during just our everyday training exercises up here.

"And I don't care how good a pilot you are," he adds, "up here, you're eventually going to have a bad night flying. It doesn't matter if you're a two-thousand-hour pilot, or you're a six-thousand-hour pilot; eventually, you'll have a bad night."

Regardless, Zullick plans to remain in the Coast Guard "as long as they'll have me," he says. "I never want to leave Alaska."

Stationed now in Sitka, Zullick and his pals fly over the 400-mile-long, 20-million-acre archipelago of timber-covered islands and intermingling sea that composes southeast Alaska, patrolling the territory from Ketchikan and the Canadian border in the south to the ancient Tlingit fishing village of Yakutat in the north, which has a population of just five hundred or so people.

To be a chopper pilot in this part of the United States, claims Zullick, is an experience in extremes. "It's either the most beautiful place you'd ever want to fly in your life, and you think you're absolutely stealing a paycheck from the taxpayer, or you are flying at night in a blinding snowstorm, with wind trying to strip you from the sky, and it all becomes a kind of living death."

But to hop aboard an H-60 on a clear blue day in late August and join Zullick on a patrol to the northernmost end of Air Station Sitka's "area of responsibility" (AOR) is to experience southeast Alaska in an intimate way that not even the original gold miners of 1898 could have dreamed of. On such a day, the stunning beauty of the inland islands, channels, mountains, rivers, and sea surrounding Sitka are captivating, and together, comprise a biological wonder, so abundant in fish and wildlife and so remarkable in its natural diversity, that many people in the continental United States have difficulty believing that it even exists.

We begin our flight fully fueled, lifting off from the circular helicopter pad that sits next to the base's only hangar, a giant building that stands a good sixty feet high and covers an area more than three times the size of a professional basketball court. Both landing pad (just a circle painted at the end of the asphalt runway) and hangar are no more than a couple of hundred feet from the unrestrained waters of Sitka Sound.

As Zullick powers into the sky, the broad blue circle of vibrant, sun-kissed sea that opens wide before us is so intensely colorful and filled with light that it seems almost tropical. The waters of the sound are interrupted only by the gleaming flashes of waves breaking over several reefs in the distance and along the shores of scores of tiny tree-studded islands scattered across the sound.

These waters are teeming with salmon and halibut, and rockfish and sea lions, and oozing with microbiotic life. Once, when Zullick was fishing with his wife, Debra, from the back deck of his cabin cruiser near the entrance to the sound, a pod of frolicking humpback whales began rolling and sounding all around them. The curious mammals eventually drew so near that Zullick and his wife could nearly reach out and touch them; so near, in fact, that they could feel the fine mist of the whales' exhaled breaths sprinkling down upon them.

Some fifteen miles in the distance, the robust waters of Sitka Sound wash up on the rocky, kelp-inundated shoreline of Kruzof Island. A lush green carpet of hemlock forest climbs sharply from atop the hundred-foot cliffs that line the beach there, rising up the magnificent volcanic face of 3,201-foot-high Mount Edgecumbe, a giant, Fuji-like volcano that wears a caved-in caldera for a crown.

Far from the summit, the trees give way suddenly to a high-mountain border of brilliant green meadowlands, which finally surrender to the gray-black slopes of eroding ash. Flying along at two thousand feet on such a rare and perfect day, Zullick can count numerous Sitka deer—their bodies fat from grazing in the warm summer light, their horns in full velvet—lying contentedly in the meadowlands.

Zullick heads north, cuts across Salisbury Sound, and sweeps into Slocum Arm on Chichagof Island, a place chopper crews often refer to as "bear alley."

"A lot of times," he says, "you'll see brown bears up in there. Typically, at that time of the year, a lot of sows with their cubs, and the loner boars [the males]."

These bruisers usually prefer to be off alone, and, in their prime, they can weigh in excess of one thousand pounds. Bolting suddenly, they can reach remarkable speeds, even over broken ground, in just seconds. A German shepherd dog, for instance, can catch a grown man sprinting all-out in about five steps; a brown bear, some experts claim, could catch the same dog in about the same distance.

In between mating seasons and winter solstices, a bear's only purpose in life is to fatten up enough to enable him to survive the long-lingering snows of winter. This the powerful, gluttonous creatures do with abandon.

They seem content to feed on the fresh white roots and stems of swamp grass that inundate the tideland marshes at the mouths of numerous streams and rivers in southeast Alaska. These chest-high grasses sometimes spread out for a thousand yards across the muddy deltas. Their stalks are charged with a sugar content so rich that bears have been known literally to step over spawning salmon swimming upstream to reach this, their favorite delicacy. And it is here that Zullick finds them, brown bears feeding in the dazzling, almost blinding, beauty of the emerald green grasses of summer.

These days, the "A,B,C" islands of Admiralty, Baranof, and Chich-agof are almost overrun with brown bears. "Baranof, on which Sitka sits, has its own sizable population," says Zullick. Each year a few of the 40,000 brown bears that live in Alaska wander down into the city limits of Sitka itself, as well as numerous other villages in the state. Those that refuse to leave are routinely shot.

Zullick searches Lisianski Inlet for seine boats making sets in the inlets, or off some point. To him, the sight of the long white strings of small, closely arranged buoys circling out from the boats and back again is a romantic vision. There was a time, as a young pilot, when the grass always seemed greener. In his spare time, Zullick used to enjoy walking along the docks past the boats and take note of their colors and study how they were rigged and try to memorize their names as well.

"And then I'd see them out on the grounds," he says, "and, flying over them at three hundred feet, I'd sometimes see their seine nets full of what looked like thousands of salmon, the weight of which some-times nearly pulled the boats over. And I'd say to myself, Man, wouldn't it be great to be a fisherman? That's the life for me!"

Given to occasionally severe bouts of self-examination, at such times Zullick would have to remind himself that the brutal truth of the matter was that he worked for the government, and he would question himself: Had he become nothing more than a bureaucrat with wings?

Just *look* at those guys down there, he'd think. There they are in the thick of it; man against nature; men working with their hands; guys getting dirty doing guy stuff.

Today, a far more seasoned Zullick knows that the reality playing out below is far different from such visionary notions. Clad in rain gear, a fisherman takes a precarious stand on a slippery, bobbing deck and, among other duties, repeatedly coils a dripping seine net aboard for twenty, thirty, forty, even fifty hours without sleep or a cooked meal. He or she will labor all too often under the thumb of some coffee-induced maniac—the vessel's skipper—while the hydraulic, pulleylike block twenty feet overhead rains down a brownish red hot goo of mu-tilated jellyfish.

At such times, a fisherman will feel no small envy for those adventurous flyboys he sees cruising along on their way to some important rendezvous in their spotless cobalt blue jumpsuits, riding shotgun over the land, pounding across the sky as if they owned it.

As Zullick closes, now, on the picturesque little fishing port of Pelican, population 105, he must be careful to keep a close watch out for any float planes that might come darting out of the narrow mountain passes of Admiralty Island. They carry mail to the villages, transport fishermen or boat parts to clandestine spots in any one of thousands of remote bays, and deliver teams of timber cutters out to the logging camps.

Bald eagles, weighing up to ten pounds and occasionally sporting a wingspan of seven feet or more, can be a problem, too, though their numbers are usually at their height during the spring herring spawn. Then the sky seems to be filled with them, "as thick as seagulls," according to Zullick. "I've hit two of them over the years," he adds, in a tone filled with regret. "They hit the windshield. Both times we were lucky; they glanced off and went up through the rotors. You can see where they hit, because there's a big smudge mark. Typically, you get blood and entrails trailed all over the aircraft," much the way a human body would react if struck by an 18,000-pound metal object traveling at 150 miles per hour.

Commonly, on such a flight, Zullick will spot bald eagles cruising past far below. Set on an entirely different course, they pass on, seemingly oblivious to the strange contraption passing by overhead. The dazzling white of their heads makes them readily identifiable, standing out starkly against the dark blue backdrop of the sea and the deep forest green surrounding Pelican.

Not so long ago, having survived several years as a deckhand working aboard king crab ships out of Kodiak, I caught a ride on one of those float planes into that romantic little port of Pelican for no more reason than just to see the place, and to celebrate, along with several score of other loggers and fishermen, the Fourth of July. With the heart-pounding radiance of a million ambient stars filling the night sky above our tents, a golden river of tequila flowing across the carved wooden counter at Rose's Bar nearby, and the desperate hormonal abandon of our proud youths goading us madly on, no insanity was left out.

Still bound for Yakutat, 125 miles farther up the coast, Zullick flies northwest from Pelican, out across Icy Strait and Cross Sound, then past the lighthouse at Cape Spencer.

The years when Alaska's commercial fishermen derby-fished for halibut are gone now. As recently as 1996, however, the season was open to anyone with hooks, bait, and a boat that would remain afloat. During the last few years of what were soon reduced to forty-eight-hour openings, and before the individual fishing quota (IFQ) system went into effect, as many as four thousand boats from all over the state participated in the opening.

Often ignoring even the most threatening of weather conditions, they raced to sea in an effort to compete against the bigger boats, and thereby garner a fair share of the coveted flatfish. The feeling was (and rightly so) that a fisherman *had* to fish, or miss out entirely. As a result, numerous lives were lost each season.

Whether one agrees with today's IFQ permit system or not, it does allow those lucky enough to own one the ability to wait for calm seas and more or less pick the weather in which they choose to fish. These days, Zullick might see thirty or thirty-five commercial boats actively fishing during a single day of patrolling.

It is here, north of Pelican, that the mainland coast of Alaska takes on a wild, often cruel appearance, with boulders the size of dump trucks sitting surfside at the bottoms of cliffs, and full-length trees sixty feet or more lying half-buried in the gravel where they washed ashore.

The mountain range in the distance seems to rise to greet our approach. This is no illusion. Starting just inland from the Gulf of Alaska, the Fairweather Range rises higher and faster than do mountains on any other shoreline on the face of the earth. With no warning at all, the land goes from sea level to the crest of the St. Elias/ Fairweather Range, with pinnacle peaks standing more than three miles high.

By comparison, the residents of Colorado are known to refer with some pride to the Rocky Mountains rising from the plains nearby. Although the Rockies do, indeed, stand 14,000 feet high, they rise a comparatively modest 9,000 feet from the mile-high plateaus upon which Denver sits. In contrast, Mount Fairweather stands like a massive sentinel beside the sea, rising 15,320 feet, and Mount St. Elias to the north of it soars 18,003 feet, with fellow mountain peaks poking up out of the spectacular glacial ice fields that surround them.

Coast Guard chopper pilots are occasionally called upon to fly into this uninhabited and inhospitable region. They use the glacial ice fields as flyways. Rising gradually as they go, the ice fields stretch away into the mountains, sweeping inland for scores of miles, eventually losing their way among the lonely, nameless crags and vast perennial snowpack that stretches out in all directions as it nears the unmarked border with Canada.

Zullick's flight along the coastline soon brings us to the stunningly beautiful glacial waters of Lituya Bay, which comes into view to the right of our aircraft. At the mouth of the bay, two sand spits trail out so far into the water that they nearly close it off. The bar conditions here, created when the outrushing tide stacks up against an incoming swell, have claimed many adventurous souls over the years.

Still, the place is captivating, if not enchanting. From the air, one can see a definite line where the clear green glacier water meets the dark blue of the sea. If the tide is right, you can peer down through the water and make out the ocean bottom several hundred feet below.

At the head of Lituya Bay, where the glaciers calve as often as they please, the air is so filled with light that the bergs themselves also appear to be almost translucent, inviting one to gaze right down into their blue pearlescence. The white radiance of the snow that still coats the top half of the mountain range directly above them is almost blinding to the eyes. Jutting out of the sea and soaring overhead, the mountains are so savagely wild and rugged in appearance, and so monstrously large relative to anything human, they feel threatening.

In sublime contrast, the glacier waters at the head of the bay are tranquil, and lie so still they create a kind of haunting perfection. The flat turquoise water floods the eyes with a visual feast of pure color.

And the line where the water touches the shore proceeds so evenly and unobtrusively that the brightly tinted water looks like some gigantic chunk of blue-green gemstone that has been cut whole and set neatly into place.

It was here, in the summer of 1958, in this impossibly beautiful setting, that one of the largest landslides (and accompanying waves) in the history of the world took place. Much like the displacement of Spirit Lake during the eruption of Mount Saint Helens, the effect on water and land, and on those unlucky enough to get caught in its path, was cataclysmic. The wave that ensued washed an adjacent point of land clean of both timber and earth, leaving only a bare rock stratum up to the seventeen-hundred-foot level.

At the time, the crews of three salmon trollers, which were resting quietly at anchor, were carried out across the bay by the unexpected wave. Carrying the remnants of broken trees, and clouded with the black soil it had consumed, the wave rolled out across the ten-mile length of the bay, picking up the fishing boats and tossing them about like toys caught in the whirlpool of a bathtub drain. While two of the vessels and their occupants were spared, the third boat was apparently pulverized when it was washed across what, only moments before, had been dry land. No trace of either the boat or her crew was ever found.

Withdrawing from the bay, Zullick points our H-60 north up the coast, resuming his mission. On his right, the jagged ridgeline of the St. Elias/Fairweather Range juts up into the sky like white rows of wolves' teeth. Several times during the years I crewed aboard fishing boats plying this stretch of coastline, I saw the setting sun drench these mountain peaks and glacial valleys with resplendent spectrums of crimson and pink.

Zullick has seen it, too. "At times like that," he says, "it literally looks like another planet."

Twenty miles farther up the coast, we come to Cape Fairweather itself. It takes just eight minutes for the H-60 to cover the distance. Yet, even on the most pleasant of trips, Zullick finds that, just to be safe, he must occasionally detour as far as a mile around cat's-paw winds or miniature williwaws he sees ruffling the surface. These pent-up bursts of invisible air stack up in the mountain passes and come rushing down their slopes at incredible speeds, tearing at the ocean surface and rending anything in their paths. At their worst, these unpredictable bursts of mountain-borne fury have been clocked in Alaska at no less than 150 miles per hour.

Directly offshore from here, fifty miles due west, lie the legendary waters of the Cape Fairweather Ground. Though often a land of beauty and wonder in summer, during the long, dark months of winter, this area becomes a no-man's-land of storm-driven winds, freezing spray, and ocean fury. Seventy-foot seas and sustained storm winds of 130 miles per hour are not at all that uncommon, says one longtime meteorologist.

Lloyd's, the high-risk insurance brokerage based in London, England, has reportedly had to pay out millions in claims when rogue waves washed dozens of storage containers the size of freight train boxcars off the stacked decks of seven-hundred-foot-long cargo freighters, creating havoc as high as eighty feet above the vessel's waterline.

Once, when a winter storm trapped several bush pilots in Lituya Bay, they staked their planes to the ground in an effort to ride it out. Even then, they reportedly still found it necessary to climb back inside and actually fly the planes to keep them from being blown away.

Now the mountains that have been paralleling us for more than sixty miles suddenly recede inland, and the land along the shoreline levels out into a wide, sprawling country as flat as a midwestern prairie. Here, Zullick drops down to an altitude of perhaps seventy-five feet and flies abreast of a gorgeous stretch of sandy beach, moving along the clean white line of unending surf. Just inland from the beach, a peninsula stacked high with storm-washed sand parallels the shore for miles, rerouting the entire Akwe River before allowing it to turn and flow into the sea.

As Zullick moves ahead, his eyes scan for any telltale signs of tire tracks, which might reveal where a poacher's plane has touched down, secretly carrying hunters inside Glacier Bay National Park (where hunting is strictly prohibited).

An avid outdoorsman himself, Zullick finds the urge to hunt here understandable, for a large population of moose live in the area. Zullick can locate the tall, long-nosed, silly-looking creatures at will, feeding across the valley floor.

Now a brown bear bolts suddenly up the beach, trying to outdistance the strange *pup-pup-pup* sound pursuing him. His path is almost identical to Zullick's, and as the helicopter closes on him, the fleeing creature splashes through the thin glaze of water at the mouth of a small stream, then continues on in his flight, revealing with each new stride a kind of explosive grace as waves of insulating fat roll violently along the length of his powerful, heaving body.

The sleek, dominating form of the H-60 sweeps past the bewildered beast like a Ferrari through a stop sign. For chopper pilots such as Russ Zullick, such sights are common. And he assures me that he has also seen wolves here a number of times, as well as deer and emperor geese and foxes. "God, it's heaven," he says. "And once in a great while we'll even catch sight of one of those rare silvertipped glacier bears."

Zullick's flight carries us over the gleaming waters of ironically named Dry Bay, and past other free-running rivers such as the Alsek, the Ustay, the Dangerous, and the Situk. Along with the Akwe, these rivers all drain into a massive and more or less continuous lowland marshland that is ten miles wide in most areas and more than fifty miles long. This lowland provides the sustenance for teeming, undisturbed populations of bear and moose, beaver and waterfowl.

Now, in late summer, the mouths of the rivers and streams are choked with spawning salmon waiting upon that mysterious internal signal to move upstream. Each time Zullick's chopper passes over, the salmon react to the moving shadow it casts as if some giant winged predator were sweeping down on them. They ripple the water as one body, exploding in a flurry of restlessness and panic. As one who has stood nearby when this has occurred, I can attest that the sound they make as they sprint away is a kind of hissing flutter as thousands of dorsal fins slice synchronously through the crystalline water.

Here lies a virtual wonderland of undisturbed wilderness. Lush green swamplands sprawl for miles, bordered by stands of weather-stunted spruce trees and interlaced with scores of rivers and streams, all creating an ecological macrocosm that remains unblemished by man. And this continues right up into Yakutat Bay, the waters of which border the tiny, ancient Tlingit village of Yakutat.

Flying upstream past the village, the final moments of Russ Zullick's guided tour carry us into Disenchantment Bay, where the Hubbard Glacier calves. It is here that one can occasionally catch a glimpse of the milky white, almost mythical-looking beluga whales that can, on occasion, be found grazing across its jewel green waters.

CHAPTER 6

"There are places here where no man in the history of the world has ever stepped," says Russ Zullick, safely on the ground once again, back in Sitka. "I love to get back off the beaten trail and go deer and goat hunting in the Annahootz Mountains. But the average citizen needs to realize that the terrain is so rough in this part of Alaska that if someone were injured and lying down unconscious and unable to draw attention to himself, he'd never be found. This is a rain forest. People forget that there is a thick canopy down there. I can't see through those trees."

Here in southeast Alaska, nature challenges all who infringe upon her. The land is extremely rugged in places, and often impassable; nature imposes certain brutal realities upon all who venture forth.

For much of the year, near-freezing winds and tidal currents cold enough to incapacitate a person in seconds are there to greet all varieties of mariners, fishermen, campers, and pilots. Many people, while plying the savage beauty of Alaska's wilderness, have come to know only too well the risks involved.

Here, life-and-death struggles occur with unsettling frequency. Those who ignore the canons of outdoor safety or who violate the unforgiving laws of nature do so at their own peril. As a result, even in these supposedly modern times, hypothermia remains the leading cause of accidental death in the state of Alaska.

Through the years, more than a fair number of anecdotal life-and-death struggles have taken place in southeast Alaska; like the time, on what began as a pleasant outing on a sunny morning, Gearhart Hiller motored down the length of Wrangell Narrows and out into Sumner Straits in his small outboard-driven canoe. He did not notice the trail of seawater leaking in until too late. When ensuing waves completed the swamping, Hiller was left under darkening skies to drift through the chilling currents and cling, as best he could, to the side of the wave-washed canoe.

There was no reason at all for Richard and Sharon Sprague to be motoring along that particular section of the coastline area. As a practicing dentist from Petersburg, Richard often commuted by boat with his wife to provide dental services to those in need in several of the local Native American villages. Earlier that day, after he'd finished caring for his patients in the Tlingit fishing village of Kake, he and his wife had decided to take an alternate route back to Petersburg. Only providence, they will tell you, could have orchestrated such a coincidental encounter.

By the time they came upon Hiller, and pulled him aboard their sixteen-foot Boston Whaler boat, he had slipped so far into the late stages of hypothermia that he was not only unable to speak, he could barely move; his stiff, cold body mimicked the advance of rigor mortis.

Then there was the time, in that same area, when a man in a skiff found himself dead in the water and being carried out of Wrangell Narrows. Using his head, he managed to help his girlfriend to safety on a channel buoy before being swept away into the night by the fierce rushing tides there, never to be seen again.

There is the tale of the commercial fisherman from Sitka who got caught without a survival suit in a sinking skiff while trying to cross open water near Haines. The story one Coast Guardsman told me was that the fisherman clasped his arms around the nearest buoy with such resolve that, although nearly unconscious from the cold by the time his rescuers finally reached him, they were hardly able to pry his fingers apart.

And there is the story of the teenage girl whose boat sank not far from Sitka. When her male companion drowned during the long swim through the icy waters to a nearby island, she was left to fend for herself. She survived without food or shelter or any way to build a fire. Ten days passed before disbelieving searchers discovered her—gaunt and emaciated, but nevertheless alive.

Though I was never able to substantiate it, I was told of a hunter who shot a deer and ended up spending several nights and the accompanying days stranded on the side of a cliff on a mountainside not far from Wrangell. By skinning the animal and using its pelt as an additional protective garment, the crafty hunter was able to endure forty-mile-per-hour winds and avoid the flesh-numbing inundations of pelting rain. And, I was told, he coolly conserved enough bullets so that when searchers finally did draw near enough, he was able to call attention to himself.

Some years ago, Petersburg's own Nancy Zoic found herself on a sinking seine boat near Glacier Bay. Her heroic boyfriend insisted that she don the vessel's only survival suit. As a result, she was the only one in the crew to make it to a nearby island alive. Then she spent ten days and nights huddling in the November cold before a U.S. Coast Guardsman named Mark Hackett, riding shotgun aboard an H-3, spied a pair of orange crab buoys "walking up the beach," as he put it. Nancy Zoic had created something "bigger, brighter, and different," he recalls, and, as a result, she managed to draw attention to herself and was rescued.

One notable story involved a thirty-one-year-old super-athlete named Nick Frangos. He was considered the iron man of health and vigor, a cardiovascular wonder, the U.S. Coast Guard's athlete of the year in Alaska in 1989. Then one day, the dinghy he and fellow Coastie Norm Dornbirer were paddling flipped over near Juneau, a short distance offshore, and both men promptly drowned. Soon thereafter, the Coast Guard initiated a survival training course for all Coasties who work aboard boats plying Alaska's waters.

Survival expert Dug Jenson is one of several instructors in the Sitka area who teach these classes. He commonly refers to the same flesh-numbing waters that struck down these two fit and popular young men as "Kryptonite." Today, all Coast Guardsmen who come to Alaska aboard either a cutter or buoy tender are required to take the course. Completing it is a notable accomplishment, and carries with it certain bragging rights.

"It's like serious boot camp," says Jenson. "There's anxiety there, as well there should be. It's the hardest thing most of them say they have ever done in their lives."

On the first day of his weeklong class, Jenson generally begins by asking one simple question. "Has anyone here ever lived in a rain forest on an island? No one ever raises their hand," he says. "Yet they are all sitting on Baranof Island in the middle of the southeastern Alaska rain forest."

If not prepared, airplane crash victims and ship castaways alike quickly find that the high-tech safety bubble in which they've always existed is suddenly gone. For some, it is too much. In a real emergency, those who panic usually die.

Jenson teaches that human beings are physically best suited for the balmy waters of the Caribbean. When caught in the Alaskan wilds, they need to know how to improvise and prioritize and govern their decisions using the "survival rules of three," says Jenson. "A human being can live for three minutes without air, three hours without shelter, three days without water, and three weeks without food."

The Coast Guard personnel he trains in advanced survival techniques are not coddled. Jenson is aware that, although these people have received a good deal of training regarding surviving in water, they have had virtually no training having to do with surviving in the mountains. Once they've grasped the fundamentals, they're dropped off together by an H-60 helicopter out on Kruzof Island. Then they begin hiking up the seven-mile-long trail that winds its way up the backside of Mount Edgecumbe.

Eventually, Jenson leads the men away from the main trail and out into the stunted, weather-tortured trees on the backside of the mountain. Near the top, he deliberately disorients them. Then he disappears into the brush, returning, in due time, to keep tabs on them from afar. Participants are left for several days to sleep in a shelter built with their own hands. In their semihypothermic state, they must scrounge for food and materials as best they can. Not until the third day are they allowed to build a fire. Trainees are taught that it is not necessary to have a fire to survive. "Is it nice? Yes," teaches Jenson. "Is it required? No." The Eskimo get along quite nicely without them.

During these outings, Jenson has seen grown men crack. As a backup, he carries along a handheld radio.

"Improvising is the key," he says. "The folks that do come back don't think like a one-bladed knife, but, rather, like one of those Swiss knives with all the many blades. You've got to get in there and tweak it and change things to your advantage." People who do nothing are people in denial. If their behavior is left unchallenged, they will often stand back and watch themselves die.

Flexibility in one's thinking is essential. "If you think brittle, you'll break," he says. "Wise men learn from their own mistakes. Wiser men yet learn from the mistakes of others." A garbage bag, a handheld radio, and a week of learning and preparation in a survival training class can make all the difference.

CHAPTER 7

In 1986, during the turbulent month of December, a local man named Jim Blades and his six-year-old son, Clint, both close friends of Dug Jenson's today, became key players in a desperate encounter while fishing commercially out on Sitka Sound. This tale of fatherly love and Coast Guard heroics has taken on a kind of legendary status over the years.

In 1982, Jim Blades, who had been felling timber in Wyoming, decided to quit his job and set out for Alaska. The early 1980s were special times in the Big Bear State. If an able-bodied man stepped off the ferryboat just into port from Seattle, people were literally waiting there to hire him. They were, in fact, quite desperate to find laborers. Some employers even went as far as walking back and forth along the rows of seats in Ketchikan's movie theater, soliciting help.

Blades found work near Whale Pass, in a logging camp run and owned by a man named Gildersleeve, one of the last of the staunch, never-give-an-inch independents. Some of the old-growth trees they felled were nine feet thick at the stump.

As it turned out, Jim Blades was handy, the kind of man Alaska has always welcomed. Master of but a few trades, he nevertheless possessed a sound working knowledge of many. By laboring side by side with people who knew their crafts, he had become an accomplished stonemason. He had acquired a solid understanding of the principles of both plumbing and electrical wiring, and he knew how to pour concrete, frame and roof a house, and put up Sheetrock. He could fell timber, drive heavy equipment, and repair the machines he ran, as well.

Since Alaskan residents are allowed the right to salvage ten thousand board feet of free timber per person each year (more than enough to build an ordinary house, and have firewood galore), Jim Blades would eventually construct a sawmill and cut his own lumber, all he might need.

During those robust days, Blades often found each year at tax preparation time that he'd accumulated as many as fourteen W-2 forms during the previous twelve months.

It was during a trip back home to Wyoming that Jim Blades met and proposed to his future wife, Jill. Giving her a hard time, he told the ebony-haired, God-fearing young woman that she had good teeth and that she would be quite useful at softening the hides of any animals he might trap. Three months later, they were married in the First Baptist Church of Pinedale, seventy miles south of Jackson Hole.

Jim Blades didn't want his wife to be disappointed when she got to Alaska, so he billed the place as one where there was much hardship, bad weather, and privation. He made it clear that there weren't any igloos where they were going, and that it rained all the time—the only difference in the seasons being the temperature of the rain.

When Jill finally arrived in southeast Alaska, Jim was pleased to find that she liked it. During their first few years together, they lived on False Island up in Peril Strait, some fifty miles from Sitka. With an abundant supply of halibut, salmon, codfish, and trout close by, and with game laws allowing the harvesting of six deer per person per year, there was never any shortage of either fish or venison in the Blades's home.

While Jim hunted for Sitka deer, trapped for martin, or fished for salmon and halibut, Jill lived the life of a self-sufficient frontier woman. She eventually gave birth to two boys, Clint and Curt. During the tiring, but contented, years that followed, she home-schooled her kids. Raising them in a place surrounded by a burgeoning population of free-roaming brown bears, she always kept a loaded rifle close at hand.

They had the entire island to themselves. And with bald eagles nesting nearby and killer whales and sea lions cruising past, it proved to be an idyllic beginning to a devoted partnership and a successful marriage. From the living room of their floating home, they could watch brown bears feeding on the roots of the swamp grass at the head of the bay. One morning, the Blades awoke to find five land otters playing on their front deck. For several hours, the whole family watched the otters preening one another's fur in the morning sun. Several dove off the deck, caught fish, dragged them back to the deck and ate them. Others took turns peering through the bottom of the sliding glass door at the strange human creatures inside the house.

Given how idyllic their life was, Jim Blades would shrug off questions when pressed as to why someone would choose to home-school their little ones forty miles from town, in a place with almost no radio contact, no neighbors, and no emergency medical care. "Oh, we were young," he says. "We didn't worry about that stuff."

The raft supporting their home was a rectangular creation of lumber twenty-five feet wide and forty feet long, composed of logs bound together with cable. Also perched on the raft and tied securely in place were a little shop, a sauna that ran off of freshwater piped down from a nearby creek, and a generator shed. Jim Blades built them all on skids (timbers with tapered ends), the house included, so that if he desired, he could drag them off the raft and ashore anywhere the landscape permitted.

Jim's boat, the F/V *Bluebird*, was only twenty-six feet long—small by commercial salmon-trolling standards—but it had a deep draft and, when under way, drew close to four feet of water. Eventually, when the family did decide to move in closer to town, they tied their home to the stern of the *Bluebird* and towed it along behind them as they made their way through Peril Strait.

Ten miles from Sitka, five miles from the nearest road, they discovered a quiet cove shrouded in old-growth timber that pushed right down to the uppermost edge of the high-water line. It offered near-total protection from the notorious southeast winds that often strike the region.

Checking further, they found that the pristine anchorage had fresh running water, plenty of game, and a deep channel that allowed passage during even the most severe tidal fluctuations. And they could soak in the warmth of the sun during its rare appearances and gaze upon the famous Alaskan sunsets to the west. So they dropped anchor in the heavily forested arm of that wild and solitary bay and, once again, set out to make it home.

During the summer months, Jim Blades made a good living trolling commercially from the *Bluebird* for both king and coho salmon. During the rest of the year, whenever the weather permitted, he long-lined for bottom-feeders offshore, specifically codfish and red snapper.

The boat's trolling poles were twenty-five feet long and made of spruce wood. When the boat was under way, the poles were stored upright, tucked in tightly against the wheelhouse. When fishing, Jim lowered the poles, secured them, and extended them out on either side of the *Bluebird* at a forty-five-degree angle, providing stability to the small vessel, in much the same way a balancing pole aids a gymnast during a tightrope walk. Over the years, Blades had become so sensitive to the feel of his boat that, while trolling, he could often determine the weight of the salmon striking the lure by the trembling transmitted to the hull through the poles.

Jim Blades often took his son Clint on fishing excursions. Though only six years old at the time, the youngster could already be counted on to contribute to the work effort in a meaningful way.

Just before Christmas, while fishing for codfish near Cape Edgecumbe on the far edge of Sitka Sound, only a dozen or so wilderness miles from home, Blades and his son encountered the exceptional.

From the outset, the fishing that day had been excellent, and Clint and his father were quickly caught up in the excitement and steady action of pulling fish after fish aboard. They hooked, landed, cleaned, and iced some six hundred pounds of ling cod. At a $1.70 a pound, Blades would pocket about $1,000 for the day's work. With

Christmas only two weeks away, such a profit would be a welcome boon.

It was only 3:00 P.M. when another long December's night in the far north fell upon them. The advancing darkness and the lucrative day of fishing set Jim Blades to figuring. I should run back in now, he thought. It was a judgment call, but with two intimidating reefs, Low Island and Vitskari Rocks, lying between him and home, he hesitated.

Smooth swells twenty to thirty feet high had been rolling through the area all day, but with no wave tops capping them, riding over them had been no problem.

Fatigued as he was, and with no working radar on board, he decided not to attempt the two-hour run back into town. He and Clint would catch up on their sleep and pick up where they'd left off on the fine fishing first thing the next morning.

I'll just ride it out here in the lee of St. Lazaria Island tonight, he decided finally.

Jim Blades radioed his wife and told her of his decision. He might have trouble with his anchor dragging on the rock bottom there, but he wanted to sit out the night behind St. Lazaria Island anyway and wait for dawn.

Jill wasn't exactly crazy about the idea but said she would leave the final decision in the matter to her husband.

"Okay, then, take care," she radioed. "Love ya! Talk to you in the morning," she added, signing off.

Jill switched off the radio, shut off the lights, and climbed up into the loft of their one-room A-frame cabin. Then, as her three-year-old son, Curt, quietly crayoned in his picture book on the bed beside her, she sat and read.

"Daddy will be home in the morning," she told him.

B lades would have been hard-pressed to pick a more picturesque spot. Located on the farthest edge of Sitka Sound, St. Lazaria Island is a bird sanctuary, the breeding ground of literally millions of seabirds and a National Wildlife Refuge since 1909. The protected anchorage behind it is a favorite of local fishermen.

As he dropped anchor in the lee of the island, countless gulls and murres and comical-looking tufted puffins looped noisily out from their cliffside dwellings before returning again to their precarious perches. St. Lazaria is only a few miles from Cape Edgecumbe and the Fuji-like form of Mount Edgecumbe rising up on the island of Kruzof.

Generally, Blades knew, there were telltale signs that warned a fisherman of an approaching storm as much as a day in advance. Usually, he would detect some cat's-paws, the strange moving islands of rippling water where gusts of wind touch down as if pawing at the ocean's surface. Under such circumstances, one might expect a storm by the following morning.

On this night, however, there was little evidence of approaching danger. It looked to be a decent night to lay up and ride it out. But several hours later, sudden thirty-mile-per-hour gusts of wind arrived without so much as a hint of warning. They, in turn, were followed by punishing gusts of thirty-five and then forty miles per hour. Within minutes, a blast of wind approaching seventy miles per hour came hurtling around the island's granite cliffs, roaring through the spruce trees and imprinting the water before whistling off through the *Bluebird*'s rigging.

As the seas rose into breakers, the *Bluebird* began to shift restlessly at anchor. Jim Blades found himself surrounded by the close yellow glow of the ship's cabin light; beyond that lay a larger theater, a seamless curtain of impenetrable darkness.

Now the swirling wind began making bizarre course changes. Blinding volleys of jetting snow shot past them. Jim knew then that he'd been caught out in the open by an intense little storm cell, the type Alaskan meteorologists often refer to as "bombs."

This doesn't look good, he thought as the abrupt rock formations of St. Lazaria Island rose and fell before him. Then Blades turned to his son. "Clint, go put on your survival suit," he said.

Working the hydraulics from inside the *Bluebird*, he winched his anchor back aboard and got under way. He wanted to escape the gnarly breakers now surging up and down on the cliffs before him. Following his compass, he idled slowly past the cliffs and through the slapping seas in the lee of the island.

As the storm intensified, the craggy rock shoreline of the island in front of him disappeared altogether in the blinding blizzard. Amid the disorienting flurries, Jim Blades tried to calculate where the protruding rocks had been and to navigate accordingly.

Caught in outside waters, without radar, running in the blind, Jim Blades fixed his eyes on the only dependable navigation device he had left—the little red compass light mounted on the panel in front of him.

He was feathering the throttle, trying to maintain his course, going the way that he thought he should be going, when the pitching *Bluebird* crunched down on a pinnacle of rock. The pointed crown of the Volkswagen-sized boulder pierced the wooden hull of the boat. Then came the echoing crunch of wood rending, much like the sound of a sledgehammer striking a watermelon. Blades threw her into reverse and floored it. Pivoting, he bolted anew. Seconds later, seeking his escape through the vision-obliterating snow squall in the opposite direction, his beloved *Bluebird* plowed bow-first into the cliff face of St. Lazaria Island. Bringing the boat around once more, Blades once again reversed his course. He was now certain that he knew the way out. As he motored ahead, waves exploded against the cliffs on one side and roared in among upright pillars of rock on the other. Passing nervously by the rock upon which his boat had previously been impaled, Blades slipped gladly into deeper waters.

With the destructive sounds of the impact still echoing in his ears, Jim Blades didn't even bother going below for a closer inspection. He knew that the ship was sinking and that they had very little time. As if to reaffirm this belief, the automobile horn that he'd cleverly rigged to his bilge alarm sounded. He grabbed the wire and tore it free, silencing the blaring noise. Then he grabbed his radio mike and called for assistance.

"Mayday! Mayday!" he called. "This is the fishing vessel *Bluebird*! The fishing vessel *Bluebird*! Mayday! Mayday! Mayday!"

"Fishing vessel *Bluebird*, this is the U.S. Coast Guard, Sitka," came the quick reply. "Sir, please give us your name, your location, and the condition of your vessel."

"Sitka Coast Guard, this is the fishing vessel *Bluebird*," he replied. "My name is Jim Blades, and you had better send someone out to get us, because I'm sinking fast here off St. Lazaria Island. I hit a rock pretty hard. I've got my six-year-old boy on board with me here. I don't know how long we'll be able to remain afloat. Over."

As the Coast Guard gathered information and rushed to prepare for the mission ahead, an anonymous voice of a fellow fisherman sounded over Jim Blades's CB radio.

"Hang in there, Jim!" encouraged the voice. "You're going to be all right. Just keep jockeying."

Blades found comfort in those words.

To rescue swimmer Jeff Tunks, on duty at the USCG base in Sitka at the time, the Mayday sounded urgent. The situation was obviously critical. Pilot John Whiddon informed Tunks that they would debrief while en route to the scene.

With thirteen years of aviator experience under his belt, Cmdr. John Whiddon would do the flying, while Lt. Greg Breithaupt would ride shotgun as his copilot. Tunks would go as the mission's rescue swimmer. Carl Saylor would run the hoist, and Mark Mylne would ride along as their avionics man.

It took Tunks and his crewmates just eighteen minutes to roll out the H-3 helo, fuel it up, load it up, and prepare for liftoff.

The model HH-3F "Pelican" helicopter (or just H-3, as most Coasties refer to it) is a large, powerful, and very dependable workhorse of an aircraft. It has two jet engines and a semiamphibious hull that can be used to land on water to facilitate a rescue, so long as the weather and conditions are relatively calm. If the rotor blades plow into a wave in heavy seas, however, the aircraft will flip over and fill with water as quickly as a capsized canoe.

That night, it was raining furiously outside. A building wind blowing in off the sound was driving the inch-an-hour rainfall horizontally.

Sheets of it were inundating the area, tumbling across the airfield's apron and out across the ramp.

While the helicopter's jet engines were warming up, and before her main rotor blades were engaged, Tunks sat in the rear cabin, looking out through the side door of the H-3. From there, he could see the long rotor blades extending out from directly overhead. Now, in the gusting winds, the long, flat blades began leaping up and down like diving boards bouncing in the wind.

The blades of the helicopter had only just begun to turn, when a gust of wind rolled in off Sitka Sound, pounding against the metal sides of the hangar nearby and scooting the eleven-ton helicopter several yards across the runway.

"We've got a boat sinking off St. Lazaria Island," said Commander Whiddon, climbing into the pilot's seat and strapping himself in. "We're going to go out and see how we can help."

Sitka Sound in winter, Tunks knew, is a brutal place. The seas are often short, choppy, and unforgiving. Should a mechanical failure force them down on this night, there would be no backup. Of the three choppers stationed at the Sitka base, one was currently down for repairs, and another was on patrol well north of them, outside of Cordova. Only theirs remained.

They had hardly risen clear of the circular helicopter pad when their loran-C computer shut down. Whiddon rose to the standard altitude of three hundred feet, where, in the cooler atmosphere, he encountered a wall of swirling snow. He found it both disorienting and hypnotizing, and, ultimately, blinding. Nevertheless, Whiddon continued on, closing determinedly on their destination. As he did so, he encountered fierce storm winds tearing around Cape Edgecumbe and accelerating down off the steep slopes of Mount Edgecumbe itself. They were closing on St. Lazaria Island when they were beseiged by the battering ninety-mile-per-hour gusts.

Under favorable conditions, a pilot might hover within fifty feet or so of the ocean's surface and those he hoped to rescue. But on this night, at an altitude of seventy-five feet, Whiddon found that he was being pelted not only with blowing snow but freezing sea spray, as well.

Shortly, the face of the radar screen outside became so coated in ice, it ceased functioning altogether. Worse yet, the gale-force winds were driving into them with such velocity, and in such irregular bursts, Whiddon knew it would be impossible to maintain anything like a stationary hover. With his navigational equipment now dead and only his altimeter and horizon-leveler instruments to guide him, Whiddon flew on.

"*Bluebird!*" radioed John Whiddon as his eyes searched the inky void all around. "This is Coast Guard rescue helicopter one four eight six. Do you read me?"

"Yes, I hear you," replied Jim Blades.

"*Bluebird,* I need you to key your mike and count backward for me from ten to one. And keep counting. As you do, we'll try to track you down using our DF [direction finding] equipment. Over."

"Roger that," said Blades. "Ten, nine, eight, seven, six, five, four . . ."

Glancing outside, Blades noticed seawater creeping up his back deck. This is not looking good, he thought.

"Well, guys—we're here. Where you at?" Blades radioed finally.

"We're doing our best to find you," replied John Whiddon.

"Give me another DF count," Whiddon radioed.

Whiddon could tell by the interference—the amount of static caused by the surprising power of the storm cell—whether they were gaining or losing ground.

At first he sounded close, then he seemed to fade away.

CHAPTER 8

J im Blades knew that his always-dependable *Bluebird* was sinking. Dying partnership or not, he hated the idea of going back inside the ship's cabin, each time, to answer the radio; like any fisherman, he abhorred the idea of getting entombed inside the sinking hull.

Wind-whipped flurries of cascading snow were tumbling unabated out of the coal black night when Blades opened the back door and shined his handheld spotlight downwind of the boat.

"Do you see that?" he radioed Whiddon. "Do you see my light?"

With their visibility limited to just a few hundred feet, none of the searching eyes on board the helicopter could see a thing. Then Carl Saylor spotted a tiny glint of light shining through the swirling snowfall off to their right. But as he watched, it soon disappeared. Jim Blades's spotlight had shown itself as the foundering *Bluebird* crested over a wave, but the seas were so large that each time it did, the F/V *Bluebird* would disappear entirely into the yawning pit of the wave troughs, taking the light with it.

"Pilot, this is the flight mech. I think I see a flashing light," radioed Saylor.

"I don't see it yet," shot back Whiddon. "Give me a heading."

80 \ *Spike Walker*

As they drew closer, copilot Greg Breithaupt spotted it, too.

"We've spotted you, *Bluebird*!" said copilot Greg Breithaupt. "Yes, we see you!" He paused. "We'll be on scene in two minutes!"

Using full power, Whiddon motored upwind toward the foundering vessel. Drawing nearer, he could see that she was riding low in the stern, with wave after wave pummeling her. The *Bluebird* was pitching wildly as she drifted up and over the long-rising swells. With her bow banked at a forty-five-degree angle and her stern constantly awash, Whiddon could see a man and a small child in orange survival suits snuggled in close to each other, clinging tenaciously to the back of the wheelhouse.

From the chopper's side door overhead, rescue swimmer Jeff Tunks could see that Jim and Clint Blades and their beloved *Bluebird* were getting the "hell beat out of them," as he put it. The fishing boat looked minuscule amid the burly storm waves lifting and tossing her. The waves themselves were covered with gray-white streaks of windblown foam, stretching in thin layers across the slate black surface. Yet wherever the chopper's floodlight touched down on the otherwise black face of the surrounding sea, it illuminated the world below in a brilliant circular swath of color and life—the green of the water glowing with an almost phosphorescent intensity.

Tunks could feel Whiddon fighting to maintain an even flight plain. Lowering the rescue basket from their wind-jousted helicopter onto the tiny gyrating rectangle of the *Bluebird's* back deck looked impossible.

The gusts were williwaw blasts of cold mountain air roaring down off the slopes of Mount Edgecumbe. Cooled well below freezing by the altitude, gathering tremendous energy and speed as they descended, the accelerating winds struck the helicopter and shook it to its rivets. At one point, the H-3 helicopter dipped so low that it nearly impaled itself on the twenty-five-foot-high cedar trolling poles that rose up on either side of the wheelhouse.

Whiddon, Tunks could tell, kept putting forward and up control commands into the flight stick, but the helo kept sliding back and down. Tipping as far as twenty degrees from side to side, they were often forced to hold on, as if riding a bucking bronco.

Then an exceptionally powerful gust of wind, well in excess of 110 miles per hour, struck the helicopter, driving them back. Whiddon fought to bring the nose down and regain control, using all the power the aircraft possessed.

"You're backing down!" shouted Carl Saylor.

As they plummeted toward the water, Whiddon and Breithaupt glanced over at each other, exchanging a look that said, This is it! Whiddon was certain that they were about to crash. It was one of those instinctive feelings. They were going in.

Yet John Whiddon felt too caught up in his duties to be scared. Oddly, a sense of peace and calm settled over him, and the message he internalized was one of acceptance, one that said, This is just the way it is.

Whiddon had three boys and a loving wife, to whom he was devoted, waiting at home just across the bay. They were all safely ashore now—a world apart. Then his mind seized upon the memory of his good friend and flying partner Pat Rivas. Pat was a superb pilot and a wonderful human being. Back in the early 1980s, they had flown alongside each other on a number of missions in Alaska. And they had made a difference. Their most notable effort was being part of the largest medivac operation in U.S. Coast Guard history. Working with their airborne comrades, they employed a relay system and were able to pluck more than five hundred survivors off the cruise ship M/V *Prinsendam* when it caught fire and began sinking far out in the Gulf of Alaska. Just ten months later, Pat Rivas and his entire crew were killed in that infamous crash in Prince William Sound, when their tail rotor chipped a wave, toppling them from the sky.

So this is how it all ended for Pat, thought Whiddon as he, his crew, and the weather-beaten helicopter carrying them careened out of control.

Both Whiddon and Breithaupt were yanking up, pulling "full-collective," on the horizontal arms mounted on the sides of their seats.

Waiting for the H-3 to respond was a painfully slow process. They were just fifteen feet from striking the water itself when the wind gust released them.

Heart in throat, Whiddon turned to Breithaupt. "Boy, let's never do *that* again," he said, forcing out a chuckle.

For the rest of the crew, Whiddon's comment proved to be an aptly timed tension breaker.

"Let's get back up there and get these guys," he told them.

"Damn straight!" replied Jeff Tunks from the rear cabin.

Now Whiddon found that he nearly had to max out the engine to move ahead at all. Slowly, however, flying into winds that fluctuated between 90 and 115 miles per hour, he inched the helicopter forward.

Hoist operator Carl Saylor worked to conn Whiddon back over the the sinking *Bluebird*. "Forward and right three hundred," he said. "Forward and right two hundred. Forward and right one hundred. Hold."

The floodlight shining down on the *Bluebird* created an amphitheater effect. The boat was taking on water and riding ever lower; then, as Jeff Tunks watched, a storm wave broke against the boat, sending up an almost dazzling light-filled spray over the *Bluebird*'s entire length.

Jim Blades hurried back inside and grabbed his mike. "How do you want to do this?" he radioed.

"Sir," replied Breithaupt, "the only way we're going to be able to execute this SAR operation is if you get your son and get off the boat."

To Tunks, Jim Blades's voice sounded so concerned with saving his son's life that he was sure the man would have gladly eaten a bucket of nails if that would have helped.

"Okay," said Blades.

"Hang on, Clint," Jim Blades told his son. "We're going to have to get in the water now."

The elder Blades found that he couldn't get the zipper on his survival suit to work properly. Some months before, he'd broken that very zipper and had gone to great effort to have it replaced. The person who had repaired it, however, had failed to put back the two-inch whistle that had always served as a handle and was normally attached to the tiny metal zipper flap itself. Now, wearing the the suit's clumsy two-fingered Gumby gloves, Blades found that despite all his efforts to prepare for just such an emergency, he was unable to pull the zipper the entire way up and lock it into the all-essential position directly beneath his chin.

As Jeff Tunks watched from the side door of the helicopter above, Jim Blades gathered up his son and walked out onto the pitching back deck of his boat. Clipping his son's suit harness to his own, he then stepped off the vessel's stern and into the tossing sea.

Their predicament, Tunks could readily see, soon went from bad to worse. For although Jim Blades and his son had dutifully abandoned ship, the prevailing winds quickly blew them in against the hull of the *Bluebird,* pinning them there.

After a half-dozen more attempts, Whiddon became convinced that the plan to basket-hoist the pair from the water unassisted would not work. When their efforts to lower the basket failed once more, Whiddon turned to rescue swimmer Jeff Tunks, who was seated behind him in the rear cabin.

"Jeff, we're not going to be able to complete this rescue without you. Do you want to give it a go?"

"Yes, sir. I'll give it a try," replied Tunks without hesitation.

"Do you think that you can get them?"

"Yah, I think I can. Let's give it a shot."

"Okay, then, Jeff, why don't you go ahead and get ready."

Hardly a year old at the time, the Coast Guard's rescue-swimmer program was still in its infancy. A swimmer wore the basics: two fins, a mask, a snorkel, a wet suit, a harness, and a knife.

Tunks was still prepping for the into-the-water deployment at hand when the F/V *Bluebird*'s bow rose sharply into the air and slipped stern-first into the waiting sea. With little Clint Blades still riding on his chest, Jim Blades lay on his back and stroked urgently away from the boat and any possible entanglements.

Jeff Tunks followed the lights of the ship's cabin as it descended perhaps twenty, even thirty feet below the surface. It was, Tunks said, "Just blazing all the way down." Tunks found it quite dramatic, even touching, to see the Bladeses' entire living and everything they were about sink out from under them.

Little Clint Blades had said nothing as his father carried him down the sloping deck and stepped off into the water. Clint's suit had arms but only a single mummylike compartment for his legs. He was lying on his back on top of his dad's chest, sea-otter-style, when the first breaking wave rolled in over them.

"Clint, keep your mouth closed and hold your breath!" Jim Blades yelled to his son. "Hold your breath until the wave passes!"

Then everything went black. Jim Blades felt the cold wash of the wave water stinging his face, and the invisible currents pulling at them. As they tumbled through the surging space, the elder Blades was certain that had he not strapped his son Clint to himself, he would surely have lost him.

Back on the surface again, Blades could feel the chilling sea water flooding in through the neck opening of his suit. He was quite aware of the advancing stages of hypothermia and the paralyzing immobility that ultimately accompanies it. Though he would not go down without a fight, Blades was certain that he had a limited amount of time. If the rescue team didn't get to them quickly, he'd soon be dead, and his son Clint would drown, too, strapped to him as he was.

Then, as he waited, he glanced to one side and caught sight of his boat careening down the face of a wave, white smoke trailing from her stack.

Jim Blades could already feel the cold robbing him of his strength and his ability to resist. He studied the chopper struggling overhead and soon realized that the erratic and unpredictable winds were making rescue virtually impossible. "God," he prayed, "could you please slow the winds down just a little. We're in a real jam here. I don't believe my son and I are going to survive this without your help."

CHAPTER 9

After a quick but precise final run-through of the rescue swimmers' checklist, flight mechanic Carl Saylor signaled Tunks forward. Tunks took a seat in the doorway and snapped on his gunner's belt (safety strap) to keep him from tumbling out. Then he slid the four-inch-wide, four-foot-long loop strap down over his head, shoulders, and arms. Theoretically, the strap would allow Tunks to extend his arms overhead and slip free of it whenever he chose. He then pulled his mask snugly into place and bit down on his snorkel's mouthpiece. With finned feet dangling out into space, he gathered himself for what looked to be a wild descent.

Barely three years prior to this, on a bitter cold night, during a driving winter storm off Cape Hatteras, North Carolina, thirty-six crew members were left to survive as best they could in the icy seas after being forced to abandon the sinking freighter *Marine Electric*.

When the pilot of an H-3 Pelican finally located them, he found the waves too high to attempt a landing on the water, and dozens of seamen scattered across the crowning seas. Though the flight mech was repeatedly able to place the rescue basket in close proximity to those struggling in the water, in the end, he and the others aboard the helicopter could only watch as, one by one, no less than thirty-three of the severely hypothermic survivors fell unconscious and died.

Ultimately, Alaska's own LCMD Kenneth Coffland (now retired) would play an instrumental role in helping wrestle something redeeming from the ruins of this tragedy and others. Subsequent hearings, investigations, and inquiries into this deadly incident explored the key shortcoming in the link between the Coast Guard crews in the air, and those imperiled souls in the water below.

As a result of the efforts of Coffland and many others, Jeff Tunks knew, just ten months before, the U.S. Coast Guard had gone "operational" with the rescue-swimmer program.

"Prepare to deploy the swimmer," ordered Whiddon.

"Okay, deploying the swimmer," replied Saylor.

Then came the token signal for which Jeff Tunks had so intensively trained—Carl Saylor's one tap on the chest. In response, Tunks released his gunner's belt and gave Saylor the standard response, a thumbs-up.

Jeff Tunks could feel the harness tighten under his arms as Saylor, working the hoist controls, lifted him into the air. As he swung out the door, Tunks heard the log-shredding power of the mammoth storm waves exploding along the shore of Kruzof Island, several thousand feet away.

"Swimmer going down," radioed Saylor.

"Swimmer going down," reiterated Whiddon.

Now Tunks took in the panoramic scene one hundred or so feet below him and saw precisely what he was "fixin' to get into."

He could see Jim and Clint almost directly beneath him, and he found himself thinking, This is going to be fairly simple. I'm going to disconnect, and then I'm going to gather them up and drag them to the basket and put them inside. Once they're safely aboard, they'll drop the basket back down to me and I'll crawl in myself, and we'll be out of here.

But in what seemed no more than a snap of a finger, Tunks found himself being dragged backward through the waves as another gust swept the chopper downwind. With so much tension suddenly seizing him under his arms, he quickly discovered that he had no way of releasing himself from the harness strap now holding him fast.

Whiddon gunned the engines, bringing the reverse odyssey to a halt, but not before dragging Tunks close to a hundred yards from the Bladeses. Finally able to slip free of the body strap, he free-fell into the sea, submerged briefly, then resurfaced and glanced quickly around. The Bladeses were nowhere in sight.

Above him, Tunks took in the "magnificent" vision of the H-3 aircraft "exuding power" and the large black USCG letters stenciled across the helo's white belly. He could see that, for all her power, the H-3 was being buffeted—its nose up, then down—and was shimmying from side to side, as if its 22,000-pound weight was inconsequential.

Tunks tried to call out to the Bladeses, wherever they were, hoping that in spite of the roar of the helicopter above and the breaking seas, they would hear him. Strangely, however, he couldn't make a sound. Tunks had never experienced anything like this. Perhaps it was the tremendous surge of adrenaline coursing through his system. Regardless, Tunks was forced to accept that he was unable to express so much as a "single blessed word."

Tunks performed a frantic 360-degree turn, searching for the man and his son, but it was pitch-black out, and the waves rolling through the area were so high that he was unable to visually hit upon them.

From the uncertain position of the helicopter overhead, it was clear to Whiddon that Tunks had become disoriented and that he no longer had any idea where the Bladeses were. Then Whiddon struck on an idea. He swung the searchlight away from Tunks and shone it down on the Bladeses.

Tunks took in the powerful column of the aircraft's floodlight as it swung to point somewhere in the distance. The shaft of light seemed to imply that Jim Blades and his son were several hundred feet away. Though Tunks could not see them, or communicate with Whiddon, he was certain that the end of that light was where he needed to be, and he began to move in that direction.

It was not a previously choreographed signal. "He didn't know to do that," John Whiddon later recalled. "It was one of the miraculous things that happened that night."

Moving along, his head completely above the water, Tunks used his arms only to steer him and his flipperlike fins into the oncoming storm waves. He swam up to the top of one wave and down to the bottom of the next. En route, he was roughed up severely when several of the waves broke over him. Peering intently as he passed over the top of one wave, he saw the searchlight beam bang off the reflective tape as the Bladeses simultaneously crested over a distant wave.

Feeling both grateful and relieved, Tunks urgently sprinted ahead in order to prevent any possibility of losing them again. When he finally closed on them, he swam up behind the drifting pair, grasped Jim Blades by the back of his suit, and swung him around. And suddenly he found himself staring into the youthful face of six-year-old Clint Blades. The boy possessed a serenity that Tunks had not expected, a kind of grace under pressure, which, given the present set of circumstances, seemed inexplicable.

Tunks would forever remember the moment. The boy seemed very peaceful. Tunks had a little boy, too, and he realized that he had to do everything that he could to get the boy and his father out of there.

"How are you doing?" shouted Tunks.

"We're hanging in there," Jim Blades replied, even though he was certain that he wouldn't be able to get into the basket under his own power. "Do you think they're going to be able to get us out of here?"

"Not to worry. We do this all the time," replied Jeff Tunks reassuringly, stretching the truth more than a little.

"Okay, now," explained Tunks. "We're going to get the basket over here, we're going to put you in the basket, we're going to hoist you up into the aircraft, and everything's going to be fine."

Several minutes later, the rescue basket landed in the water, well off from them. Immediately, Tunks grabbed the Bladeses and started dragging them toward it. They were closing fast on it, when the helicopter struggling to hover overhead was abruptly blown back off the site. The basket sprang from the water and shot into the sky like a missile being launched.

For the next few minutes, each time Tunks saw the basket land in the water in anything like a stationary position, he'd immediately start hustling toward it, towing the Bladeses along behind him.

Half a dozen similar attempts ensued before the gyrations of both basket and man finally coincided. Tunks could feel another sudden surge of adrenaline flooding his system. He grabbed Jim Blades by the back of his body harness, pulled the basket close with the other, and floated the Bladeses near. Then, just as he had been trained, he rolled them up and over his hip and set them down inside the basket in one seemingly effortless movement.

Tunks could see the hoist operator, Carl Saylor, crouched in the side doorway of the helo. He was waiting for Tunks to climb into the basket, as well. There was no room left, however, so Tunks pushed the basket away, lifted his right arm, and gave Saylor the thumbs-up sign.

Jim and Clint Blades sprang from the water as if weightless as Carl Saylor "two-blocked" the hoist, bringing the basket up at top speed. As they rose, the Bladeses began swinging violently below the chopper. Tunks could see how Commander Whiddon, climbing frantically in the H-3, was doing everything possible to make sure the precious cargo below cleared the wave tops. It turned out to be a beautiful hoist. Jim Blades and his son rose clear of the sea and ascended to the side door of the helicopter, untouched by further calamity.

As he watched them rise, Tunks was suddenly struck with a euphoric sense of accomplishment at having successfully completed one of the first high-seas rescue-swimmer operations in USCG history. "Yes!" he howled aloud.

And just as suddenly, he felt himself breaking free of the fears that had bound him. He had full confidence in his crewmates, and as Whiddon and his helicopter danced across the skies and Carl Saylor rushed to lower the basket to him again, Tunks experienced a resolute faith in the final outcome. They'll get me, he thought as he drifted alone over the pummeling seas and through the darkness. I'm going to be fine.

Inside the helicopter, Jim Blades still did not feel safe. The rattling, wind-battered machine that carried them felt no more substantial to him, he said, than "a bunch of spare parts all flying in formation." Furthermore, it was agonizing knowing that Jeff Tunks was still in the water and that they were having real trouble trying to fish him out.

As Tunks drifted in closer to the craggy, abrupt, sheer rock cliffs lining Kruzof Island, Whiddon flashed his floodlight along the shoreline. Even from the water, Tunks could see the ponderous storm waves gathering themselves in the shallows and crashing against the cliffs. He was certain that there was no way he could survive an attempt to reach shore through such a surf.

But Tunks also knew that with thirteen years of flying under his belt, Commander Whiddon was probably the finest stick-and-rudder pilot at the base in Sitka. With Lieutenant Breithaupt seated beside Whiddon as copilot, Tunks could not have imagined being caught in such a predicament with better people sitting up front. Nor could he think of more competent men than Carl Saylor on the hoist and Mark Milner on the radio.

After three or four more missed attempts to drop the rescue basket close to him, Jeff Tunks reached overhead and managed to snag it with an arm as it swung past. Sinking the basket with the weight of his body, he swam into it, wearing fins, snorkel, and all. He came to rest on his buttocks on the floor of the metal cage. Doubling over into a ball, he rose up only long enough to give Carl Saylor another thumbs-up before crouching back down again.

Abruptly, a gust of wind of a hundred miles per hour or better plowed into the hovering chopper and sent it reeling. Completely helpless to rise, barely able to keep the aircraft in the air, Whiddon struggled to regain a semblance of control.

In the mayhem that followed, the rescue basket was jerked from the water and launched into the sky like a recoiling paddle ball. With Jeff Tunks huddled down inside, the otherwise-hollow shell was jerked about on the end of the cable line like a knot on the end of a whiplash. Tunks was jerked around so violently that he nearly collided with the bottom of the helicopter itself.

As the accelerating chopper fled backward at more than sixty miles per hour, there was a "massive explosion" as the rescue basket collided with an oncoming wave. The water struck him from behind, knocking the wind from him and ripping both his mask and snorkel from his face. Tunks hadn't even seen it coming.

It was then that John Whiddon caught the unsettling vision of Jeff Tunks out his front window. His favorite rescue swimmer was being dragged along behind them. Both basket and man bounced across the water like a skipping rock, and wherever they touched down, white explosions of sea spray erupted.

Coming off the previous collision, Tunks and the basket would arch down and forward, flying through the broad wave troughs on the blunt end of a pendulum swing before hitting the crown of the next wave. Tunks plowed into three consecutive waves before Whiddon was able to instruct a climb. The third wave proved to be the culmination of his ride. Tunks hit so hard that Whiddon could actually feel the helicopter shudder.

"Oh my God! Did you see him hit that wave?" barked Carl Saylor.

I've killed him, thought Whiddon.

Jeff Tunks felt the basket start to capsize, so he clutched at the steel meshing of the floor to prevent himself from being tossed out.

"Bring him up!" screamed John Whiddon.

When Jeff Tunks was finally yanked aboard, he was choking on some saltwater he'd inadvertently inhaled.

"Swimmer's in the cabin, sir. Ready for forward flight," reported Saylor triumphantly.

Tunks crawled across the heaving floor and pulled himself up on to the troop seat. Then, looking over at Jim Blades and his son Clint, he once again gave the thumbs-up sign, which they returned.

"Jeff's all right," Carl Saylor told Whiddon. "He's swallowed a lot of water, and he's bruised, but otherwise, he's all right."

With the fishing boat *Bluebird* destroyed but her shivering survivors safely on board, Whiddon turned the H-3 toward home.

At the time Jim and Clint Blades were aboard the sinking *Bluebird,* Jill Blades and her son Kurt were talking quietly. Then a freakish blast of wind rocked the house. Jill could hear the cables tethering the house to the shore cinch up tight and groan under the strain as the house swung out across the water.

Jill hurried down out of the loft and threw open one of the portholes her husband had so cleverly built into the living room walls. The wind and rain were blowing straight into her face, driving against the outside walls, pelting the windows, and sending a stream of seawater up over the outside deck, under the front door, and across the cabin floor.

Oh my word, Jill thought. Jim's out in this?

She hurried over to the CB radio, switched it on, and tried to reach her husband, but to no avail. She was clicking through the channels when she caught the sound of her husband's voice on Channel 16. He was talking to a Coast Guard helicopter pilot. The rescue of both her husband and son, she quickly surmised, was already under way.

"Are you guys going to get here pretty soon?" she heard Jim ask the Coast Guard. "Cause my decks are awash."

Jill refused to panic. As the wife of a man who made his living on the sea, she was acutely aware of the inherent risks such a life involved. Besides, her husband was a strong, resourceful man who could fix or repair virtually anything. Turning to her son Kurt, she said, "Daddy's in trouble, honey. Got to start praying."

With her head bowed, she began. "Oh, Father God, I just ask that you be with them out there tonight. Protect my little boy. Protect my husband. And bring them back safely to me."

Then Jill Blades struck on an idea. Switching channels, she used the radio to call Laura and Ben Hubbard, members of her church, and they began a prayer chain that quickly branched out into the community of Sitka.

"Mom," said little Kurt, "when Dad and Clint get back, I'm never going to let 'em go out in a storm again."

Then Jill Blades caught the voice of the Coast Guard pilot on the radio. "Okay, we're coming up over the top of you," he said. Suddenly, all communications between the pilot and Jill's husband ceased. For the next twenty minutes, nothing more was heard from either of them.

Jill Blades had been all right up until that time. But now she felt fear beginning to well up. *The helicopter has either crashed or the boat sank, and Jim and Clint are gone,* she thought. *And they're not going to tell me, because they're afraid that I'll freak out, being out here all by myself.*

Then a friend, commercial fisherman Ottie Florschutz, radioed Jill, offering to take his fishing boat out to their houseboat and get her and her son Curt to town.

"Fishing vessel *Adeline* to *Bluebird*," he began. "Jill, do you want me to come out and pick you up?"

"No, Ottie," she replied. "I don't want anybody else out in this stuff. It's really howling out here. The only thing is—I just wish they'd tell me. If they're dead, I just want them to tell me that they're dead, so I know. I just gotta know what happened."

It was then that the voice of a member of the Coast Guard came over Channel 16.

"Mrs. Blades," the man said.

"Yes?" she replied.

"We got them."

"Thank God!" she yelled, loudly enough for all to hear.

"I didn't know if God was going to make me a widow," she later told me when I visited their island home in Sitka Sound. "I didn't know what was going to happen, because I know that some people don't come back."

Book II

Into the Storm

CHAPTER 1

For free-spirited young deckhands, trappers, gold miners, and footloose tramp-loggers following their star from one camp to another, as well as all those eccentrics who have followed their westering spirits about as far as the physical boundaries of the United States will allow, the panhandle of southeast Alaska, and Sitka in particular, may be as good a place as any to come to terms with the naïveté of that kind of individualism and the vast natural resources that are often required to sustain it.

Working in the invigorating sweep of Alaska's fishing grounds and forests, many of these hard-drinking rogues live on the fringes of society and have chosen to turn their backs on the state and federal politics that will inevitably govern their world. They view life with a kind of proud obstinacy, and as staunch individualists, they care not at all for most politicians and their endless strategies. These intractable characters look upon them more or less with contempt, regarding them, one fisherman told me, as "slightly above a child molester, and well below a horse thief."

Caught between the legal rulings handed down by these lawmakers, and the Coast Guard who must enforce them, fishermen continue to do what they have always done, and what many believe they were born to do—catch fish. For within the chest of a dyed-in-the-wool fin-chaser beats the heart of a hunter. Each day, they arise and begin their satisfying labors, all the while suffering hangovers and enduring liens imposed on them for back child support, and dodging the eviscerating pen of some meticulous IRS accountant, hoping it will all work out, willing to face whatever comes. They are the men and women who refuse to fit in.

Few individuals I have met fit this mold better than Mike DeCapua (pronounced "*Dee-cap-poo-uh*"), a local fisherman and the titanium-tough survivor of arguably the most harrowing high-seas helicopter rescue in the history of the U.S. Coast Guard. During the months of tracking down those involved in the deadly incident, chasing leads, making phone calls, and pounding the graveled streets of remote villages throughout southeast Alaska, I'd always hoped to run into Mike DeCapua.

For several months, during the heart of the severe winter of 1998–99, I lived in a remarkable southeastern village of three thousand people called Petersburg. Hiking into town through four-foot snowdrifts and along her freshly plowed streets, I'd often arrive before sunrise to have coffee with a group of local fishermen at the Homestead Cafe. Then I'd wander along Wrangell Narrows at the water's edge, where I'd often happen upon waterfowl feeding in the shallows, and bald eagles in the trees, and watch the tireless currents pushing hard against the red steel channel buoys. Once, I spied an iceberg as large as a dump truck drifting down the narrows, with an indifferent harbor seal perched contentedly upon its bright blue mass.

Eventually, I'd wander out into the fresh, clean air of the countryside into a winter wonderland of natural encounters. And I remember seeing snowflakes as big as silver dollars falling with an almost luminous effect against the dark green backdrop of the hemlock forest.

One day, after returning to my cabin, the home of Lynn Staake, a local gillnetter (who allowed me to house-sit for her while she bathed in the ninety-degree waters of some South Pacific lagoon), I checked the phone book, but I found no listing for DeCapua. The operator insisted that he did not exist.

It was in Sitka that I found him. Pack on my back, breathing deeply and inhaling the sweet-smelling aroma of the sea, I came upon Mike DeCapua one afternoon the following May down on one of the city's romantic waterfront docks, not far from the Totem Bar & Grill. Mike was standing on the back deck of the F/V *Judith* at the time, drunk on his feet, peeing prodigiously over the stern railing. I'd just begun to introduce myself, when he interrupted. "You're the guy who writes those books!" he yelled, obviously impressed, pointing at me with his free hand.

"And you're the man who survived the impossible," I replied.

Born in 1956, Mike DeCapua was raised in the state of Vermont. When he was five, his father took him to see the movie *Moby Dick*. To the spirited young boy, his father was a hero, a status not the least diminished by the fact that after the movie, he took Mike to see the F/V *Peaquad,* the actual vessel that they had used in making the film. Once on board, the young DeCapua raced from bow to stern, hungrily absorbing everything. Eventually, he made his way down into the crewmen's quarters, where he crawled into a bunk. It was July 19, 1961, Mike DeCapua's birthday. As young as he was, DeCapua secretly decided that one day, he, too, would live on a boat and kill fish in the sea.

Both of his parents have since died, but DeCapua remembers them as good folks, hardworking people who tried their best to bring him up correctly and give him a good life. Both parents were deaf-mutes. His father worked for twenty-nine years at the same job in a factory. As a machinist, he stood at a lathe machine all day. Though his father never complained, Mike DeCapua could see even as a youngster that he was not a happy man. He knew the dissatisfaction his father felt at being tied to that machine.

The elder DeCapua did his best by his wife and their five children. He became Mike's best friend. "We used to hang out together," says DeCapua. Regardless, Mike could feel his father's pain, and the thought of living the kind of life he had lived, the same old grind, terrified him.

Though his mother had learned to speak to some extent and could read lips, Mike's father communicated only through sign language. Using emphatic hand movements, his father would often tell him, "Michael, you're young. Go find something else to do with your life."

Perhaps taking what his father had told him too literally, Mike DeCapua ran away from home when he was just thirteen. He encountered a life on the road that varied between the bizarre and the impossible. Yet even as a boy, DeCapua proved to be a hard worker, and in the days prior to tough juvenile labor laws, he found employment wherever he roamed. He worked in the oil fields of Texas. He picked fruit all over the country, from West Virginia to Miami to the apple orchards of Washington State. Along the way, he also managed to master the fundamentals of cooking.

For a time, he lived in a commune in Texas. After attending the historic rock festival at Woodstock in upstate New York, he had hitched a ride, joining up with approximately seventy people who were traveling on three school buses. The group became known as the Stone Family. He herded cows with them in the desert in New Mexico. These were the same people depicted in the commune in the movie *Easy Rider.* People rolled through their encampment as freely as windblown tumbleweeds. Charlie Manson even stopped by for a time with about eight people before heading on to L.A.

Back on the road again, DeCapua worked as a roofer, performing sweaty, tar-slopping labor in the melting heat of the day. He picked oranges and limes in Florida, melons in Arizona, then worked as a day laborer in Texas, packing asbestos insulation inside a refinery plant. He picked mangoes and avocados in California, peas in Georgia, and carrots, potatoes, onions, apples, and cherries while working as an itinerant picker in Washington State's Yakima and Wenatchee valleys.

Over the years, DeCapua wandered home to Vermont several times to visit his parents. The feeling that stole in over him each time, however, was that he just didn't fit in. Worried about the dangers of life on the road, his father suggested that Mike apply for one of the job openings at the factory where he worked. Shortly thereafter, Mike began experiencing the same recurring dream, one in which he found himself trapped indoors, shackled to the seemingly inescapable ball and chain of his father's lathe machine, and he soon fled, setting out for distant horizons once again.

For whatever reasons, DeCapua always seemed drawn to test the boundaries of freedom, sound judgment, and danger. As a result, he was stabbed twice by a Cuban in Florida. For a time, he lived the life of a hobo, hopping aboard freight trains, which took him through Texas and New Mexico, among other places. He rode the rails with an elkhound pup who'd wandered into his tent camp somewhere in Idaho and sat down by the fire. DeCapua fed him the only things he had left, a can of Spaggetios and a long draw of beer. The dog took naturally to the strange cuisine. DeCapua named him Captain Nemo, and he and the dog became traveling partners, a bond that would last for years.

The first place Mike DeCapua visited when he emigrated to Alaska was Ketchikan, on the southernmost tip of the southeastern panhandle of the state. And he was soon smitten with what he saw. Down on the waterfront, a giant wooden sign arched over the street. It read WEL-COME TO KETCHIKAN! SALMON CAPITAL OF THE WORLD! Across the way, a twenty-foot-high fake wooden barometer pegged the record annual rainfall for Ketchikan at 205 inches. A few steps away, salmon leapt bodily from the salt waters of Tongass Narrows. He saw pontooned bush planes roar off across the water, carrying able-bodied people off to wild places and lives of adventure.

This was a land of possibility. When he awoke the next morning, he spotted the long, sheer crest of Deer Mountain standing over the oceanfront city, and he immediately set out to climb it. When he drew near to the top, he found it enshrouded by clouds. It was April 1983, and Mike DeCapua would forever recall how he literally "walked among the clouds."

DeCapua had seen the Rocky Mountains, the Appalachian chain, the Sierra Nevada, and the Sierra Madre, yet he had never seen anything quite like this. He told himself, This is heaven on earth.

Vowing never to leave the state, he found work as a roofer in Juneau and immediately began saving every dime he could. Eventually, he bought an inexpensive boat and longline gear and sailed out into the straits near Juneau, where he dropped his baited gear over the side. And promptly lost it. The only thing he brought back to port with him was his boat.

Undaunted, DeCapua went back to work onshore and, once again, set about saving money. When, after a number of months, he'd accumulated enough cash, he set sail once more. Again, he lost his gear as quickly as he set it—all of it. So bulldog-determined was DeCapua that this process might have continued ad infinitum had not the observant skipper of another boat identified his cohort's "brain-weak and stubborn-strong" condition and taken pity on him.

"Come out longline fishing with me as my deckhand," the skipper told him, "and I will teach you what to do."

DeCapua took the man at his word, and for the next three years, he proved a quick study at both long-lining and salmon trolling.

Over the next sixteen years, Mike DeCapua evolved into a highly competent and respected fisherman. Whether fishing for cod, shark, yellowfin, or salmon, he now felt at home on the ocean. "I love it," he says. "When I'm out there at sea, I'm alive. I never get seasick. Never. And I've got good deck feet. I don't fumble around much."

He readily admits, however, that if you unleash the maniac, tank him up on fifteen shots of tequila, and toss in a mixture of other extremely illegal chemicals, a man with such an unbridled temperament could wake up the next day with no memory of the previous night's events and yet find himself facing a three-to-five-year sentence at Lemon Creek (the state penitentiary outside of Juneau).

"When I'm in port, I drink a lot," he says, speaking openly of his weaknesses. "And when I sleep on the beach and wake up in the middle of the night, it can get pretty horrendous. Because I start running around with a knife in my hand, trying to find the lines I need to cut loose, 'cause I keep thinking we've run aground."

His face is weathered. His sea blue eyes are bordered by crow's-feet and give him the appearance of a man squinting into the sun reflecting off a flat plate of ocean at high noon. His hands are weathered by repeated, gloveless exposure to long knives and salmon leader, and rended by a million stainless-steel longline hooks flashing aboard.

His ragged clothes and dishevelled demeanor seem indicative of some brute beast of burden.

Yet aside from the madness, behind the rough outer appearance of ungroomed beard and shoulder-length hair, the gruff texture of voice and its dogmatic delivery, and in spite of a lifetime of hard knocks, a kindness remains.

Former crewmates of Mike's remember him as emotionally expressive, generous, gregarious, and theatric, with a robust heart as big as a pumpkin beating within.

"He liked his music, was a really hard worker, and knew what he was about on deck," recalls one friend.

Not one to allow a resentment to fester in his gut while on deck, DeCapua chooses instead to vocalize it and then move on. In short, Mike DeCapua doesn't get ulcers; he gives them.

It was in this lower, ocean-hugging leg of the Big Bear State that Mike DeCapua eventually staked his claim. Here, the similarities between this man and the country he loves abound: bighearted, generous, rugged, and extreme. He looks upon southeast Alaska as the last little corner of the free world. For him, there is no place left to go.

Over the years, he's worked aboard ships that put in at Edna Bay, Elfin Cove, Graves Harbor, Pelican, Funter Bay, and the Native American villages of Angoon, Kake, and Hoonah. He found the abundance of the land nothing short of staggering. Mike had visited the fish trap at Metlakatla, where 1 million salmon were reportedly intercepted in a single season, in a state in which upward of 350 million salmon have been known to return to its streams in a given summer.

He has seen humpback whales leaping clear of the sea in Frederick Sound, as well as black and brown bears roaming the shoreline, as common a sight as farm dogs along a country road. He's seen streams of struggling salmon so thick, one could literally traverse the water by walking across on their backs. He's seen the unending forests that cover the tens of thousands of stunningly beautiful islands that make up the vast archipelago of land and sea that comprises southeast Alaska, as well as more than his fair share of the forty thousand bald eagles that nest in its trees.

Boom or bust, he's weathered the storms, seen the mountains, and visited the glaciers. He's motored east along Petersburg's waterfront, past the clean white canneries built upon tall, almost stiltlike, creosoted pilings, and, from the entrance to Wrangell Narrows, has beheld the majestic granite pinnacle of Devil's Thumb, too.

The area roughly from Cape Spencer to Whale Bay is his favorite part of this rich area. "That's home," he says. "The abundance of seafood, the wildness of it. There's a whole lot of wilderness with no town to scar it."

Yet his favorite spot in that vast earthly heaven is, and always will be, a place called Bennett Bay, named after Larry Bennett, a famous logger from Cottage Grove, Oregon. "Bennett Bay," he says nostalgically, his blue eyes and far-off look expressing a hunger to be gone once again. "That's the most beautiful place I've ever come upon. There're mud flats there with ducks and geese. And if you're hungry, why, the place just won't let you go hungry. There're halibut right at the mouth of the bay. And there're Sitka deer.

"It's just a little bitty bay. Small boats only. A nice place to motor in and drop anchor. And I don't care what the wind is doing; there isn't enough room in there for the water to kick up. There just aren't many guys alive today who know about it.

"My favorite fishing is trolling for salmon," he says longingly. "It's just me and the skipper, the shore, the islands, and the sea. It's all very quiet, and intimate. And it's pretty much that way all year. I like to work alone, outside in the free air.

"In the morning, the skipper wakes up and fires up the engine. When the engine starts, it's probably three-thirty A.M. In this country, after July tenth, I'm psyched, because I know there're cohos [silver salmon] near. For silvers, I make chowder-thick coffee. And it's electric."

DeCapua rebels against the physical constriction of rain gear—even if it *is* raining. He wears a hat, sweatpants, a Russell sweater with hood, and boots and gloves. And though he has nothing against dental hygiene, he adamantly refuses to shave. Upon rising in the morning, he staggers out on deck and urinates over the side while holding his breakfast in his free hand. More often than not, breakfast is a peanut butter and honey sandwich.

Then he positions himself for the day ahead in "the pit," that waist-deep compartment "aft of everything," where he stands and works all day. "We get four lines on a power troller," he says, "and we put a hook about every fathom. We run forty hooks on each wire. That's a hundred and sixty hooks, total. I put out the gear and then reel in and dress and ice the fish we happen to apprehend."

CHAPTER 2

Over the years, Bob Doyle had also come to know the straits and backwaters of southeastern Alaska intimately. Originally from Bellows Falls, Vermont, the son of a machinist father and a beautician mother, he joined the Coast Guard when he was just eighteen. Soon, he was serving as ship supply officer on board the USCG icebreaker *Polar Star,* roaming the vast icy reaches of the world from Antarctica to the edge of the polar ice cap in Alaska's Bering Sea.

Later, he called Ketchikan his home port, and he served on the buoy tender *Laural,* traveling throughout much of the stunningly beautiful archipelago of timber-covered islands and inland sea that composes southeast Alaska. His ship plied the salmon-rich waters, replacing marker buoys in a myriad of backwater channels extending for hundreds of miles from Prince Rupert in British Columbia, to Ketchikan, and on to Craig and Wrangell and Waterfall, and Petersburg, as well, and as far north as Sitka, where he eventually met Mike DeCapua and served out his remaining years as chief warrant officer.

In his free hours, he enjoyed everything physical and challenging. This included mountain climbing, camping, and bear, goat, and deer hunting.

Through it all, Bob Doyle had held fast to the dream that one day he, too, would become a commercial fisherman in Alaska. When he retired in 1997, at age thirty-eight, after twenty years in the Coast Guard, he decided to remain in Sitka. He found work down on the waterfront painting, repairing shrimp pots, mending lines, tying knots, and helping people get their gear ready for fishing.

He hoped one day to get into the charter business in Sitka, taking people sportfishing as they tried to intercept some of the finest runs of king and silver salmon in the world. In 1997, for example, 150 million pink (humpy) salmon returned to the streams in southeast Alaska alone.

After retirement, Doyle soon found a job fishing for shrimp on board the F/V *Quicksilver,* working for Eric Calvin out of Tenakee Springs. The boat was also used as a dive platform, during which time Doyle tended to the air hoses of a commercial diver in search of sea cucumbers. When those seasons expired, he found work aboard another, less successful fishing boat, a vessel that shall remain nameless.

Short of money, with financial demands bearing down on him, Doyle felt increasingly discontent in his new job. He found that he was fishing far less often than many of his competitors. So Bob Doyle and his widely experienced fisherman friend Mike DeCapua set out on a hike that took them along the docks in Sitka's sprawling North Harbor. They were walking along, just checking things out, when they came upon the F/V *La Conte.* Skipper Mark Morley and deck boss William "Gig" Mork were working out on deck at the time, so they stopped and chatted.

Mike DeCapua had known Gig Mork for over sixteen years, and he respected Mork's judgment both as a crewman and as a deck boss. Mork had come from a solid native fishing family, worked like one obsessed, and, physically, was as tough as a nickel steak. Although Bob Doyle wasn't an experienced hand, DeCapua knew he was lean and hard, a "good guy with a good attitude," as he put it, and a disarming sense of humor.

Standing upright during a calm day at sea, Doyle's lean, muscular frame rose exactly six feet above the deck itself. Of Scottish descent, he had red hair and hazel eyes, and sported a rusty red beard peppered with a premature chin dusting of grayish white.

Rumor had it that Morley, the *La Conte*'s skipper, had two deck-hand positions that he needed to fill. DeCapua asked him about this straightaway.

"I hear you need a crew."

"Yah, I need two hands," replied Morley.

"Well," shot back DeCapua, pointing to Bob Doyle, "I've got a green guy here. But I'm not green. I'll teach him myself and pick up his slack until he catches on."

The skipper hadn't yet finished looking Mike DeCapua over when Gig Mork spoke up. "I know Mike," he said. "He's a good hand. And if he says the green guy's okay, then he's okay."

DeCapua was glad to have Gig as a friend. There was nothing wrong in being good at what you did; no reason to feel embarrassed over such a compliment. Like any human, however, Mike DeCapua had his own Achilles' heel. While in port, on shore leave, his affinity for alcohol had won him a reputation as a veritable wild man. Once at sea, however, all imbibing ceased, and DeCapua became the kind of able-bodied fisherman upon whom a skipper could readily depend. In fact, it wasn't uncommon for a skipper to bump a deckhand (fire him or her without reason on the spot) to make room for DeCapua on his crew. This time, however, hands were shaken and names and numbers were exchanged, but no decision was made.

That night, Bob Doyle called Mark Morley at home and reiterated that both he and Mike DeCapua were still very much interested in working for him.

"Good," said Morley. "You're hired."

As is the custom on fishing boats, the first thing the next morning, Doyle and DeCapua gathered their belongings, stuffed them into their navy bags, and moved off their respective boats and former places of employment. Then they hiked down the docks to the F/V *La Conte* and climbed aboard their new home. DeCapua took the top bunk; Doyle, the bottom. Being the senior deckhand on board, Gig Mork had the interior bed, while the skipper slept upstairs in the wheelhouse stateroom.

CHAPTER 3

The first trip out to sea on board the *La Conte* proved to be both brutal and inauspicious, as DeCapua and his shipmates spent a cold, wet, and laborious week trying to wrestle a living from the sea, turning over mile upon mile of longline gear in fifteen- to twenty-foot seas south of Sitka. They were working down off the savage, weather-flogged cluster of islands in Chatham Strait, an area that fishermen commonly refer to as the "Carnations."

It was an unprofitable, if not disappointing, maiden voyage. But Doyle and DeCapua had gotten along well with skipper Mark Morley and with deck boss Gig Mork. Besides, the F/V *La Conte* had proven to be a stable platform upon which to work. In that respect, acknowledged Mike DeCapua, it was a marvelous boat. For a longline fisherman such as himself, working on board a schooner like the *La Conte* was considered "the pick."

What troubled DeCapua most about his new home, however, was the seawater that he often found down in the engine-room bilge. In heavy seas, the bilge alarm went off incessantly, and DeCapua and his crewmates were constantly called into duty. Each time the alarm sounded, someone would have to run down and fire up the gas pump.

The little Honda engine would usually pump out the bilgewater in just minutes.

The *La Conte* wasn't any path to riches, but Doyle and DeCapua had been promised the much coveted job of "tendering" salmon aboard her throughout the following summer. Under contract to one of the canneries such as Trident Seafoods or Alaska Fresh Seafoods, the *La Conte* would be driven far out onto the fishing grounds, where her crew would buy fresh-caught salmon from the seine and gillnet fishermen. Then, icing the fish down in the *La Conte*'s holds, they would pack the cold, fresh, hundred-thousand-pound loads back to be off-loaded at one of the company canneries in ports such as Juneau, Petersburg, Ketchikan, or Sitka.

It was a prime job, one that promised an income of $150 to $200 each and every day, seven days a week. While living and eating for free on board ship, a crewman could spend the kindest, busiest, and most beautiful season of all in Alaska. Working out in the open air, with unending miles of stunning scenes of wilderness and wildlife scrolling by, a deckhand could sock away $4,000 or $5,000 a month, if one avoided the pitfalls of the bar life.

But it was January now, and Mark Morley was feeling the pressure. His crew was itching to make money. And though they would never push him to do so, he wanted to provide for his stepdaughter, Kyla, and her mother, Tamara, his fiancée, and to pay a fair share of the money to the boat's owner. Most important, if he hoped to secure future employment with the owners of other boats, he needed to prove himself—a brutal fact of life for a commercial fishing boat captain in Alaska. It came down to one question: If you weren't able to turn a profit on the vessel you previously ran, why would the next boat owner consider hiring you?

For a time, skipper and crew discussed going after some "seven-ups" (sand sharks seven pounds and over), running the dogfish into a cannery in Juneau, and coming back when the weather had improved. But buyers were offering a lavish $1.75 a pound for red snapper, the exact kind of fish swimming in renowned schools out on the exposed waters of the Cape Fairweather Ground.

Knowing Morley was short on money and that he was no doubt feeling the pressure, Mike DeCapua felt he understood what was motivating the skipper to risk a trip to the Fairweather Ground. The problem inherent in such a bold scheme, however, was that the *La Conte* had not been designed to run in outside waters. She'd been built long ago to serve as a salmon packer, one that would ply the relatively calm inland waters of southeast Alaska. Her two-story-high wheelhouse had windows little more sturdy than those of a pleasure craft. In addition, the covers to the two large fish holds on her foredeck were not sealed; the covers were held in place only because of their weight. Should exceptional waves keep her deck awash, seawater would likely find its way into both holds. Eventually, the tons and tons of seawater rising inside the *La Conte*'s half-filled holds would begin to slam destructively from side to side with each new storm-tossed roll of the boat.

Worse yet, the F/V *La Conte* did not have a life raft on board. The entire crew knew about it, and though they did not like the idea, they had, with time, gotten somewhat accustomed to the fact.

The legendary Fairweather Ground is a fish-rich area of shoal and pinnacle rock approximately sixty miles offshore from Cape Fairweather. It is here that the Tolvo Pinnacle rises out of surrounding waters five hundred feet deep to within just thirteen fathoms (seventy-eight feet) of the ocean's surface. The nutrient-rich upwelling that occurs there sustains massive populations of bottom fish.

Scott Eckels, the boat's owner, did not want the *La Conte* to venture out into open waters, recalls DeCapua. "He wanted us to fish the inside waters of Chatham Strait for gray cod or dog sharks. I knew that if we could get into the dog sharks, I could make a living. At just ten cents a pound, I'd have a paycheck. We could catch ten thousand pounds a day. Easy. I mean, no problem.

"The skipper was a nice guy. So I couldn't just say to him, 'I'm not making any money, so I'm going to quit you.' No sir." Gig Mork felt the same way. Even the best of skippers got skunked every now and then. Mork and DeCapua figured they'd see it through—"tidy up the season and go on to the next show and be friends."

Then Morley told his men that he planned to motor up to the

Fairweather Ground and do some fishing. They'd go after red snapper and yellow-eye. The prospective fishing grounds were said to support a huge biomass of fish. Though no one protested, DeCapua wasn't in the least overjoyed at the prospects of venturing out in unprotected waters, so far from shore.

Morley and his crew made good time covering the 110 miles out to the fishing grounds. They tossed out their baited gear as fast as they could set it, but then the weather started kicking up, so they were forced to run the entire way back into the beach at Graves Harbor, near Cape Spencer.

"We were way out there," recalls Mike DeCapua. "We ran with our tails tucked between our legs for eleven hours at ten knots to reach the shelter of the bay."

Throughout the entire eleven-hour leg, the never-ending racket of the bilge alarm sounded almost constantly, making sleep fairly impossible. Each time the chronically overactive alarm went off, some sleepy crewman was forced to get up, dress, go outside, and make his way along the walkway between the wheelhouse and the side railing. When he reached the stern, he'd descend into the engine room to check the water level in the bilge. More often than not, Mike DeCapua volunteered for the duty. The bilge reeked of diesel fuel, and in the gyrating space of the engine room, DeCapua would grab the lawn-mower-type starter cord of the Honda pump and crank it to life. He would remain long enough to pump out the hundreds of gallons of saltwater that had leaked in, then he'd go topside again and try to grab a little shut-eye.

As one crusty old Norwegian fisherman once said, "Sometimes there just ain't no easy way." Such was the case this night, for now it seemed that everything began falling apart. As the rain and storm winds lashed the outside of the boat, water began leaking from the galley ceiling. Those inside rushed to ignite the cabin stove and warm themselves. Although essential for both heating and cooking, the diesel-fueled stove refused to ignite, which meant there was no heat or heater, no hot showers, and no cooked meals. For those able to hold them down, cold sandwiches and cereal were their lot that night. The ship's interior and wheelhouse were cold enough that they could see one another's breath.

The next day, they left Graves Harbor and moved over to Elfin Cove, near the tiny hamlet of Pelican, to get the stove fixed. They also needed to buy some lubricating grease for the driveshaft bearing.

With their anchor finally resting on the bottom of Elfin Cove, the crew turned in. They were sleeping like the dead when, at about 3:00 A.M. on that blustery winter morning, the *La Conte* lost all power. Dead in the water, she began to drag anchor. As the boat slid out into deeper waters, her anchor floated free of the bottom, and they began drifting steadily toward the craggy shore on the opposite side of the bay. Without engine power, there would be no propulsion and no hydraulics and, of course, no way to winch the anchor back aboard.

As the skipper rushed to get the main engine started, Doyle, DeCapua, Mork, and recently hired David Hanlon scrambled to rig a tarp as a sail, which ultimately kept them off the rocks.

For a time, however, things looked grim, and Mark Morley decided to inform the Coast Guard. When the Coast Guard received the call, they began preparing to launch an all-out rescue. But then they learned it was the F/V *La Conte* that had run into trouble, not the M/V *Le Conte*, the multimillion-dollar Alaskan ferryboat that shuttles passengers throughout the archipelago of southeast Alaska—at which point, they called off the rescue.

Finally, Mark Morley managed to get the stubborn engine started and the hyraulic pump working. They reeled their anchor back aboard and motored back into shallow water, where they dropped anchor once again.

Several days later, there appeared to be a break in the weather. Morley decided to seize what he viewed as a small window of opportunity. The crew of the *La Conte* reluctantly agreed to make a second trip out to the Fairweather Ground, but only on the promise of retrieving the gear they'd left behind.

It was almost flat calm when, at about 10:00 P.M, they reached the Fairweather Ground and started checking their gear. The fishing was good to excellent, and as the night progressed, several thousand pounds of lively red snapper came flopping aboard. It was at about this time that the original plan to retrieve their gear changed. Understandably, Mark Morley now wanted to rebait the gear on board and lay it back out, along with several more skates of freshly baited gear.

"Okay," said Mike DeCapua testily under his breath. "We'll throw you out another set."

When setting out these long sections of ground line, fishermen use snap-on gear, pieces of line three or four feet long, with a baited hook tied to one end and a small stainless-steel snap-on device tethered to the other. Every fifteen feet or so, the fishermen on deck will snap these baited ganions onto the ground line as it trails over the side. The reels on many boats contain as much as forty miles of ground line. It is not uncommon for a skipper and his crew to lay out ten miles of this line at a time, running at perhaps a steady ten miles per hour for an hour or more. At chosen intervals on a given set, buoy markers and bamboo poles with flags waving from them are secured to prevent the loss of the gear should the ground line part as the gear is being pulled aboard.

The length of line, the direction of the set, and the time the gear is allowed to "soak" are decisions left solely to the discretion of the skipper. The crew of the *La Conte* had worked their way through approximately half of the four-mile-long section, when the ground line suddenly parted, forcing them to run to the nearest buoy marker.

During the twenty-minute run, Mike DeCapua noticed that the weather was kicking up, with winds blowing steadily now at twenty-five miles per hour. As they worked on through the night, the wind and seas built gradually. Soon big lumpers fifteen feet and better were rolling toward them from the stern in long, predictable swells, effortlessly lifting and lowering the 200,000-pound *La Conte* with an overpowering indifference. The seventy-nine-year-old wooden-hulled vessel seemed to take it all in stride, however.

By morning, the wind was pushing in from the west, recalls DeCapua. "We had a good twelve-foot swell running, with a good long sweep of trough between waves. It wasn't comfortable. We didn't like it. In fact, it was slamming us around pretty good. But it was January in Alaska; it was the Fairweather Ground!"

The crew of the *La Conte* moved aft then to the dimly lighted, spray-soaked compound of the bait shed mounted on the stern, where they began chopping up frozen blocks of herring bait and impaling them on hooks. Their faces were set hard to the task, and their feet were braced widely against the leap and buck of the deck, when Mike DeCapua rose up from the tangle of ground line he'd been hovering over and glanced up at the horizon. What he saw brought him up short. The entire sky was gray. Then, as the ship rose over another wave, he saw it again; a solid black line stretching across the horizon at the exact point where the sky met the sea. It was an eerie specter, an unusual natural phenomenon, one he'd rarely seen in his seventeen years at sea, and one he'd hoped he'd never see again. He froze when he saw it. For him, it had always been a vision of doom, and he felt certain at that moment that they were in deep trouble. (Though many commercial fishermen in Alaska are adamant about its existence, there is no official scientific explanation for this phenomenon.) Mike rose from his work and called out to the others. "It's time to get out of here!" he said, pointing.

Born and bred in the area of the Fairweather Ground, Gig Mork nodded in emphatic agreement.

"Mark," DeCapua yelled up to his skipper. "Do you see that black line? That means we've got really heavy weather approaching. It's time to run back in. That's death coming!"

Morley poked his head out the wheelhouse window. "No!" he yelled down. "We've just got a few more sets to make!"

"This is the Fairweather Ground!" shot back DeCapua. "Gig and I have fished it all our lives! That black line is a real bad sign! And it's coming this way! It's time to get out of here! Why don't we cut our frigging losses? We can come back later and pick up our gear."

But the skipper disagreed. "No," he said again. "We've got to get our gear up before we leave."

"Okay," said DeCapua begrudgingly.

Though forced to bite his tongue, DeCapua felt philosophic about the decision. As a deckhand, he knew, he was only a servant. His job was to take orders, not give them. Offering up such advice to the skipper was stepping out of bounds, breaking the rules by which he'd always lived.

"But the skipper just didn't understand," he says. "For me to give advice to the old man like that, for me to say that, well, that just don't happen. I would never have spoken up like that if I hadn't thought it was important. Now, I'm not saying even now that I'm mad at him; I liked the man. I just wasn't able to get through to him."

By the time they reeled the last skate aboard, the seas were twenty-five feet high. They knew that a big storm was brewing. Gradually, the black line disappeared altogether.

It's already rolled in on us, thought DaCapua finally. We're in it right now.

Through the years, Mike DeCapua and Gig Mork had fished the Fairweather Ground for black cod, halibut, rockfish, and salmon. Mork had twenty years of experience trolling and long-lining in the area in all kinds of weather, while DeCapua boasted another fourteen years. Both men knew that it wasn't just a time for prudence; it was a time to flee!

Now DeCapua decided to climb up the ladder on the outside of the wheelhouse to try to reason with the skipper.

"No," reiterated Morley again. "We're going to stick it out and pick up one more set."

DeCapua knew that the skipper was betting that the wind and seas would calm down. This is not good, he thought, returning to his work.

In general, the crew felt that the sooner they got their gear coiled back aboard the *La Conte* and stowed away, the sooner they could "get the hell out of there" and start beating a path toward town.

When the waves grew higher still, Morley decided to quit for a time, in the hope of better weather. Dripping and exhausted from work, Mike DeCapua crawled into his bunk and abruptly fell asleep.

CHAPTER 4

DeCapua awoke three hours later, only to discover that the winds had increased to at least fifty knots and the seas had grown into rollers thirty feet high. He climbed into the wheelhouse then and watched as Mark Morley drove the *La Conte* over them. With skillful aplomb, the skipper calmed the straightforward soaring and plunging of the bow by quartering up and moving across the face of each wave at a forty-five-degree angle.

Sensing for perhaps the first time the monumental gravity of their predicament, Morley began steering the *La Conte* on a beeline course for Cape Spencer. Soon, however, the skipper found himself locked in a life-and-death struggle, fighting for every inch gained. Over the next few hours, the best the seventy-seven-foot *La Conte* could muster as it plowed ahead was one-quarter of a knot. On land, one could crawl faster. They were, in fact, barely moving.

As the storm continued to gather, the wind and seas checked the *La Conte*'s every move. Eventually, no matter how hard the skipper tried, the aging vessel could make no headway at all. Then, for the first time, they began losing ground.

With darkness approaching, the waves showed no sign of halting their muscular climb. "The larger they got, the bigger they grew," says DeCapua, using a fisherman's colloquialism. "Now, I've fished out among the sea mounds [mountains beneath the sea] off Seward and all," he adds, "and I've seen big seas, but this wasn't just any regular storm. We're talking frigging horrendous! The waves were banging into the frigging bow. We couldn't turn and run with it because we didn't want to end up in Russia, or China, or some damned place."

Deck boss Gig Mork and skipper Mark Morley took the first wheel watch together. Every half hour, whoever was on duty at the time would run below into the engine room to check the water level in the bilge, the grease level on the driveshaft, and the oil level in the main diesel engine. As always, this also entailed firing up the Honda pump and sucking out the seawater that had invariably accumulated in the bilge.

DeCapua had been on his feet, working and hauling gear, for nearly twenty-four hours by that time. Bob Doyle, Gig Mork, and Dave Hanlon had already had their naps, and DeCapua was hoping to grab a little shut-eye himself. But no sooner had he lain down than he felt someone shaking him awake. It was Bob Doyle. His voice had an edge to it. "Mike, you've got to get up. It's getting serious out there," he said.

Bob Doyle had always felt comfortable on the ocean, high seas or no. Standing on the galley floor of the sharply pitching *La Conte,* he'd even managed to brew some coffee, but there was something exceptional taking place outside, and he wanted to be on top of it. Besides, he needed someone to follow him outside and down into the engine room to check the bilge.

DeCapua rose and shook himself awake. He agreed to accompany Doyle, but first he wanted to check on things in the wheelhouse overhead. DeCapua climbed halfway up the stairwell and, at floor level, poked his head into the room. In that instant, he could feel the desperation. Climbing fully into the wheelhouse, he stood watching as gale-force winds of over eighty miles per hour went screaming past and lumbering forty-five-foot waves lifted and tossed them. Worse yet, the mammoth seas seemed to have tapped into some inexhaustible source of energy, appeared to be mounting without end.

Built for kinder seas and protected passages, the *La Conte* did not have the powerful, far-reaching floodlights that the larger king-crab boats and longline vessels had mounted on their masts. On clear nights, these ultraefficient beams of light could illuminate the sea a thousand feet away. But the *La Conte* had no such mast lights. The men in her wheelhouse could see almost nothing, and were relegated to feeling their way blindly up the long, steep slopes of the approaching waves.

In the wheelhouse, Gig Mork found himself fighting to hold ground as he squinted out through wintery inundations of blowing snow and spray. As he moved ahead through the smothering darkness, each time he felt the rising approach of a wave, he'd back off on the throttle. That way when the wave crest finally did sweep past underneath them, the free-falling bow wouldn't crash down quite so hard into the wave trough on the other side. Regardless, each time he crested over a wave, the bow went into a free fall, followed by a jarring impact as the whole vessel plunged into the jet black valley below.

DeCapua said nothing. Leaving Morley and Gig in the wheelhouse, he retreated back down the ladder. He came upon Bob Doyle and David Hanlon in the ship's galley. Hanlon, forty-eight, was a respected, lifelong Alaskan fisherman who'd come from a well-known Tlingit Indian family. DeCapua found both Hanlon and Doyle were holding fast to the kitchen table there, bracing themselves as the *La Conte* pitched sharply beneath them. Hanlon was seasick, something that could happen to anybody. Both DeCapua and Doyle felt a certain empathy for the man, along with a kind of guilty gratitude that they weren't suffering from the same miserable, body-weakening affliction.

"As soon as I get to the beach, I'm getting off this thing," said DeCapua. "I don't care. I like Mark, but I sure as hell don't plan on doing this again. I've had enough. If we make it through this, as soon as this ship pulls into port, I'm quitting. That's it."

Doyle and Hanlon were quick to agree.

"When it lifts, that is," said Hanlon.

It was 6:30 P.M. and well past dark when DeCapua pulled on his Uniroyal deck boots and joined Doyle to check the level of water down in the engine room. For safety reasons, Morley had ordered that no one was to go out on deck alone. Bilge inspections would be carried out in pairs, employing the buddy system.

With Doyle following along behind him, DeCapua worked his way out the side door and along the walkway leading to the stern and the door that led down into the engine room. Feeling his way along the outer wall, he was assailed by the strong winds and soaked by bucketfuls of drenching seawater exploding off the sides of the ship. He moved blindly through the night-blackened space, placing his feet here and his hands there instinctively, in patterns that had already become familiar to him. When he found the door handle and jerked it open, the dripping pair entered the comparative quiet of the ship's interior.

It seemed to Mike DeCapua that he had only just begun his harried descent, light-footing it down the stairway that led into the engine room, when he plunged into the icy jolt of waist-deep seawater. The sudden shock of the frigid Gulf of Alaska waters took his breath away. His hands clutched at the handrails in an effort to bring both himself and Bob Doyle, who was now backpedaling beside him in the water, to a halt.

DeCapua's sleep-numbed mind fought to come fully awake and deal with the sudden reality of the flooded room before him. It was an ugly sight. The water was rising fast. If it continued, it would soon begin shorting out the *La Conte*'s electrical circuitry. In the gyrating confines of the engine room, a lone flickering lightbulb swung back and forth from the ceiling overhead, casting shadows over the scene, while seawater, leaking in from the deck above, trickled from the ceiling.

Each time the boat pitched, the heaving flood of seawater would shift, slamming up against the riblike interior wooden braces of the *La Conte*'s hull. The seawater was already halfway up the main engine and was threatening to drown her and fill the entire engine room as well.

"Sweet Jesus!" said DeCapua, already heading up the stairs with the news.

"Holy God!" exclaimed Doyle.

Turning to DeCapua, he said, "Mike, get up into the wheelhouse and wake everybody up! And get Gig down here now! Go let them know! Go let them know!" He paused, then added, "And please, tell them to send out a Mayday." He also told DeCapua to get the EPIRB (emergency position-indicating radio beacon—pronounced *Eee-purb*) going.

"Will do!" said Mike DeCapua, disappearing up the stairwell.

When DeCapua reached the wheelhouse, he said, "Man, we've got to deploy the EPIRB!"

"What?" asked Gig Mork incredulously.

"We're going down. We're taking on a lot more water than we are pumping off this thing. The pump has stopped! The way the water's coming in down there, something must have broken loose somewhere along the line!"

Gig Mork eased back on the throttle. A moment later, Mark Morley was standing in the pilothouse.

"Keep us turned into it," ordered the skipper. "I'm going below to take a look myself."

Bob Doyle was still trying to start the normally dependable Honda pump when Mike DeCapua returned, with Mark Morley and David Hanlon in tow.

DeCapua grabbed the handle end of the cord and gave it a yank. The engine turned over with a disheartening sound. There was absolutely no compression or spark. Subsequent efforts served only to validate his initial impression. Seawater had lapped over the four-stroke gas engine, dousing both plug and points. They'd have to be thoroughly dried out before the pump would start. Useless, he thought.

Bob Doyle snagged a pair of five-gallon buckets as they floated by. With one man standing in the water and the rest scattered along the stairway to the top, they formed a bucket brigade, feverishly relaying pails of water up the stairwell and dumping them out on the stern end of the deck.

While Mark Morley tried to control the *La Conte*'s leaden movements from the wheelhouse above, the bailing below continued unabated. As they worked, the cold tide of seawater rose up the ladder. One by one, the bailing crewmen rotated out of the relay line just long enough to don their survival suits and return again.

In an effort to lift morale and boost confidence, Bob Doyle tried to encourage his shipmates. "It's not gaining on us!" he announced. "It's making a difference, guys! It's not coming up any higher!" In truth, with all the water sloshing about, Doyle wasn't sure if they were holding their own or not. Their only chance was to neutralize the invading waters long enough to allow the Coast Guard to arrive.

If we want to stay alive, thought Mike DeCapua as he worked, we've got to keep this old girl under us alive. If she dies, our odds go way down.

When Bob Doyle returned wearing his survival suit, he leapt down into the water of the flooding engine room and relieved DeCapua. "Now go get on your own suit!" he yelled as he bent and began bailing furiously.

Moments later, DeCapua returned, giving Gig Mork a chance to don his suit.

As the *La Conte* pitched up and dived down under them, those on the stairwell braced themselves as best they could. With no railing to hold on to, Doyle wedged himself into a semisecure position at the top of the stairs by bracing his buttocks against one wall and the top of his head against the opposite wall. In this way, he freed up his arms so he could pass the buckets of water along as quickly as they appeared.

The F/V *La Conte* had been built in the shipyards of Seattle back in 1919. Some eighty years before, skilled hands had taken fresh-cut planks of oak wood and fashioned them into a double-planked hull. But eight decades was a long time, and the *La Conte* had seen more than its fair share of storms and shipyards.

Because she had been built to pack salmon on the largely protected, inside waters of southeast Alaska, neither the engine room nor the fish holds belowdecks had watertight bulkheads separating them. One continuous compartment ran from stem to stern. If left unchecked, a break anywhere, either in the fiberglass fish holds extending down into that compartment or in the double-planked hull itself, would eventually result in the engine room flooding and the vessel itself eventually sinking.

Probably no one will ever know for certain the source of the influx of flooding seawater. Perhaps a piece of plumbing had sheared off somewhere in between the live-hold tanks up forward. Or perhaps a length of dry-rotted plank that had gone undetected in the yard work done the summer before had now given way. What is certain is that there was a sudden letting go. The volume of water rushing in was indicative of a complete structural failure, and in spite of their best efforts to bail and pump the inundating waters back overboard, the water continued to rise.

"That's about enough of this shit!" DeCapua announced loudly, certain now that the *La Conte* would soon sink. "Man, it's no use. The water's coming up too fast. We're going down!"

"It's a lost cause," agreed Gig Mork. "We gotta go get prepared. We need to be worrying more about how we plan to get off of here alive!"

When Mark Morley appeared again on the stairwell to survey the scene, he saw Gig Mork standing in water up to his armpits. The flooding tide was now lapping at the chest-high bank of batteries. Seawater five feet deep was washing over the top of the main engine, but the engine itself refused to quit.

Then, as Morley watched, the water crashing about inside the engine room drove into Gig Mork, slamming him against the bulkhead. "Stop bailing!" the skipper ordered. "And get out of the engine room!"

Throughout all the furious bailing, the crew of the *La Conte* had been fully aware that at any moment their ship could roll and entomb them, carrying them into the hull-crushing depths below. The moment they heard those words, the crewmen standing in their bulky orange survival suits bolted up the stairwell in a stampede.

When skipper Mark Morley climbed back into the wheelhouse, he grabbed the radio mike and began sending out distress signals. "Mayday! Mayday!" he called. "This is the fishing vessel *La Conte*! We're out on the Fairweather Ground right near compass rose, and we're going down! The vessel is sinking! We've donned our suits. We're getting in the water. We're abandoning ship." But there was no reply.

Boom! . . . Boom! . . . Boom! sounded the storm waves in a long, slow cadence as, one after another, they reverberated against the hull of the F/V *La Conte.*

Weighed down by the growing burden of the flood of seawater filling her, the *La Conte* began to falter. The best that skipper Mark Morley could do was to keep her nose into the oncoming seas. Then, as she lumbered ahead, her bow and foredeck began to scoop up the oncoming waves. Each time her bow rose from the brackish sea, untold tons of seawater spilled from her foredeck, offering up the image of a submarine rising.

"Look," shouted Bob Doyle, "we've got the EPIRB!"

"It goes with us!" shot back the skipper.

"I don't believe this!" said Gig Mork as he helped Morley activate the EPIRB.

The state-of-the-art 406 EPIRB would send up a pulse, broadcasting on a supersecure satellite channel. If the battery was sufficiently charged, the Mayday message would be picked up by one of several satellites circling the globe some 530 miles out in space, and relayed to the Coast Guard just seconds after its activation.

With feet braced wide and backs turned away from the wind-flung spray, the crew of the *La Conte* assembled again on the vessel's exposed foredeck. Dressed now in hooded survival suits, they gathered in front of the wheelhouse in the soft glow of light reflecting down from the bridge two stories above. They squinted in the stinging spray and yelled to be heard as winds of eighty miles per hour and better shrieked through the rigging overhead.

"We are going to stick together!" shouted Morley for everyone to hear. "We're going to tie ourselves together with rope line and abandon this vessel together." The decisiveness of his words had a calming effect on the terrified crew. "Someone needs to go get some buoy balls!" he added.

Bob Doyle and David Hanlon leapt to the task. They climbed the ladder alongside the wheelhouse and felt their way in the dying light to the buoy setups and rope line stored on the roof.

The *La Conte* was riding much lower in the bow now, and as each wave drove in over her, seawater crashed across the slanting deck and raced around the wheelhouse in divided rivers of swift-running lather. As the *La Conte* swayed heavily underfoot, her terrified crewmen checked to see if one another's survival suit zippers and inflatable collars were in good repair.

Mike DeCapua knew that they were in big trouble. The ship's lights and electrical systems would soon short out, and given her sluggish movements, the *La Conte* herself could roll at any second. When Bob Doyle and David Hanlon returned with the buoys and line, DeCapua went to work.

He set out to tie everyone in a line. "They had two-fingered Gumby suits," he recalls, "while my Imperial suit came with articulated fingers; that's why I tied the knots. I put a quick ring around each of my crewmates and a quick half hitch with a figure-eight back over it. I spaced us about a fathom and a half apart, then tied us all together with a sheep-bend knot. And I put a granny half hitch on the back side of each sheep-bend. Then I used a sheep-bend again to tie a crab buoy on each end of the bunch of us. It was sinking line, lead line three-eighths of an inch thick. Tough nylon cord. I used up about sixty feet of rope line altogether."

DeCapua worked furiously to tie the five of them securely in place, while allowing a reasonable amount of slack for each to move about or escape, if it became necessary. The sequence of tethered fishermen turned out to be Bob Doyle on one end, followed by Mark Morley, Mike DeCapua, Gig Mork, and David Hanlon.

As her belly filled with water, the *La Conte* continued to settle. Although completely submerged now, her main diesel engine still refused to die. But the shifting tonnage of seawater flooding the vessel's interior served to destabilize her, and she soon began listing to starboard. With no way to counterbalance the weight and regain control, she began drifting sideways to the storm, entirely vulnerable to the elements that would soon destroy her.

CHAPTER 5

Everything seemed so unreal. And as the crew stood tethered together, the rolling ship, racing deck water, and blowing spray created a world of sensory overload and stifling fear. The men were staggered by the unpredictable undulations of the slanting deck, and they finally retreated to higher ground as the flooding seawater threatened to wash their legs from under them.

Now waves began striking the exposed perpendicular sides of the *La Conte* with the booming violence of clapping thunder, launching tall geysers of drenching spray that were instantly swept away and sent hurtling across the face of the sea at ninety miles per hour and more. The vaporous explosions dwarfed the ship and stung the exposed faces of all those who had not turned away or protected themselves with a sheltering hand. With only the circular patches of their faces showing, the five crewmates checked their nooses, knots, and suit apparatus for the final time as they prepared to abandon ship.

Everyone was cognizant of the fact that no one had responded to their Mayday call. They had, however, succeeded in switching on their EPIRB. Its small blinking light gave proof that it was indeed transmitting a signal, broadcasting their urgent plea on its supersecure military satellite channel.

DeCapua could feel the long, steep shadow of a dimensionless groundswell rising unseen underneath him. Every ten seconds or so, the EPIRB's strobe light would blink, offering up a brief chinking flash of white light.

Still nauseous from seasickness, David Hanlon was having trouble getting his suit to fit snugly in the area around his neck and shoulders. DeCapua was still helping him pull the hood of his suit into place when the *La Conte* listed sharply to starboard and the gathering waters began pouring in over the side.

"We've got to get off this thing!" called out Mark Morley, shouting in order to be heard above the wind and waves. "Climb up on the leeward side! We don't want it to flip over on top of us!"

Mike DeCapua and his crewmates were shuffling up the deck when the *La Conte* began to roll in a slow, belabored acceleration onto her starboard side. The moment DeCapua and the others felt her start to go, they moved quickly up the ever-steepening face of the deck.

"Now we are going to step off this vessel," instructed Morley, "and we're going to do it together! We're all going over together! On three!"

Mike DeCapua's heart felt as if it might just beat its way out of his chest. He and the others had backed up to the highest point of the sloping deck and now stood silently waiting. It took fifteen seconds or longer for the perilously deep wave trough, one perhaps a thousand feet long, to pass. They were waiting on the highest point of the sloping deck, near the portside railing, when the *La Conte* heeled completely onto her side. Now, with the ship's deck standing on its side, completely vertical, they climbed onto the high ground atop her portside railing.

"One! Two! Three!" shouted Mark Morley as the five terrified crewmen fled overboard.

Not so very long ago, I was happily asleep in my bunk, thought

Mike DeCapua as he stepped off into the icy forty-two-degree waters of the Gulf of Alaska, certain of the inevitable ordeal that awaited him.

Most met with an unexpected jolt as their feet and behinds impacted with the sizable protrusion of the ship's keel as it pivoted back toward the surface. The five crewmen went under briefly, bobbed to the surface, gulped oxygen, and paddled furiously away from the foundering hulk of the *La Conte*.

Turtled over onto her starboard side as she was, with her engine still running and propeller still engaged, she looked like a wounded duck kicking spasmodically—dead, but still swimming.

An undetected wave plowed into them, smashing the crew against the keel and wooden underside of the ship's hull, and exploded over the vessel's entire length. The wave drove the men under, and DeCapua and his crewmates were down for several seconds before they were able to once again gain the surface. The impact ripped the state-of-the-art 406 EPIRB from Bob Doyle's hands. Designed to float, the EPIRB came with a long length of line attached to it. As it washed away, it became momentarily entangled with the *La Conte*'s long steel mast slanting out of the water nearby, and for a time, Doyle found himself essentially tethered to a sinking ship.

The moment he managed to free the beacon from the sinking wreckage, he paddled furiously away. Dragging it along behind him, he joined the others, who now had distanced themselves from any further entanglements with the sinking ship.

Then the *La Conte* righted herself. She rolled back toward the men in the water, and for a time, her tall mast stood upright, reaching into the scouring black heavens, trailing seawater from every limb.

DeCapua could see the lights of her wheelhouse shining in the dark. "You could look right inside her, and everything looked clean and dry and in its proper place," he recalls. Below that, he could see the even alignment of portholes, filled with yellow light. Then the *La Conte* seemed to languish evenly in the water, leveled herself out with a final touch of dignity, and sank on the spot.

As the *La Conte* slipped into the depths, her golden lights took on a greenish tint, a coloration that darkened progressively. DeCapua felt that in some strange way the ship was now beckoning to him to follow.

"Look!" said Mike DeCapua. "Look at that! There's smoke still coming out of her stack! She's forty feet down and the main engine is still running!" Then came a belching rumble and the stench of diesel fumes as exhaust gases bubbled up out of the water all around him. Mike DeCapua thought it an "eerie vision, haunting to behold," he says. "It scared the hell out of me. I expected her to grab me somehow and pull me down with her. I was worried about the malevolence of the boat. And when I saw the smoke from the diesel engine that was running underneath the water, that was unnatural."

DeCapua and his buddies watched in silence then as the lights of the ship descended. Her light-filled portholes and rectangular pilothouse windows shone with a distinctive glow before vanishing altogether, leaving DeCapua and his drifting crewmates to face the night alone.

With the flashing EPIRB floating on the end of a length of line fifty to one hundred feet away, there was scant light. DeCapua found that he couldn't identify anyone. Then something erupted from the surface nearby. Even with all the wind he could still hear it. *Whuff! Whoosh!* He quickly surmised that they were wooden pallets that had floated free of the *La Conte,* a ship that was now being carried along by the currents directly below. They arose dangerously out of the invisible depths, advancing with a mindless stealth, accelerating as they climbed, before exploding through the surface. We're right in their path, thought DeCapua pensively.

"Okay, let's keep the flock together!" yelled Mark Morley. "Everyone sound off! Is everybody okay? Is everybody all right?

"Mike?"

"Yah!" replied DeCapua.

"Gig? Dave? Bob?"

One by one, the crewmen yelled in response.

"Good." Morley paused; then his voice rose again. "Oh damn! I

think I tore my suit getting off the boat." He paused again, as if searching to locate the tear. "Does anybody have a leak in his suit?"

Only silence followed. Morley himself had struck hard against the
boat's keel. "Well, I do. I think I tore a hole down by my knee. I'm
taking water in through the leg of my suit. I'm getting a lot of water
in, and it's cold."

Doyle swam to him then. He checked out Morley's submerged
legs as best he could, and around his face and the zipper of his suit
as well. Everything seemed all right, undisturbed. He even caught
the flash of the strobe light reflecting off the surface of Morley's
reading glasses; in spite of it all, they were still sitting neatly in place
on the bridge of his nose. "Mark, I can't seem to find anything,"
Doyle told him finally. "The seal around your face seems okay. And
your zipper is up."

In his mind, however, Bob Doyle red-flagged the moment. During
his twenty years with the Coast Guard, he'd donned survival suits hundreds, if not thousands, of times, and he knew he would rather have
his ribs broken or just about anything else than a leak in his suit—
because he knew that a survivor's only hope out in the open ocean was
his suit. And one couldn't survive for long with that icy Alaskan seawater pouring into it.

This isn't so bad, thought Mike DeCapua after the first few minutes.
People live through things like this all the time.

No one could have guessed at the size of the monstrous hulk of
free-running ocean until it crested and broke fully down upon them.
Sixty miles from shore, the huge storm wave buried the five crewmen
of the fishing vessel *La Conte* under tons of frigid sea. Now they found
themselves trapped inside the churning body of the wave itself. The
overwhelming force of the rushing currents sent the hapless fishermen
careening through the depths in violent somersaults, and they fought
to hold their breath and gain the surface.

"This frigging wave was huge!" recalls DeCapua. "It was a rogue.
That first wave had a big, growling comber that rolled right in over us,
sucked us up, and began to tumble us about inside the 'washing machine.' When I was inside that wild vortex there, before she coughed

us up, that's when I got scared. We came up coughing and sputtering, choking and gasping for air. Some were groaning. I swallowed a lot of seawater."

DeCapua sought to quell the fear rising within him. I don't want to die like this, God! he prayed. I'm trying to hang on here.

CHAPTER 6

When Lt. Bill Adickes walked down the short distance from his office and stepped into the Operations Center in the remote Coast Guard outpost in Sitka, Alaska, things were already abuzz. Only minutes before, their SAR satellite had picked up a hit—an emergency frequency pulse—coming from a 406 EPIRB located 120 miles north and 60 offshore of the tiny Tlingit fishing village of Yakutat out on the Fairweather Ground in the Gulf of Alaska.

Typically, upon receiving a signal from one of the more primitive systems, such as the relatively low-tech 121.5 emergency locator transmitters, the Coast Guard would allow the satellite to make several more half-hour passes around the earth before launching an all-out rescue mission. With the older transmitters, it took time as well as a certain detachment to proceed rationally, a nerve-racking task, given the tragic circumstances that might be unfolding offshore. Impassioned as those in the USCG were about saving lives, it was essential to process the information gathered as unemotionally as possible.

But the 406 EPIRB system, Adickes knew, emitted an extremely reliable signal, with a low rate of false alarms. There was no need to wait for confirmation; no need to wait for the satellite to make another pass. The decision was made to launch immediately.

Born in Seattle, Bill Adickes moved with his parents to the Los Angeles area when he was just a boy so that his father could fly jets. His father was working full-time as an airline pilot for Pan Am when Bill joined the Marine Corps. Bill Adickes did his basic training in Quantico, Virginia, received his officer training in Virginia, too, and then was shipped to Pensacola, Florida, for flight training.

Fresh out of flight school, he completed two shipboard deployments. One was served on the aircraft carrier USS *Okinawa* in the Persian Gulf, flying combat assault helicopters. Officially, Adickes was there to maintain the right of free navigation in the Persian Gulf and the Strait of Hormuz. But the real reason for the military presence, Adickes knew, was to keep the oil flowing.

In 1989, Adickes joined the Coast Guard. His first assignment was a four-year tour piloting helicopters out of Clearwater, Florida, chasing drug smugglers and learning the rudiments of search and rescue. Then, in 1994, he was given the prestigious duty of flying rescue missions out of Sitka, Alaska.

On this night, Adickes would sit in the left seat, serving as copilot, commander, and navigator. Lt. Dan Molthen would take the right seat, the one reserved for pilots.

Lieutenant Adickes was a choice pick for the mission at hand. In 1997, Adickes had been awarded the Distinguished Flying Cross (pilots refer to it as simply the DFC)—the highest military medal a pilot can receive during times of peace—for being the copilot and navigator during a wild high-seas rescue that saved the lives of two of the three fishermen of the sinking F/V *Oceanic*.

Not surprisingly, the highly decorated Adickes did not think of himself as the world's best pilot. Like all of the pilots assigned to duty at the base in Sitka, he approached flying in southeast Alaska with what he called a "tremendous amount of caution." He felt responsible for his entire crew, and as a seasoned pilot, he was acutely aware of his own limitations.

So critical is navigation in Alaska, the ranking officer on board generally performs that duty. In every other military branch, the aircraft commander does the flying, and the copilot does the navigating.

As a copilot, Adickes had to resist getting bogged down in the details. Throughout a mission, he strived to take a look at the big picture, thinking and planning, without trying to fly the aircraft at the same time. And Dan Molthen was such an excellent pilot, he knew he wouldn't have to worry about that end of things.

Raised in the San Francisco Bay Area, Lt. Dan Molthen was one of three children. He caught the bug to fly from his father, who started flying in 1945 in the navy. The elder Molthen eventually became a dentist, but his love for planes and flying continued. Throughout his son's childhood, he built model airplanes and built and flew remote control planes, as well.

He also owned a helicopter-flying business, and he often took his son Dan flying out over San Francisco Bay and along the California coastline north of there. From the outset, Dan Molthen loved flying; he thought it was the "neatest thing in the world."

No stranger to dangerous duty, after graduation from the U.S. Naval Academy in Annapolis, Maryland, Molthen earned his wings in the navy flying H-3s off several destroyers and the aircraft carriers *Eisenhower* and *Roosevelt* out of Norfolk, Virginia. He further sharpened his skills serving as a navy helicopter flight instructor in Pensacola, Florida, before joining the Coast Guard and being reassigned to Elizabeth City, North Carolina, where he met and married his wife, Theresa.

Now, as a front-line Alaskan chopper pilot, Molthen was no newcomer to dramatic high-seas rescues. Through the years he'd flown hundreds of missions, and he had been directly involved in such well-known Coast Guard helicopter rescues as that involving the F/V *Collisto* only the month before. Along with fellow pilot Cmdr. Doug Taylor, he was awarded the DFC for his heroics.

Molthen was sitting in the wardroom of a small cabin on a rocky knoll overlooking the hangar when the call came in. "We have a four-oh-six EPIRB going off," came a voice over the intercom wired into the cabin. "Put the ready helo on the line."

The state-of-the-art H-60 helicopter would be flown by Lt. Dan Molthen, and copiloted by Lt. Bill Adickes, two of the finest helicopter pilots in the military today. Their chopper would carry no extraordinary provisions. Facing the "big unknown" 120 miles northwest of Sitka and 60 miles offshore, they'd lift off with the standard issue of just three Mark-25 flares (of short duration), two Mark-58s (of longer duration), one life raft, one flight mechanic, and one rescue swimmer.

Minutes later, as Adickes and Molthen taxied out to the runway, it was apparent that the weather was atrocious, the raging spawn of a 984-millibar low gripping the region. Inside Sitka Sound, Adickes knew, he wouldn't have to face the full fury of the storm. But there was normally some protection behind Mount Edgecumbe. Molthen and Adickes lifted off into what looked to be a typical January storm in southeastern Alaska, with the wintery mixture of Sitka hail, snow, sleet, and rain coming at them sideways.

Adickes chose to use the procedure for a zero-visibility departure. This hinged upon picking up the signal from the nav-aid beacon mounted on an island directly across from them in Sitka Sound. They quickly discovered, however, that the storm had knocked the beacon off-line. They would be forced to rely on their GPS (global positioning system) and the aircraft's radar.

Born and raised in the state of New Jersey, Rich Sansone had come along as the crew's rescue swimmer. A bundle of lean muscle and can-do energy, Sansone was just eighteen when, fresh out of high school, he joined the Coast Guard. Boot camp was tough, but nothing could have prepared him for the second boot camp, the one set up just for rescue swimmers. Its brutal regimen continued unabated for sixteen weeks! By comparison, the boot camp that all Marines must attend lasts just six weeks. When Sansone started out, there were six aspiring rescue swimmers in his class. Three dropped out. Rich Sansone was one of the three who graduated.

In the past, Sansone had launched out on a number of EPIRB cases. Usually, he knew, they turned up absolutely nothing. Often as not, long flights and a great deal of risk and effort resulted only in finding a boat floating at anchor, her crew sound asleep, and the EPIRB either drifting nearby or strapped to the vessel's wheelhouse, still in place, but accidentally activated.

"Hey, hey," Sansone joked. "This EPIRB probably just fell off some boat. There's no way in hell anyone is going to be out here fishing. Nobody could be that dumb."

Dan Molthen leveled the H-60 off at one thousand feet.

Molthen well knew that Alaska is different from any other place pilots might fly in the United States. Flying throughout the long winter nights among the endless mountain ranges in Alaska requires precise navigational skills. Fly too close to stormy waters and their helo could "chip a wave" and auger in, falling into the sea like a dropped stone, as Lt. Pat Rivas and his crew had done just up the coast in Prince William Sound. More recently, there had been a crash down off Coos Bay, on the Oregon coast, where a storm had knocked a Coast Guard helicopter out of the sky and into the sea, once again killing the entire crew.

In spite of the weather, however, Dan Molthen felt hopeful. This isn't so bad, he told himself. We can do this.

"Mr. Adickes," radioed Sansone, upon learning that they were going more than sixty miles offshore. "Are we going to have cover out there?"

"Well, the C-one-thirty out of Kodiak couldn't get in the air," replied Adickes.

Now, as Molthen and Adickes headed out across Sitka Sound, they could only sit and watch the storm building around them. When they first got airborne, the wind was blowing at thirty knots, with higher gusts. As they proceeded out the mouth of the sound, however, the wind-velocity gauge showed forty knots, then fifty.

Twenty or so miles from their landing pad back on Japonski Island, Dan Molthen "turned the corner" around Cape Edgecumbe and, suddenly carried along by a powerful tailwind, sprinted north up the coast. As they flew on, the wind rose to gale force—60 knots—and beyond. The faster they went, the worse the ride became.

Normally, Molthen knew they would travel toward a given scene at

150 knots (165 miles per hour). But riding a tailwind with gusts topping 70 knots (77 miles per hour), Molthen found himself closing on his destination at 220 knots (240 miles per hour), an unheard-of speed for a helicopter.

As they drew closer to the fixed point marked by digital numbers on their computer screen, the weather continued to worsen, and the helicopter began pitching up and down. Molthen felt himself leaping across the pitch-black sky in a gut-wrenching set of acrobatic maneuvers.

Even for the notorious Gulf of Alaska, it was a savage winter storm. Calling upon his own past, Molthen thought it felt quite similar to sailing into the eye of a hurricane, and he found himself sharing his concerns with Bill Adickes, essentially asking, "At what point are we going to say this is beyond our capabilities?"

Now and then, a crew member in back would check to see how they were doing. With fourteen thousand hours of flying time between them, Adickes and Molthen were sensitive to their crew's concerns. The men, they knew, wanted some reassurance that their pilots weren't going to get in over their heads, that they weren't going to go and do something stupid. They wanted to know that their pilots could bring them back from wherever they were going. While the men trusted Adickes and Molthen, on this night they were understandably concerned about self-preservation. No one on board had ever been out in weather anywhere near this bad.

As Molthen flew on, Adickes kept tabs on the weather, working with a handheld Jepson computer, commonly called a "whiz wheel." The gadget, nothing more than a circular slide rule, is used by navigators to calculate fuel consumption and range possibilities in any given situation.

For a time, both Adickes and Molthen wore their NVGs (night-vision goggles), but they weren't able to see anything except the snow and hail hurtling at them. The hail struck their windshield with the pinging clack of small rocks. Then a maniacal gust of wind would sucker punch the helicopter and send it reeling.

"Hey," radioed Rich Sansone. "Is this ever going to calm down?"

"No, Rich," replied Adickes. "It's probably going to be like this all the way out."

With all the changes of course and variations in altitude, Adickes found he couldn't hold his Jepson computer steady enough to read it. Mentally, then, he estimated their fuel burn: with the anti-icing system in the helo blades, the engine intake, and the cabin all running, how much fuel would it take to complete the mission? If those systems are turned on and Molthen is driving this helo at 98 percent of recommended torque, it's probably going to burn fourteen hundred pounds of fuel an hour, he figured. Flying against seventy- and eighty-mile-per-hour winds on their way back would dramatically increase that rate.

The optimum air speed for conserving fuel, Adickes knew, was 129 knots, although a pilot would never fly that slowly en route to a scene where people might be drowning or were in imminent danger. In such cases, he'd fly the H-60 at maximum speed on the way out, then choose the most efficient combination of speed and distance for the journey home.

A copilot could get overwhelmed by endless suppositions about the countless possibilities awaiting him. The prudent mind closed at the reality that should their helo crash, no rescue would be possible. As the flight continued, Adickes kept running the scenario in his head, asking himself, Does the plan we had still apply here? Does it still work? What's my backup plan?

It seemed only minutes had passed since they'd turned the corner at Cape Edgecumbe and felt the tailwind launch them on their way. Then Adickes noticed how much sooner they would be arriving on the rescue scene.

"Good God," he told Molthen, "we're going to be there in just fifteen minutes!"

"Rescue checklist part one for a basket hoist," Lieutenant Adickes told his crew. "Let's get that ball rolling, so that if we do find ourselves in a hoisting situation when we get there, we'll already have the preliminary steps completed. We need to get some flares ready. And get the computer set up so that we can immediately mark the point on the screen and begin conducting a Victor-Sierra search revolving around that point."

There was always a remote chance that they'd be facing a hoisting situation, so Adickes tried to lay the scenario out and have his men fill in the blanks. He had to keep them thinking, he knew; otherwise, they were going to just sit there and be terrified.

Then Molthen heard a faint sound coming from his headset. It was the pulse of an emergency radio beacon transmitter sounding off somewhere in the sleet and darkness a thousand feet below. At first, he could barely detect the fragile beacon, but as the distance between their helo and the transmitter shrank, the *beep-beep-beep* pulse spilling from his headset became amplified.

"Hey, we've got something!" declared Adickes and Molthen almost simultaneously.

The sound of the alarm echoing inside the chopper was both loud and unsettling, something akin to the warbling sound of a European police car's siren.

"Okay, we have the tone," said Adickes. "We have the needle pointing to it. Getting closer. But we're going to need to come down to where we can see the water."

"We're not going to see anything unless we drop down," agreed Molthen. "Okay, I'm leaving one thousand feet and coming down to three hundred feet," he said, pausing.

"Passing nine hundred."

"Gotcha," replied Adickes.

"Passing eight hundred."

"Gotcha."

As Molthen descended, he kept his eyes glued to the attitude indicator. The wing-shaped horizontal bar stared back at him from a blue backdrop, while the top half of a little red ball stuck up like a miniature sunrise directly behind it. Nose the helo forward, and the display darkened. Point her nose up, and the blue jumped out at you.

Chances were that this would turn out to be an accidental activation, another ghost chase. But there was always a chance that a fisherman with radio trouble or a mechanical problem might have switched his 406 EPIRB on as a way of communicating to others that he was drifting without power and, with winds and seas building, was going to need some help.

But hopefully, thought Molthen, all we're going to do here is locate the EPIRB, and nothing else. Then we can all go home.

They were still descending when, at about 350 feet, Dan Molthen started "pulling power" (meaning, increasing power) in an effort to slow their descent. This leveled them off at about three hundred feet. As he flew on in search of the source of the sound, Molthen could feel his adrenaline kicking in.

"Getting closer," said Adickes. "Getting closer. Getting closer." Suddenly, the direction-finding (DF) needle he was watching swung to point, pivoting around 180 degrees, and began pointing directly behind them.

"Oh crap, the needle swung around," said Adickes. "We just flew over the top of it. Mark point. Mark. Mark. Mark."

Lieutenant Adickes punched the datum button on his computer screen, marking that location as the epicenter around which they would conduct their search. With the aircraft history recorded, they would now be able to trace every leg of their flight on their aircraft's state-of-the-art GPS—dependable to within about the width of the chopper itself.

Now, as his helicopter sped downwind, Molthen began the indelicate task of turning the helicopter around. He would loop out and around and then swing in downwind of the drifting, blinking EPIRB. Then, flying into the wind, he'd make another pass, searching the mountains and valleys of the waters below at a far slower and more advantageous speed.

"We need to turn around," said Adickes.

"Okay, I'm going to start turning left now," replied Molthen.

"All right. Go ahead," said Adickes.

Just then, rescue swimmer and radioman Rich Sansone went "lost comms." All communications with the entire civilized world had just vanished. He tried repeatedly to raise a response, switching from channel to channel and testing his luck on every frequency available.

"Pilot," he radioed, "we have lost comms. I've tried Kodiak on all frequencies, and the comm center in Juneau on all frequencies, and no luck with them."

"Keep trying."

"Roger, sir."

In this case, going "lost comms" meant complete isolation under the worst-possible conditions. Having flown through the area on several occasions since being stationed in Sitka, Molthen knew that there had always been a dead spot there. The area in between Yakutat and Cape Spencer was known as "the black hole of communications." Through the years, it had caused big problems for fliers and mariners passing through the area.

Molthen had only just begun making his teardrop turn when he felt the wind strike the helicopter's exposed side. It swept him sideways downwind at breakneck speed. The wind carried them for several thousand feet before Molthen was able to complete the turn and get the chopper's nose turned back into the wind. Then he came fighting his way back upwind toward the swelling sound of the mechanical beeper and whatever else might possibly be awaiting them there.

Lt. Dan Molthen slowed to seventy knots. Not yet within sight of the water, he had only his computer readout to tell him how fast he was approaching. The digits on the GPS computer, however, seemed locked in place. Apparently, he quickly surmised, he was flying into a seventy-knot head wind and, in effect, was in a hover, gaining little, if any, real ground. It took appoximately fifteen minutes to work his way back over the object signaling in the water.

"I still can't see anything," said Bill Adickes. "Why don't we try two hundred feet."

"Okay, let's go to two hundred feet," replied Molthen. "I'm leaving three hundred feet. I'm setting my RAT OUT [radar altimeter warning alarm] to one hundred and eighty feet."

"Gotcha. Leaving three hundred feet. Coming down to two hundred feet." Adickes paused. "Hey, I can see the water."

"Yep, I see it, too," said Molthen. He allowed himself only a momentary glance, and in the next instant, he shifted his concentration back to his instruments.

"Boy, Dan, those waves look awfully big," said Adickes.

The seas were mountainous. It was an ocean gone mad. Storm winds had blown unchallenged across more than one thousand miles of open Gulf of Alaska sea, creating waves that averaged over sixty feet in height, moved at nearly 50 miles per hour, and sported wave troughs that, on occasion, stretched for over 1,200 hundred feet from crest to crest. By comparison, if one were to stand on the top of one end of the Rose Bowl in Pasadena, California, just one of these wave troughs would sweep down to the playing field and arch up again to the top of the opposite end of the stadium.

Their gigantic size and breaking fury were enough to give any pilot pause. Worse yet, the sea appeared to possess limitless energy and came powering out of the darkness without warning, often from different directions. Surfers in the winter on the north shore of Hawaii often refer to such waves as "mackers," because they strike with all the subtlety of a Mack truck.

Adickes and Molthen observed the watery mayhem from their precarious perch two hundred feet above. The storm waves passed through one another, sometimes canceling one another and other times stacking up on one another, creating massive anomalies of pyramiding seas commonly referred to by fishermen as "rogue" waves.

Now, more than ever, Molthen hoped to make quick work of locating the tiny floating transmitter and, with the vessel and crew long gone, sprint for the safety of harbor and home.

CHAPTER 7

I 'm getting water in my face," coughed out Dave Hanlon. "I can't keep my head up! I can't keep my head out of the water!"

Somehow, during their rush to abandon ship, Dave Hanlon and his crewmates had failed to inflate Hanlon's all-essential neck collar.

Gig Mork swam to Hanlon, grabbed him, and pulled him back across his stomach and chest. Then he looped his left arm down across Hanlon's chest and held on, using his right arm to maneuver.

When the next monstrous wave found them, DeCapua could feel it sucking them up into the curl of its wave crest. "Oh Lord, here we go again!" he yelled aloud. "I'm so sick of this!"

The worst part for DeCapua was getting sucked up in the curl of the wave. There, inside, in the cold, suffocating darkness, tied to one another on a twisting leash approximately thirty feet long, those unlucky enough to be present forfeited any semblance of control.

As the flooding sea submerged them, DeCapua felt himself being slammed bodily into a crewmate's back; the flailing foot of an unidentified comrade struck him in the ribs with the effectiveness of one trained in the martial arts; someone's head collided with his own. To keep from involuntarily inhaling the seawater into his lungs, he held his breath through various levels of oxygen deprivation as he tried to locate the surface, reminding himself all the while not to panic.

As the wave powered along, it kept DeCapua and his buddies trapped inside. That was the terrifying part, not knowing when, or even *if*, the mad vortex of swirling water was ever going to relinquish its hold. Through dozens of such disquieting excursions, DeCapua was certain of one thing: he and the others didn't physically escape from such a wave; *it let them go.*

There was only one thing that DeCapua feared more, and that was the thought of getting washed out of his rope loop and coming up all alone out there.

"Sound off!" he yelled when they surfaced again. "How many we got? How many we got? I'm here."

"I'm here, too," called out Gig Mork.

"Yes!" piped in Bob Doyle.

"Me, too!" added Mark Morley.

"That makes four," shouted DeCapua. "Where's Dave?"

"Hanlon!" yelled the skipper. "Dave Hanlon! Are you with us?"

A silence ensued.

"Yah, I'm here," he said finally, but for several seconds, they were left to wonder.

They had barely gathered themselves and finished their roll call when another free-running slab of ocean began to lift them. Up and up they drifted, with G-forces similar to a never-ending elevator ride pulling at them. Then came a deafening roar from far overhead as the approaching wave broke fully down upon them.

DeCapua involuntarily swallowed several mouthfuls of the flat-tasting saltwater before drifting back to the surface again.

"It was Mark Morley who broke the silence," recalls DeCapua. "He's the one who cared for everybody."

"Is everybody here?" shouted the skipper. "Sound off!" he yelled again.

The response from each crewman was immediate. "Mike!" "Gig!" "Bob!" Then silence. Something was wrong. David Hanlon hadn't answered.

"Dave!" screamed the skipper in a frantic, demanding tone.

"Yah, I'm here," came back Hanlon's tired voice.

Hanlon's voice surprised Mike DeCapua, because it rose out of the darkness right beside him.

"Hey, look," shot back the skipper. "The next time we holler, answer immediately! All right? Because we need to know where in the hell you are! We're trying to keep track of one another out here!"

No more than a half hour had passed before the steady leaks around the hood of David Hanlon's survival suit and the leg of Mark Morley's suit began to catch up with both of the men.

Survival suits are designed to keep a survivor upright and lying on his back, with his or her face in the air. But both Hanlon's and Morley's suits were filling quickly, and the progression of their hypothermic states in the near-freezing wash now sloshing about inside their suits was forcing both men onto their stomachs.

Now, approaching him from behind, Bob Doyle swung an arm over Mark Morley's shoulder and, just as Gig Mork had done with David Hanlon, drew him back onto his lap and chest. The unavoidable reality, however, was that each time a wave washed in over the men, neither Gig Mork nor Bob Doyle was able to hold on to his struggling crewmate. When another trampling wave again released them, Hanlon came up hacking roughly, offering up clear evidence that he'd inadvertently inhaled some seawater. Morley fared slightly better, coughing lightly, then fell silent.

Along with the camaraderie, the EPIRB provided a kind of unexpected solace, for every ten seconds or so, it would emit a staccato flash of brilliant white light, a pulse, actually. As they drifted through the pummeling seas, strung out along a thirty-foot-long chain of rope and bodies, Doyle noted how the howling vacuum of spray screaming past them filled every centimeter of surrounding space, bombarding them like a swarm of insects.

As each wave approached, the deafening roar seemed to break through to new levels of barbaric intensity. Profane shouts were heaped one on another, and sometimes finalized by a simple "Look out!" followed by another collapsing wave.

This is more than just seas, thought DeCapua. God's out to kill us!

Some waves would carry them higher and higher, without ever actually cresting. Sliding down the face of one of these waves was a little like experiencing the rush of a wild carnival ride. The crew members even had occassion to verbally taunt the wave gods.

"Is that the best you've got, Poseidon?" yelled Bob Doyle. "Oh, no, no, no! I didn't mean it. Just kidding," he added, feeling superstitious about having offended the Greek god of the sea.

Tied last in line behind his shipmates, Bob Doyle rode up the astoundingly tall face of one wave. Then, as Morley, DeCapua, Mork, and Hanlon popped over the top, they began a near free fall down the opposite side of the watery mountain. As his crewmates descended, Doyle found himself being dragged along across the water and flung over the top of the wave—whiplashed through the air as if weightless.

Then it became an amazing ride that involved a seventy-five or eighty-foot vertical drop down the backside of the monster wave.

On such a night, and completely aside from the life-and-death struggle at hand, if a fisherman happened to be in the right place and chanced to look in the correct direction at the precise moment when the strobe light flashed, he might capture a snapshot vision of his crewmates caught in midstruggle in a position that defied the laws of gravity—their ranks frozen in place up the steep black face of a wave, or, just as likely, the flash of their bodies, halted in midair, as they tumbled through space off its folding crest.

The sound of the waves accelerating toward them from far overhead filled their ears with a deafening roar that rose octave upon octave, until their hearts beat with a furious paranoia.

Gig Mork was holding on to David Hanlon across his left side and had just locked arms with Mike DeCapua on his right when the curling face of a wave perhaps seven stories high fell on them. As the roar of the wave descended upon them, Mork could sense the terror in Mike DeCapua, because when Mike locked elbows with him, he did so with the strength and urgency of a death grip.

"Hold your breath!" Mork screamed as the roaring wave descended.

The mammoth rogue, weighing fifteen hundred pounds per cubic yard, slammed down upon them with the concussive sound of dynamite detonating. The initial force of the wave stripped both Hanlon and DeCapua from Gig Mork's arms, driving the men perhaps thirty feet below the surface.

Alone in the dark, underneath the water, Mork held his breath. Lost in the dark body of the wave, with the pressure in his ears building, he struggled to remain calm. Though he felt certain that his survival suit would eventually carry him back to the surface, Mork wasn't at all confident that he could hold his breath that long, especially with everybody kicking, scrambling, and cartwheeling through the currents all around him.

When he surfaced again, he drew in deep, long lungfuls of the wet, cold air and checked to see if he was still tied to his crewmates inside his own rope loop. Then he began searching for David Hanlon. He could hear him choking nearby and called out to him. He grabbed Hanlon's rope line and pulled him near.

"Dave, come on," urged Mork. "We've got to swim! Goddamn it, we've got to keep swimming!"

"My suit's leaking in around the neck," replied Dave Hanlon exhaustedly, almost unable to catch his breath. "And I can't keep my head above water. I keep getting water in my face. I just can't keep my head out of the water."

With each ensuing wave, Hanlon's condition seemed to worsen. He was in pretty bad shape, even with Gig Mork's efforts to do all he could to look after his shipmate.

"Hey, here, come on," Mork told him, pulling him up and across his own chest once again. "There. How does that feel?"

"That's better," said Hanlon gratefully. "I'm doing fine now."

Each time another wave folded down on them and tore them apart, Mork would resurface and fight to shake off the ill effects of the latest trouncing. Then he would immediately set out to relocate the wrenching, seasick Hanlon.

David Hanlon was lying on his back on top of Gig Mork, with his head clear of the water, when another hopelessly large wave dropped on them, burying both men.

Choking, Mork surfaced.

Bob Doyle began to call for the others. "Mike! Where are you?"

"I'm here," came the slurred but valiant voice of Mike DeCapua.

"Gig?"

"Here!"

"Mark, is that you?" asked Doyle, drawing him in close and slinging him across his lap.

"Yes," came the skipper's groggy reply.

Gig Mork was searching intently for David Hanlon when Doyle called out, "Hanlon!"

When there was no reply, Gig Mork and Mike DeCapua joined Doyle in the unified call: "H-A-N-L-O-N!"

The darkness seemed to swallow the name. Perhaps he was caught up in the tangle of lines directly beneath them, they reasoned. They searched frantically under and around themselves for any sign of the man, but they encountered only the slippery seaweed feel of the rope lines sliding through their hands and across their legs and feet.

Then, a single blink of the strobe light illuminated the hazy form of a buoy drifting away. Doyle spotted it as it moved through the gray-white inundations of spray, beyond the outermost edge of the light. Then he noticed that the buoy on the far end of the human chain was missing. It would be a long shot, but if Hanlon was attached to the buoy, and could somehow stop his suit from leaking, he stood a solid chance of surviving.

"Dave! Dave! Hanlon! Where are you? We're over here! Over here!" called Mork and his crewmates again and again. But they heard nothing, and never saw him again.

In the hours that followed, DeCapua and the others often called out for Dave Hanlon: "Dave! Daaaave! We're over here!" But there was never any response.

"I'm so sorry for bringing you guys out here," said Mark Morley suddenly, his sad voice and regretful tone rising out of the darkness only inches away. "I wish I would have listened to you guys. I'm so sorry."

He then began talking about his fiancée, Tamara, who was four-months pregnant at the time. He wanted to be there when their son was born.

"Hang in there, man!" DeCapua yelled back to him. "Don't give up! Don't give up! Keep on fighting!"

"I don't know if I can!" replied Morley. "I'm awfully cold. My suit's leaking badly."

"Man, you've got to pull through," DeCapua told him. "You just gotta!"

Losing David Hanlon had come near to breaking the skipper's heart, DeCapua knew. Also weighing heavily on him was the realization that more of his men might very well die, as well. This reality, DeCapua felt, was almost too much for the man.

Morley must have felt more than a little bewildered at how suddenly and completely his love for, and childlike vision of, Alaska could have gone so hellishly astray.

As a youngster growing up back in Michigan, he delighted in going fishing with his father. Mark took naturally to the outdoors. Together, Roger Morley and his son spent a good deal of time together investigating the marshlands bordering nearby Lake Erie, jigging for walleye and salmon, and catching as many as sixty-five perch during a single day.

Anyone could see the boy's big heart. And let a TV documentary on Alaska flash over the screen, and the wide-eyed youngster would yell, "Momma! Come quick. Look! It's Alaska!"

In the years to come, Mark Morley grew up into a solid young man, with a reputation for being both a hard worker and a generous human being. Once he bought his parents a garage door opener; another time, he showed up on Christmas Eve carrying a dishwasher.

His real gift, however, was his ability to fix anything, turning a hand successfully at carpentry, plumbing, and auto body work as well.

Then one day, just after his thirty-second birthday, his boyhood obsession seemed to sprout wings, and he suddenly announced to his father that he was quitting his job.

"Dad, I'm going to Alaska," he told him.

"Mark, you can't be serious," replied his father.

The elder Morley hated to see him go. His son, he knew, didn't get upset about the little things, was popular at work, and easy to get along with. Yet he was attracted to the life on the edge. Risk-taking was the key element that was missing.

As one might expect, when he arrived in Sitka, Morley took instantly to the place. And Tamara Westcott.

"Mom, I found her!" Mark told his mother, Edna Fantozzi, soon thereafter. "I've found the perfect girl. She's strong, and she's a redhead."

Only the Sunday before the *La Conte*'s final journey, Mark had called his father in Michigan using a cell phone. He was down on the docks working on board the *La Conte* at the time, trying to prepare her for the upcoming journey.

It was a "tough show," he eventually confided, "not making any money, so far, and all."

Now, in an effort to protect and warm themselves, Gig Mork, Mike DeCapua, Bob Doyle, and Mark Morley decided to draw in closer to one another. They locked arms and huddled together as best they could.

Mike DeCapua had struggled to keep his face and hood seal clear of his long brown hair in order to remain dry and to see. Often, he found it blind going, but when the silvery EPIRB light blinked, DeCapua caught, in its camera-like flash, the image of his shipmates clustered around him. It was the fellowship they shared that had sustained them; by now, each of them had come to know the value of it.

"So look, boys," called out Bob Doyle. "It's going to be awhile, but the helicopter is going to be here. We've got the EPIRB working. You guys don't worry. 'Cause I'm telling you, I know the guys at the Sitka Air Station. I know them, and they're going to be here. I've worked in

Antarctica. I've been around, and the best pilots there are anywhere in the whole world are either up in Kodiak or right here at Sitka. They are the best there is: that's why they're here!"

Such encouraging talk lifted their spirits.

CHAPTER 8

owering upwind, Molthen began what is called a "Victor-Sierra search" of the area. Using such a flight pattern, or grid, Molthen would fly out from ground zero and return to it again and again, flying like a bee in a pattern similar in design to the curve of a flower petal sweeping out and back. In so doing, he would ensure that he'd cover the same general area of ocean again and again, as opposed to the long, straight, back-and-forth ladder search commonly used during the daylight hours by the four-engine C-130 turboprop planes.

As in most search and rescue operations, luck would play a part. Searching the slopes and valleys in the dark in such seas meant a short radius of vision. Everything would likely depend upon someone on board looking down at exactly the right place, at precisely the right time.

A raft would be a lot easier to find than a person in the water. According to USCG data, there is only a 5 percent chance of spotting a person in the water in broad daylight with moderate seas running, a statistic that is dramatically enhanced by on-site assets such as a flashing EPIRB light or one of the new strobe lights that can be purchased and attached to a survival suit itself.

On a night like this one, however, the odds of locating an individual survivor or even a group of survivors unless there was a life raft, EPIRB, handheld radio, or strobe light to draw attention to them were infinitesimal.

Piloting a helicopter forward into gusting eighty- and ninety-mile-per-hour winds produces a loathsome, body-jarring flight. Ask a pilot to initiate a stable hover over those he intends to rescue, and several things will happen. First, the wind will drive up the nose of the H-60. As a result, the tail rudder will dive down, and the chopper will rise, exposing its entire underside to the brunt of the wind and causing it to be blown back off-site. If left uncorrected, with her weight pitching back on her tail, the chopper will be swept backward and, simultaneously, will plummet, crew and all, into the sea.

As the pilot of the H-60, Lt. Dan Molthen now faced the challenge of his life. It was important, he knew, to fly as close as possible along the grid lines indicated on the computer screen. Otherwise, there would be no way to ensure that he had either covered the area or gone over the same area twice. So he bore down hard, flying as close as he could, trying to achieve the impossible goal of perfect flight.

Heading upwind, Molthen struggled to maintain an altitude of approximately two hundred feet. Nevertheless, in making his approach in to hover, he began oscillating wildly through the night, rising and falling in leaping vicissitudes one hundred feet and more within just seconds. One moment, the helo's nose would pitch violently up, and he'd climb up into that battering storm; in the the next, the nose of the H-60 would dip forward and down, and he'd find himself free-falling toward the ocean.

They were staggering upwind when, in the mist of the snow and sleet pummeling them, Bill Adickes caught a glimpse of a light with his NVGs. It was just a single flash from the strobe light mounted atop the floating EPIRB, yet it was everything. And from that moment on, Adickes kept his eyes glued to the spot.

"Dan, come right ten degrees," he ordered. "I'm sure I saw a light. I'm certain I did."

Molthen obeyed, instantly adjusting his course.

"Come right another ten degrees," said Adickes. "Keep heading in that direction, and we'll see if we get more flashes."

Then a tiny point of light flashed in the lens of Dan Molthen's NVGs. Molthen knew that with the illumination as low as it was at that moment, sparkles sometimes appeared in the lens for no good reason, inexplicably rendering the goggles useless. Then, in between the bombarding slopes of the skyscraper waves, he, too, captured the tiny momentary flash of the strobe light.

"I see it," said Molthen steadily, readjusting his course.

There was no sign of any boat. If there are people in the area, he thought, they'd most likely be drifting somewhere nearby inside a life raft. Aw, he speculated further, it's probably just another EPIRB that fell off a boat, and the ship is returning safely to town—like we should be.

But neither Bill Adickes nor Dan Molthen was prepared for what they saw next.

"I see something in the water!" said Adickes.

With winds of eighty miles per hour and better now trying to push them back, they battled closer. As they drew nearer, they caught the stark sticklike reflections of retrotape coming from the area near the floating EPIRB.

Adickes and Molthen could hardly believe their eyes.

"I don't know, but I think I see a raft," said Molthen. "Hey, turn on the big light and let's have a look-see," he added.

The powerful 1.5-million-candlepower "night sun" was mounted on the helicopter's underside; in clear weather, it was capable of lighting up an entire football field at one time. But when it flashed to life, it reflected back off the snow and spray, and they were promptly blinded by it. Engulfed in a complete whiteout, with all visual cues and external references instantly wiped out, Molthen was left with total spacial disorientation.

"Turn it off!" he snapped, and the light clicked off.

Molthen placed his right thumb on the searchlight switch mounted atop the collective stick and flicked on his smaller, secondary spotlight, one with less than a twentieth of the power. It had a small Chinesecoolie-hat-shaped control that allowed a pilot to point the beam of light in any direction he desired. Though Molthen could see somewhat better now, he still couldn't make out exactly how many men there were. Then the reflective tape glued to the material of the survival suits below caught his eye again, and Molthen took in the vision of the arms of at least two survivors waving frantically up at him.

"I think we've got at least two people in the water," said Molthen, returning now to his instruments.

"I think there're more than two," replied Adickes, peering down through the windshield's "chin bowl" at his feet with his night-vision goggles. He could see people coming in and out of view, and chunks of reflective tape. He knew suits often came with a long strip of tape attached to each shoulder. He counted at least eight of the strips, perhaps more. The survivors had somehow managed to remain huddled together, which, he silently acknowledged, was an extremely smart thing to do.

"I'm pretty confident there're at least four people down there," said Adickes finally.

Man, this is going to be tough, thought Molthen. There really is a boat out here! We've got eighty-mile-per-hour winds, and God knows how large the seas are. And if we have any kind of mechanical failure and are forced to ditch this helo in this weather so far from land . . . His mind closed off at the thought.

Under normal conditions, Molthen would have gone down to within fifty feet or so of the water, established a controlled hover, and proceeded with the rescue. On this night, however, that would be impossible. At one hundred feet, they were barely clearing the tops of the waves.

As soon as Molthen reached anything like a stationary hover, a gust of wind would plow into the helo and sweep it backward at fifty miles per hour or better. Then Molthen would have to dump the nose down thirty degrees and apply full throttle just to pull out of the backward cycle and begin inching his way back. Thereupon, the wind would abruptly relent, and they would find themselves screaming forward. In spite of the thousands of hours of flying time accumulated over more than twelve years of flying, it was all an accomplished pilot like Dan Molthen could do just to keep the helicopter out of the water.

"Get me over on top of those people," Adickes told Molthen, cutting him no slack. "That's who we're here to save."

"I'm trying," shot back Molthen.

Molthen, Adickes knew, was struggling to maintain both airspeed and altitude. He was being forced to move the highly sensitive controls three-quarters of the maximum distance just to remain in the air. Equally troubling were the countless particles of snow and spray swirling around the helicopter. It was giving those in the cockpit an intense sense of vertigo, called "the leans." This created the visual illusion of moving in a direction when in fact they were not. Such a phenomenon was both distracting and deadly. Several times, neither Molthen nor Adickes could determine the direction in which their aircraft was moving, and, as a result, they very nearly crashed.

Stress, anxiety, fear, panic. It isn't that a pilot doesn't ever have those feelings, but after years of flying, he or she learns to deal with them. At such times, pilots will instinctively run back to the fundamentals beaten into their brains all through their flight simulator training. The "what if" procedures, which, month after month, they had practiced but, in the real world, had never actually used.

When threatened with losing control of his ride, a pilot has to revert back to the fundamental skills he was taught: Fly by your instruments. Stay glued to them. No matter what your body tells you, believe in your instruments. Watch your altitude indicator. Watch your Doppler radar scanner. Check your GPS, your compass heading, your ground speed, and your attitude and altitude readouts as well. They will see you through.

Even when your gut feeling tells you that you're rolling upside down and about to dive into the sea, if your attitude indicator says you need to make a left turn adjustment, then you must make a left turn.

Ignoring the autokinesis of balance going on in his inner ear, a pilot has to say to himself, Even though I feel this is wrong, I'm going to take the stick and move it to the right. I'm going to move it to the right and level out the winds, even though I feel that by doing so I'll be turning that helo upside down.

Digress from this, and you face the growing likelihood of becoming another morbid statistic, like the jet pilot caught in bad weather who believes he's fighting to gain altitude when, in reality, he's upside down, flying straight into the ground.

Molthen pulled back slightly on the cyclic, but as he slowed in an attempt to hover, the H-60 started bouncing around the sky. In spite of that fact, he flipped up his NVGs and swung the small searchlight around until he could look down again on those awaiting rescue.

In the rear cabin, flight mech Sean Witherspoon slid open the side door and leaned forward to survey the scene. Rescue swimmer Rich Sansone joined him there. They could make out a ragged row of people in orange survival suits, their heads cocked to the side, waving up at them as they rode over the tsunami-sized waves below.

"Good God, there really *are* people in the water," said Sansone in total disbelief. "We've got people down there!"

"Roger that," said Molthen.

Sansone felt determined to help them. Regardless of the fierce seas, he wanted to get into the water himself. He felt certain that he could make a difference down there with the survivors, whoever they were.

"Sir," Sansone radioed to his officers in front. "Would you consider using me in this situation? Should I dress down?"

"Hell no," said Adickes. "Rich, there is not a snowball's chance in hell that we're going to deploy you in a sea state like this."

Sansone decided to dress down regardless, just in case.

Molthen worked the helo's controls to try to establish a stable hover and to remain somewhere near the survivors so they wouldn't lose sight of them. It was a constant struggle to maintain both altitude and stability, to hover close enough to attempt the rescue and yet not end up in the water themselves.

Now it was time to attempt the hoist.

"Target in sight," said Molthen. "Conn me in."

The instant Sean Witherspoon pushed the rescue basket out the door, the storm winds stripped it away, sweeping it horizontally back toward the tail rotor blades.

To compensate for the sharp slant of the hoist cable playing out behind them, Molthen was forced to creep forward into a position well ahead of the survivors, and in doing so, he effectively stripped himself of all visual references. Overall, the hoisting cycle proved to be a miserable failure. They rode across the sky, rising and falling and twisting on a wind-tortured course that forced Molthen to concentrate more on survival than on snatching helpless victims from a savage sea.

With snow, spray, and rain obstructing their view, and without the flares, Molthen knew there really would be no way to tell where the nighttime started and the wave began. They would need to deploy some flares to facilitate a reference for hovering and to keep them from flying into one of the invisible black slopes of one of the gigantic waves. For a time, the drifting flares would provide fair warning of the otherwise invisible approach of "monstrous pitch-black waves moving out of a pitch-black night."

"Crew, we need to toss out some flares," said Molthen, knowing full well that there were only five such flares on board.

A chopper, Molthen knew, had to be in forward flight and clear of the area once the saltwater-activated flares were tossed out, to avoid the missile projectile they initially sent up. Therefore, he moved ahead, swung in, and dispersed three of the flares. Flying past those waiting in the water below, he then allowed the helicopter to slide back downwind of them again.

"Rescue checklist part two for basket hoist of survivors," said Molthen.

"Rescue checklist part two is complete," replied flight mech Sean Witherspoon. "Ready to hoist."

"Begin the hoist," said Molthen.

"Basket's going out the door," said Witherspoon. "Basket's going down."

A rescue basket is a stainless-steel cage that is surisingly short. It's about half the length of the standard ambulance stretcher, but much stockier and deeper. Made of stainless steel, the basket is 45 inches long, 25 inches wide, and 14 inches deep, and weighs about 40 pounds. The peak of the arc, where the hoist cable attaches, is about 38 inches above the floor. Round chunks of buoyant foam are wrapped around horizontal crossbars at each end. As it comes to rest in the water, the basket, under ideal conditions, will lie semi-submerged, theoretically allowing easy access and egress.

At first glance, a rescue basket looks a little like the protective cage on a go-cart, but without the wheels.

The message that Dan Molthen was hoping to hear from his flight mech was "Basket is approaching the water." Instead, there was a lengthy pause.

"Basket's going back! Basket's going aft of the aircraft!" reported the voice.

"As soon as we got the basket out the door," Witherspoon would later recall, "it started flapping in the wind like a piece of confetti. Everything I'd been taught about high-seas rescues went out the door that night.

"This isn't going to work," Witherspoon radioed the pilots up front.

Adickes decided to intercede. "Crew, we may or we may not be able to do this," he began. "So let's everybody just keep our heads. We're going to take this one step at a time, very methodically and very slowly. If we succeed, great. But that's how we're going to approach it. We're going to treat this like other events that we've been a part of. And we'll see where it leads us."

In a clever act of cable management, Witherspoon somehow managed to lower the rescue basket past the tail rotor. But in the unremitting storm winds, the basket was soon trailing far behind them, and nowhere near the survivors. When the hoist cable began chafing on the underbelly of the chopper, Witherspoon reeled in the cable and played it back out again. When he did finally manage to lower the basket down to the water, a passing wave buried the basket and line almost up to the chopper itself. Then the hoist cable came drum-tight and literally began to yank on the helicopter. With the chopper pitching violently, and the straining cable snapping uncontrollably against the side of the aircraft, it wasn't inconceivable that the rescue basket could end up launching into the tail rotor, bringing them all down.

Dan Molthen worked to maintain an altitude of 150 feet, dividing his attentions between the instruments before him and the survivors, who were generally below and in back of him. At the time, he felt like he was "on top of the Seattle Space Needle," he recalls. "I was over here. I was over there. I mean, I was just trying to capture some semblance of station on these guys. I was just swinging back and forth, shifting each time the length of an entire football field, and doing so in just seconds. I'd have the guys right in front of me, to within just one hundred feet or so of the helicopter, and the next thing I knew, I was being blown back at least a thousand feet, to where I couldn't even see the survivors anymore! That's how fierce the winds were. And we were asking ourselves, How the hell are we ever going to be able to pull this thing off? We can't even hover the helo!"

We're here, thought Molthen, and we're going to get these guys. I hate the way I'm flying right now. I refuse to accept it. I know I can do better.

"Let's try this again," said Molthen aloud.

CHAPTER 9

The four remaining crewmen off the lost ship *La Conte* had been in the water a little over an hour and a half when Molthen, Adickes, and the crew of the H-60 arrived on the scene. Those in the water heard the chopper before they actually saw it. The roar of the jet engines drowned out the sound of waves. When Mike DeCapua first spotted the helo, it was flying into the wind, its lights flashing and its searchlights searching.

To DeCapua and his crewmates, the chopper seemed like the very hand of the Almighty. God can defeat this storm, thought DeCapua. He was certain now that they were about to jump aboard the helicopter and off they would go. We're out'a here! he thought.

"Hey, everybody," yelled Doyle. "Wave as much as possible! And hold the EPIRB up as high as you can!"

Mike DeCapua waved and rejoiced right along with his crewmates. "Wow! We're rescued, man!" he yelled. "They found us! Can you believe this? We're getting rescued!"

The chopper pilot appeared to be attempting to hold at an altitude just above the crests of the massive waves, now lumbering through the grainy swath of the chopper's spotlight. DeCapua could see that whoever was up there flying the chopper was dead set on reaching them. Frustrating as it was to everyone concerned, those waiting in the water below could actually see for themselves why they weren't able to lower the basket. Each time they sent the rescue basket out the chopper's side door, it would drop down about four feet, whereupon the blasting gusts of wind would blow it back toward the tail rudder like a kite in the wind. It was the most perplexing thing—to be so close to getting rescued and yet so far. And yet, for all the helicopter crew's unflinching efforts, time did not seem to bring them closer.

DeCapua knew that Morley, unlike himself and the rest of his crewmates, was having trouble with his suit. Ice-cold seawater had been flushing in through the hole in the knee of Mark Morley's survival suit the entire time.

DeCapua could not have known that, when immersed in water, the human body loses heat at an astounding twenty-four times the rate it does in air of the same temperature. There was no way Morley's body could keep up with the massive amount of energy being robbed by the Alaskan seawater flushing through his suit.

The medical people who dealt with similar cases called it "cold water immersion," or "immersion frostbite." Morley was, in fact, slowly freezing to death.

As DeCapua figured it, the chopper crew must have chucked a little weight into the basket, because the next time they lowered it, it descended safely below and, finally, aft of the tail rotor.

"Be careful!" yelled Bob Doyle to his crewmates. "Watch it! Watch it! If that basket does come down here and hits one of us, it can kill you! And let the basket hit the water first. Don't touch it until it hits the water, because it'll shock you. It's got to ground itself out on the water first."

Rarely did the rescue basket land very close, and the few times that it did, it quickly became immersed in the waves, and the crewmen felt that it was too risky to cut themselves loose and just swim for it. More often, when the basket made it down, it would ricochet off the water like a skipping rock, shooting ahead and burying itself in the face of an oncoming wave. Then, as several hundred feet of cable line trailing far behind the chopper came taut, as the opposing velocities of swinging basket and powering wave met head-on, the basket would break free of the water and shoot skyward once again. Under such circumstances, the forty-pound rescue basket became an object of destruction, nothing short of a flying wrecking ball rending damage, in its pendulum like swing, wherever it struck.

Sometimes, a sixty- or seventy-foot wave would bury the basket, creeping up the cable line to within what looked to be just feet from the bottom of the chopper itself. Next came the clacking roar, and those in the water could hear the pilot go full-collective as the chopper came under the strain. Then they'd see the basket explode out of the top of the wave, trailing water after it right up to the helicopter's side door.

Now, several saltwater-activated flares ignited in the water nearby, illuminating the area in a yellowish haze of soft amber light. Each time the men would crest over one of the waves, they could see one or more of the flares. Then they would go back down into the "muck and gloom" of the wave trough. Even from there, however, they could make out the silhouettes of the waves and the yellowish glow of flare light filtering over the ridges of the waves separating them.

Now, as he watched, DeCapua saw the helicopter above hovering for a few seconds in what looked to be a somewhat stable posture. Suddenly, an unseen blast of wind struck, staggering the chopper, nearly knocking it onto its side. The helo's blades dipped almost vertically as the pilot fought to gain control. Then Doyle heard the straining roar of the aircraft's gearbox and engines being torqued to levels that he strongly suspected were well beyond the recommended limits.

The pilot recovered less than the width of the main rotor blades from the water. He was trying to gain altitude, fighting his way up the long, sloping face of the wave, when, just as he crowned over it, another williwaw struck. The hollowing force of the winds funneling out of the stadium-sized wave valleys on the opposite side, exploded over the ridge top with typhoon force, blasting the aircraft into the heavens with a wet and icy vacuum of arctic air.

As DeCapua watched, the helo reared up on its tail like a horse bucking. Then, as if weightless, it was swept backward at a furious clip, quickly losing itself in the vast, turbulent body of blowing sea spray.

During his supply-officer days, Bob Doyle had had some adventures of his own aboard ships at sea, and aboard helicopters ranging as far as four hundred miles north of the U.S. Coast Guard's base at Point Barrow, on the edge of the Arctic Ocean. He'd encountered some strong winds up there, but nothing like the kind of winds his helicopter was braving on this night.

"Oh my God," said Mark Morley, his mind fogging now from the stupefying effects of severe hypothermia. "I'm so sorry for bringing you out here."

"Hey, Mark," shot back Mike DeCapua. "We're still going to get out of here. There's the chopper. Just hang on. They're a-coming. Just hang on."

"No, man, you guys don't know. I'm so sorry. I should have listened to you."

"No, no. You can't think of that," said Doyle, patiently scolding him. "You've got to hang on."

"Mark, work on staying alive," said DeCapua. "Devote your energy to something else, buddy!"

Caught up in the late stages of hypothermia, his body temperature already slumping easily into the eighties, Morley spoke with a hopeless resignation. He regretted the things he hadn't been able to do yet with his fiancée, Tamara. "Tell my lady that I love her."

Like many who fish in Alaska, Mark Morley wanted to buy some property in the wild and live out away from the common herd. He planned to build a log cabin for Tamara and the little ones. "He had every detail set in his mind," she says. "He knew exactly how it was going to be, and exactly what it would look like."

They were leaning toward buying a beautiful piece of wilderness property about thirty miles outside the village of Haines on Lynn Canal, just down the line from Skagway, once the gateway to the Klondike gold fields. It was there, in 1898, that Jack London climbed up and over the forty-mile-long Chilkoot Pass, built a raft, and floated to Dawson down the Yukon River. And it was there, in 1886, that Tamara's great-grandfather had been born and had as a young man worked for the railroad on the train carrying miners and adventurers over White Pass. Once, during a visit to the small town of Skagway, she'd even discovered his name in the historical registry of the Arctic Brotherhood Association.

For now, however, they would remain in Sitka. In between fishing trips, Mark and Tamara often made excursions together into the wilderness that still surrounds the town. Once, they hiked up to Bear Lake. Another time, they climbed to the top of 2,900-foot-high Harbor Peak. On other trips, they traveled by skiff to Deep Inlet and Silver Bay and hiked ashore, making their way around the waterfalls, past the cliffs, and on through the lush green forestland that carpets so much of southeast Alaska.

Morley kept a picture of his bride-to-be in the *La Conte*'s wheelhouse. Though not a particularly religious man, he kept another card posted alongside it—a picture of a young sailor wrestling with a chest-high wheel out on the exposed poop deck of a sailing ship of old. Behind him stood the image of Jesus, with one hand resting on the youngster's shoulder and the other arm outstretched and pointing the way.

Due to the widely held fisherman's superstition that it was bad luck to set off on a fishing trip on a Friday, Morley had tossed off the *La Conte*'s lines, setting sail from Sitka Harbor on Thursday.

"Hey, baby! You're my world! You know that?" he told Tamara over the telephone. "Take care of my babies." And then he was gone.

CHAPTER 10

J ust two days before they left Sitka, Mark Morley had taken Tamara and her nine-year-old stepdaughter, Kyla, along with Bob Doyle and his eight-year-old son, Brendan, out whale watching on Sitka Sound on board the *La Conte*. It was a sunny winter's day, clear, brisk, and cold, and Brendan had had a great time. He got to sit on Mark's lap and drive the boat. Feigning the need to attend to other things, Morley soon went below, leaving father and son to take the boat out alone.

Throughout the voyage, Tamara and Mark openly lavished affection upon each other, and Kyla had responded in kind. To the delight of everyone on board, they soon spotted a whale—a number of them, actually. They were humpbacks—a few feeding adults out of an estimated thirty thousand that presently migrate, in search of food and safety, from Baja, Mexico, to their favorite feeding grounds along some 33,000 miles of coastline in Alaska, and then back again.

In the relative calm of a beautiful winter day, an astute whale watcher can spot them by searching the sea for the thin black line of their backs, or the slow, dignified flip of their tails, or, even more likely, from their blowholes, which gush spume several fathoms into the air.

The whales moved along in a casual ballet, rising and spewing and sounding. On such a pleasant day, their spray lingered on behind them, offering up a soul-cleansing vision of brilliant white. It was the kind of day when one might also take in the colorful sheen of a miniature rainbow making a brief appearance in the dissipating mist.

Six feet tall and weighing in at 210 pounds, Morley was powerfully built. But he was no iron-pumper. His strength came to him naturally, through a lifetime of hard work and robust living—hunting, camping, and fishing, both commercial and sport.

Old-fashioned, but meticulous about how they wanted to do things, both partners brought to their relationship strong personalities. When they first moved in together, Mark and Tamara often came to logger-heads. "But he was a sweetie," Tamara would later tell me, "and we worked it out."

Tamara saw herself as practical, organized, and loving, but she was prone to dwell on outstanding bills. Morley took a more relaxed approach to life. On occasion, his attitude was even zany. "You can't let that get to you," Morley had told her. "There are always going to be bills."

Once, when he was working on the *La Conte* in port, he tried to work out a method whereby he could talk to Tamara on the phone and still keep working. "He was down on the boat, and it was snowing. He was baiting up gear when he called me," she recalls. "And he said, 'I sure hope no one comes down to the boat.' I wanted to know why. Apparently, he'd duct-taped the telephone to the side of his head."

Morley also knew that his fiancée had been pregnant with twins. She had lost one, but the other fetus was, by all indications, quite healthy.

Now as he drifted, Morley occasionally voiced the doubts he had about surviving his predicament. But Bob Doyle felt he understood. He knew that Morley was in a bad way and was trying to face the important issues in his life as best he could. And as he continued to carry Morley across his lap, Doyle did his best to dispel the skipper's fears. In a calm but forceful manner, he would speak into Morley's ear, encouraging him to keep in the fight. "Well, come on now, Mark," Doyle told him. "We're all in this together here. The Coast Guard's found us, and they're going to get us. There's no doubt about that. You've just gotta hang in there."

CHAPTER 11

Inside the H-60 Jayhawk helicopter overhead, Molthen was busily trying to imitiate the motion of the survivors. When they'd go up, he'd rise with them, and when they started getting smaller, he'd move toward them. Molthen was beginning to feel that things might just work out.

An hour of sweating effort later, however, left Molthen feeling somewhat desperate. And he thought to himself, We may not be able to pull this off. We're not moving fast enough toward the solution here. At this rate, we're going to run out of either fuel or strength before we resolve this.

Lieutenant Adickes's thoughts were nearly identical. We're running out of time here, he thought. We're running out of gas. And my crew is getting fatigued.

Each time Molthen managed to maneuver in close, a blast of wind would lift and shake them like a dog rending a snake, sending them reeling.

Okay, Mr. Aircraft Commander, Bill Adickes finally said to himself, this is not working. So, what are you going to do to get these people out of the water? Those people down there are freezing to death. At this point, Adickes decided to make a radical departure. He'd attempt something entirely new. It would be necessary to draw near to the serpent in order to snatch away her would-be victims.

"Let me try it from the left seat," he told Dan Molthen finally. "With goggles."

In an effort to shorten the uncontrollable length of the cable and the wild oscillating swing of the rescue basket, he'd hover down and attempt to hoist from an altitude of just eighty feet.

"If we can move in, then move out fast enough, maybe we've got a chance of getting somebody," Adickes told Molthen.

Several times, Adickes knew, they had come quite close to "losing the bubble," a term he used for crashing, augering in, buying the farm. He took the controls, thinking, God, we've been flying around so violently and all, I'm going to take this real slow and be very patient and methodical. . . . I'm going to make my control inputs very, very carefully, and I'm going to try and stop this thing from moving around so much.

In the back, Rich Sansone busied himself by calling out the altitude in an unemotional tone whenever the helicopter dipped too close. He watched the RAT OUT go from eighty feet to twenty feet in just seconds, giving notice that a sixty-foot wave had just swept by directly underneath them.

"You've got to imagine the chaos that night," recalls Bill Adickes. "We were flying in wind velocities of near hurricane force, without the large bundles of flares needed to aid station. I was catching glimpses of these people. And they were here, they were there, and then here again. Suddenly we'd get blown back a quarter of a mile. Then we'd fight to scratch our way back. Now we're thirty degrees nose up. Then we were getting blown away again. It was very difficult to pinpoint anything exactly."

Still, Adickes thought the new plan might just work. They were staggering along, trying to hoist from that altitude, when, amazingly, Sean Witherspoon managed to land the basket just fifteen feet from the survivors in the water. Adickes saw his chance. They looked to be within only moments of getting the first of the survivors into the rescue basket, when something strange occurred.

The unprecedented event unfolding before them was detailed in the unsettling, telltale movements of the flares. Instead of drifting around in the lower third of the pilot's windshield screen, the flares had drifted up to the very top portion of the window. Neither Adickes nor Molthen had even seen anything like it. The topper came when the flares just blinked out overhead, which meant that the crest of the wave was now above the height of the rotor system.

Adickes was concentrating on holding his hover and listening to Rich Sansone's conning commands as he took in the event. And he thought, Uh-oh, something is very wrong here.

Lieutenant Molthen had also seen the anomaly above them. It took him awhile to decipher it. The flares appeared to be floating, drifting farther and farther away. Then they disappeared altogether, and the reason they had vanished, Molthen's racing mind soon inferred, was that they were now drifting down the backside of the approaching wave. Judging by the peak of the flares' ascent, he also knew that the wave had to be above their present hover position.

At the time, Rich Sansone and Sean Witherspoon were squatting beside each other in the doorway, fastened securely to their safety straps, as the blasting effects of sea spray and blizzard snow sprinted horizontally past at ninety miles per hour, only inches from their faces. With his visor flipped down, and rain and snow striking his face, Witherspoon was hardly able to see at all. Physically, he was just freezing. He was trying, without much success, to see through his fogged-up visor and, simultaneously, keep track of the basket flying through the air, as well as watch the people in the water below.

Then, as the chopper struggled to maintain its inexact hover, Witherspoon and Sansone glanced up. The vision before them took their breath away, for they found themselves staring directly into the face of a rogue wave "at least one hundred feet high" in the very act of breaking down upon them. The foaming avalanche of cascading white water towered over the helicopter and descended toward them with the soul-shuddering power of a locomotive. The wave was, in fact, about to bury them alive. Sansone was the first to react.

"Up! Up! Up! *Emergency up!*" he screamed. "Altitude! Up! Up! Up! Take her up! *Now!*"

The frantic warnings exploded from Molthen's headset.

"Up! Up! Up!"

Concurrently, Molthen and Adickes watched from the cockpit as the collapsing wave approached.

"*Oh-my-God!*" said Adickes, his voice rising with each word.

Pilot and copilot reacted without thinking. They grabbed their respective collective sticks mounted alongside their seats and yanked up on them at the same moment.

"Oh God," prayed Molthen aloud.

"Up, up, up!" the crewmen screamed.

"I'm trying!" called back Dan Molthen. "I've got an armload of collective here, and I'm trying!"

Sucked down in front of the wave by an invisible downdraft, the powerful H-60 rescue helicopter refused to budge. As if caught in a cycle of slow death, they watched the growling wave come thundering down upon them. The chopper's twin turbine engines revved high under the load. The transmission box whined under the impossible strain like an incoming artillery round about to explode. To Sean Witherspoon and Rich Sansone, the feeling was one of being stuck down there with the consuming force of the wave about to swallow them whole—helicopter blades, rotor, tail section, cabin, and crew.

An H-60 allows a pilot to be fairly ham-handed and to fly his or her way out of most types of trouble with awesome amounts of power—almost four thousand shaft horsepower with which to climb out of danger.

Bill Adickes went full-collective, nose down in an effort to gain all the altitude he could, but he found that he was unable to free himself of the imposing downdraft. The roaring white mountain of breaking sea was about to wash inside the cabin itself; the helicopter began to break loose from the gripping suction. The wave surged past no more than five feet beneath them, missing their tail rotor by even less.

Adickes would be forever grateful to Rich Sansone for initiating the warning that saved their lives.

The sudden blast of wind that held the helo in its grip is known as a williwaw. Such a powerful anomaly of nature is normally created when storm systems move in against one of the fencelike mountain ranges in Alaska. As the already energetic forces press in over the mountains and are squeezed into the narrow mountain passes, they accelerate dramatically, creating fierce unharnessed blasts of turbulent air that break out, exploding with dumbfounding power, destroying anything in their paths.

On rare occassions, when high storm winds create such an extreme sea state, the same thing may occur. On this night, winds racing through the bowl-shaped contours of the wave troughs produced an avalanche of accelerating turbulence, creating wind vacuums in their howling descent, and upwellings in their rush to exit.

The departing forces tore the wave tops off the waves themselves and launched spray across the face of the sea, creating a bellowing vacuum of sea spray several hundred feet deep. It is the same kind of turbulence that pilots encounter when flying in mountainous terrain. When storm winds rush over a ridge or mountaintop, they take off, accelerating down the slope of the mountain, following the contour of the land as they go. Over the years, hundreds of single-engined airplanes whose pilots were unlucky (or unwitting) enough to get caught flying in such conditions in Alaska have been destroyed and their passengers killed when the planes flipped upside down, had their wings torn off, or were batted from the sky. The only way to overcome such explosive wind accelerating across the surface of a wave is with lightning-quick reflexes, luck, and—if one has access to it—pure, unadulterated power.

Adickes and Molthen were feeling grateful at having avoided the "big crunch." But just then, as they rose up and over the crest of the wave, another punishing jolt of williwaw fury came ranging out of the wave valley and plowed into them. Adickes had lifted the nose of the aircraft only slightly, when suddenly it rocketed backward. He had never known a helicopter to get pushed back so fast. The sixteen-thousand-pound machine went hurtling backward as if launched from a slingshot. Adickes could see the crashing waves peeling out from under their feet, flipping past underfoot. He feared that at any second the tail rotor would clip the crown of a passing wave and they would auger in. And he thought to himself, This is not good.

Seated securely in his chair in the chopper's tail section, Sansone was tossed into a carnival-like ride. With the entire fifty-five-foot-long helicopter suddenly tipped up and knocked back on its tail, Sansone found himself seated in much the same position that the early-day astronauts once used—his knees bent and his feet planted on the near-vertical face of the floor—as he awaited the outcome.

Adickes had to execute the most radical control that he'd ever had to make in a helicopter. He was very much afraid that they were going to get into a pitch attitude from which they would not be able to recover and that he would simply fly the aircraft into the water.

When Adickes regained control of the chopper, he found himself wide-eyed and a bit breathless—and four thousand feet downwind of the survivors.

"Okay," Adickes told his crew. "We need to regroup here. We need to retreat for a few minutes and get everybody calmed down and go back to the basics."

Then, flying well above the water, he rose to three hundred feet. "I'm going to give the controls back now to Lieutenant Molthen," said Adickes finally. "And we're not going to try that again. So don't worry. We're going back to standard operating procedures."

Though Molthen was not at all happy about his partner's close call, he found it impossible to judge him. For he knew that it could have just as easily happened to him. Adickes would always appreciate Molthen's measured response. He knew that he'd "screwed up." He didn't need anybody to get on his case. He'd gotten a little too aggressive, a little impatient, and had allowed his heart for those in the water to take him to a place where rescuing them was so imperative that he was going to *make* it happen.

Part of the problem, Dan Molthen knew as he descended into battle once again, was that every time he started getting close and "in the groove," it was extremely difficult and frustrating to have to give it up and let it go. Molthen had also become aware that flight mech Sean Witherspoon was nearly exhausted now. Several attempts later, he decided to give the young man a much-needed break. "Hey, listen," Adickes told him, "this situation is absolutely horrible. We may not get these guys. But we're just going to keep trying."

For the pilots, one issue remained unsolvable: By the time they were actually able to *see* a given wave rolling toward them, it was already so close that they hardly had time to pull up.

CHAPTER 12

A s the crew of the H-60 fought to continue the rescue operation, Mike DeCapua and his crewmates did their best to hold on. "The pilot seemed absolutely determined to stay with us," recalls DeCapua. "To try and accomplish this, he maneuvered down in between a couple of those monster waves and got it into his head that he'd just ride right up over them and lower the basket to us. It must have seemed like a great idea. But when he tried to pull away, the helicopter got stuck down in between the waves. And with the flares way off ahead of them, there was no light. That was really scary. They had their basket down, and they were trying to time themselves with the seas, when all of a sudden, here comes this one monstrous mother of a wave, completely out of step. It wasn't the one they'd been counting on."

It seemed a much-deserved bit of luck for DeCapua and his shipmates when the monster wave held together and did not break down upon them, and they drifted up and over onto the opposite side. But when the tattered column of Doyle, Morley, DeCapua, and Mork peeled over the crest of the wave, they found an entirely unexpected scenario awaiting them: At this moment, the relationship between the rescue chopper above and fishermen below had somehow flip-flopped. For now, no more than thirty feet below them hovered the straining, tottering figure of the Coast Guard rescue helicopter. And they found themselves staring down into the deadly, whirling blur of the aircraft's rotor blades.

The blasting *pup-pup-pup-pup* roar of the helicopter straining to recover echoed through the tunnel-like wave troughs, producing the acoustical effect of a machine gun volley. With the chopper's "night sun" switched off, the fishermen could see the H-60's red and white navigation signals pulsing through the unsettling chop of her main rotator blades, which were spinning almost directly below.

The men slid down the face of the wave on a course that led directly into the swirling rotor blades flashing underfoot. To DeCapua, the experience was like "descending into a giant lawn mower. And we were the dandelions."

"Damn!" he yelled, backpedaling along with the others. God, please don't let those blades hit us! he prayed as his heart thundered in his ears.

Then, as DeCapua and his crewmates descended, the helicopter pulled slowly away. Sucked down again by the winds howling out of the large wave valley, and unable to climb, the pilot moved cleverly forward, exactly paralleling the progress and flow of the departing wave trough. Then the helo vanished without a trace.

"We drifted down and into the wave, up and over again, and the chopper was gone," recalls DeCapua. "It was like it just disappeared into the night."

So completely did the helo vanish, DeCapua and the others felt certain that the pilot had chipped a wave and crashed, and that his entire crew had been killed.

"What happened to that chopper?" shouted Mike DeCapua, finally uttering what all of them were thinking.

"I sure hope those boys didn't get killed trying to get to us," said Bob Doyle. "Because if they did, we're history."

"That guy has *got* to be dead!" said DeCapua.

With the helo gone, DeCapua and his crewmates found themselves in the belly of the next set of swells. Well ahead of them now, the glow of several of the remaining flares bathed their world in a thin amber veil of translucent light.

When the helicopter disappeared, the men were deprived of the sight of its ceaseless efforts, the resonant sound of its robust presence, and the bright, penetrating sweep of its scanning searchlight. Now, all that was replaced by the battering cold of an indifferent sea, leaving each survivor to face his own doleful sentiments, as well as a heavy fatigue drawing him toward slumber.

"What the hell am I doing out here?" Mike DeCapua asked out loud.

Several interminable minutes had passed when, suddenly, a thousand or more feet in the distance, the tiny figure of the helicopter rose tentatively into view. Dwarfed by the distance, the minuscule navigation lights mounted along its toylike body blinked bravely as the helo staggered into the sky.

"Oh God, he's still here!" yelled DeCapua.

He and his crewmates were so delighted to see the chopper again that they started cheering the pilot on as if he could actually hear them. "All right! What balls! He's still with us! Way to go, man! Way to go!"

"Hold your breath!" ordered Gig Mork, interrupting their jubilation, as another wave rolled in over them.

As the wave collapsed down upon them, Doyle felt more icy rivulets of seawater collecting around the perimeter of his hood and forcing their way inside. Overall, he was pleased at how well his suit had held up, but after being adrift for so long, the accumulation of seawater had filled the leg compartments and had now risen nearly to his stomach.

DeCapua, too, was having his problems. Above all, he longed for sleep. Sleep would be almost as gratifying as a hot cup of cocoa or a sweet glass of orange juice in this never-ending desert of saltwater. "I can't take it anymore," he said, closing his eyes.

"Don't fall asleep, Mike!" scolded Doyle, shaking him. "If you fall asleep, you're dead!"

The Coast Guard crew made several more resolute efforts to reach the men in the water. They deployed their last flare, but, lasting only minutes, the Mark 25 flares proved almost worthless. To those on board the helicopter, they were hardly worth the effort.

With his fuel supply running low, his flares burning out, and his exhausted crew soaked in sweat, Lieutenant Adickes forced himself to step back and be objective. What's our goal? he asked himself. How's my crew doing? How productive are we now? What's our fuel situation? Can we continue, or is it time to leave?

Paramount in Adickes's mind was his experience with the severely hypothermic crew members of the vanished fishing vessel *Oceanic* the year before. He hadn't been able to force himself to leave them; in fact, he'd been awarded the DFC for saving the lives of two of the three fishermen drifting offshore on that mean, blustery night. But in so doing, he'd been forced to run the helicopter's fuel supply to near exhaustion. The ride back to safety became a gut-wrenching ordeal, in which he was forced to navigate blindly as he picked his way through a never-ending maze of rugged islands and boulder-strewn shores to the dirt runway in Haines, with the H-60 aircraft about to flop lifelessly into the sea. He'd sworn that he'd never cut it that close again.

Ever since they had arrived on the scene, Rich Sansone had been unable to establish communications with anyone. Nobody even knew where they were exactly, or that they'd found survivors in the water, nor had they heard about the gargantuan winds and seas awaiting any who might come looking for them.

"Any Coast Guard unit! Any Coast Guard unit! This is Coast Guard Rescue six-oh-two-nine!" Each time, Sansone gave their position, detailing what the on-scene weather had been like and offering up his estimate that there were three to five people still huddled in the water. Then Sansone achieved a breakthrough when he was able to raise the pilot of an Alaska Airlines passenger jet some thirty thousand feet overhead, en route to Anchorage. Sansone described in detail the rescue operation under way. The Alaska Airlines pilot assured him that he'd immediately pass the information on to Coast Guard headquarters in

Juneau, as well as to the second USCG helicopter he'd overheard, which was already en route to the scene, coming from Sitka. It was apparently just twenty minutes away and closing fast.

Good! thought Sansone. When the boys back at their home base in Sitka didn't hear from us for so long, they launched another helicopter. Sansone took great comfort in the fact that someone was actually out there looking for them.

Rich Sansone could see that Sean Witherspoon was getting overheated and breathing hard.

"Hey, Rich, look at my hands," Witherspoon told him. "I just can't stop shaking here. I'm really cold." The flight mech had become sick and nauseous. Not long after that, Witherspoon slumped to the cabin floor and "started shaking and throwing up," recalled Sansone later. He appeared to be going into shock. Sansone had never run a hoist before. If they were to continue, he would have to somehow divide his time between running the hoist at the door and taking care of Sean Witherspoon on the floor.

Sansone debated whether or not to remove Sean's dry suit. Normally, he would have cut the suit off of anyone going into shock. No, he ultimately decided. We still aren't sure if we have enough gas to get back home. That dry suit may be the only chance Sean will have if we end up ditching this thing.

Sansone placed Witherspoon into a hypothermia bag (basically, just a big sleeping bag), leaving Sean's helmet on to protect his head from the pounding that they were taking. He also placed him on oxygen. Finally, he took Sean off ICS (intercom) so that he could no longer hear them. Sansone was covered in vomit when he radioed his commander in the cockpit.

"Sir," said Sansone, "we're going to need an ambulance when we get back. Sean's not doing good at all. We need to get him to a hospital. He's dehydrated. He's throwing up. He's shaking uncontrollably. He needs to get some fluids back in him."

Next, Sansone passed his radio up front. He would need both hands to take care of Sean. Rich Sansone felt relieved, now, that he hadn't been allowed to repel from the helicopter and go into the water. With no one left to reel him back aboard, he would have been stranded out there, praying for the next chopper to arrive. Still, he would have liked to provide a bit of encouragement to those poor struggling souls down there, and, hopefully, even facilitate their rescue. He would have taken more than a little satisfaction in that.

For Sansone, the worst part was seeing the people waving up at him and coming to the final realization that they weren't going to be able to save them, that they were actually going to have to abandon the effort and leave them behind. Equally as sickening, another helicopter crew would soon be risking their lives to finish what Sansone and his team could not.

Richard Sansone was monitoring Sean's vital signs when his patient Sean went into convulsions. To Adickes, it was indeed beginning to sound like the symptoms of shock. I need to get my aircraft back in one piece, he figured finally. I need to get my crew back . . . and keep my assets alive here, so that we can use them again on another day.

"Sir," radioed Sansone. "Sean's done. He can't hoist anymore."

Neither Dan Molthen nor Bill Adickes had ever been caught in a situation where they were forced to leave survivors in the water. For Molthen, it was the worst feeling imaginable. "Knowing that those guys were still down there," he would tell me later, "and that they were probably going to die, that absolutely sucked."

"We've got to go," asserted Adickes finally. "We can't get these guys. We have to go now. Rescue checklist part three."

This was a pilot's way of saying, "We're leaving. Pull the basket inside and stow it away. We're going home."

Adickes, too, found the notion of deserting people who were locked so desperately in a struggle to survive almost impossible to accept. He knew from experience that people caught in such a horrendous predicament often tired of the struggle; they got to a point where they just wanted it to be over. He'd seen it before—those waiting to be rescued had reached a point where they couldn't endure the suspense and the pain for even another minute, and so they just checked out. But Adickes also knew that "some people with weak physical stature and poor health often do manage to come back alive because their desire to live is so strong."

N ow the small covey of short-duration flares tossed out by Bill
Adickes's crew began to flicker and die, once again immersing
both helo and survivors in total darkness. Then, as the remaining crew
of the *La Conte* watched, the Coast Guard helicopter rose into the
night and sped deliberately away.

Mike DeCapua felt doomed. He swore aloud. "Hey, you never even
picked us up, man! You left us here! Where are you going? Wait! You're
the Coast Guard! You can't just leave us here! What the hell?" he
ranted. "Are they just going to abandon us?"

"They'll come back," said Bob Doyle. "They'll come."

"Hell, yes!" shouted DeCapua, more than happy to agree. "They're
going to come back."

"I don't think that I'm going to be able to wait that long," said
Morley flatly.

"No, no, Mark," insisted Bob Doyle. "They're going to get fuel.
They're just going to get some more fuel. Look at the weather. This is
going to be tough, but we'll pull out of this."

"Hope so," replied DeCapua, feeling frozen and dejected. "I
don't want to die here. I want to live through this. You come back,
now," he called out, nodding in the direction of the vanished
chopper.

"Doyle, do you think they'll be back?" yelled Gig Mork. "Is there
going to be another helicopter coming out here for us?"

"Oh, sure," called back Doyle. "They're not going to leave us for
long. Yah, they'll be back. They're just going to get refueled, and maybe
grab some coffee. They'll be back. I wouldn't worry about it."

Only ten minutes passed before the second helicopter, piloted by
Cmdr. David "Bull" Durham, arrived on-scene. So little time had
elapsed that when the remaining crewmen of the *La Conte* caught sight
of this chopper, they were certain it was the first helo returning for
them once again.

"All right! They've come back! They came back for us!" yelled
DeCapua. He could see the beam of the helo's spotlight searching the
waves for them.

"They're looking for us now," noted Morley in a voice slurred by the effects of hypothermia and exhaustion.

Though Mark Morley was now too done in to be of much help, Doyle, DeCapua, and Mork waved their arms and screamed, hoping beyond logic to be heard somehow, if not seen.

"Over here!" they shouted. "Over here!"

CHAPTER 13

The Coast Guard would have been hard-pressed to come up with a more competent team of flyers than Cmdr. Dave Durham, the pilot for the trip, and Lt. Russ Zullick, who was serving as co-pilot and chief navigator.

Originally from the Tampa Bay area of Florida, Durham had over twenty years of flying under his belt. He now found himself sprinting toward the Cape Fairweather Ground with a steely-eyed determination. The unthinkable might just have occurred. One of their own could well be in trouble. No one had heard from fellow pilots Dan Molthen or Bill Adickes in nearly two hours.

They were just fifteen minutes from arriving on-scene at the last known coordinates when they happened upon the USCG chopper returning to base. Flight mech Chris Windnagle spotted the navigation lights of the first helo as it passed off their starboard side.

"Your flight mech might want to listen to this," advised Bill Adickes, who was speaking to them on the radio after giving his initial debriefing. "If you get the basket down to these guys, it's just going to be luck. The only way you're going to get a survivor in the basket is if he happens to grab it as it swings past."

Chris Windnagle was listening, but he wasn't buying it. He felt cocky. He'd been hoisting survivors from precarious places for more than a decade. In fact, at that moment, Windnagle felt like he may have well been the best flight mechanic in the entire Coast Guard. I can do this! he told himself.

As the two helicopters put space between them, Zullick spoke up. "And Chris, if you start getting tired, remember, the rescue swimmer can always take a turn at the hoist."

"Sir," shot back Windnagle, "you don't have enough gas in this aircraft to tire me out!"

Russ Zullick had to smile.

Born in Sandusky, Ohio, and raised in northern Michigan, Chris Windnagle attended Michigan State, then worked construction in Pennsylvania for a year. He went into the USCG for a little adventure, and because they were involved in saving people. In the six years since then, he had never seriously considered getting out.

As an avid hunter, he had explored scores of the endless backwater bays of southeastern Alaska in an eighteen-foot skiff, and during week-long trips to hunt mountain goat and deer, he had often bathed in the heart-stopping cold of those Alaskan waters. With snowcapped mountain spires filling the skyline all around, he had lingered buck naked in the dead of winter in several of the bays as glacial ice rubble drifted past, carried out to sea by the tidal currents.

Now, without warning, they overflew the EPIRB.

"There's the strobe light, sir!" announced Windnagle.

Commander Durham tried to slow the helicopter, but before he could swing the aircraft around, they'd been blown several thousand feet downwind. They were slowly creeping their way back, when Windnagle again caught the distant flash of the strobe light. A single blip as crisp as lightning was all he could see as it passed over the peak of a swell and disappeared again.

As they drew nearer, each time the strobe light blinked, Windnagle was able to take in the blazing silver sticklike reflections of the retrotape gleaming back at him. He could see the men's heads and their arms as they waved up at him.

"Stand by to deploy the flares," came Commander Durham's steady voice.

"Chris, arm all our flares," added Zullick. "We're going to put everything out. It's all or nothing now."

"Once we get going on our drop heading, as soon as you see the people below us, just drop them out one after another, as fast as you can," said Durham.

Tall combers rolled out of the darkness and passed directly under the belly of their chopper. Durham took in their full dimension as they powered past. As far as sheer size went, he'd never seen anything like them. Wave trains seventy feet high, with an occasional one standing closer to one hundred feet, rose up and seemed to slap at them. Now as he watched, the waves spent themselves against one another in a wild and incongruous orchestration of nature run riot.

Normally, storm waves roll forth hour after hour in fairly consistent patterns, plowing ahead in the same direction as the wind. Not this night. No sooner would a pattern of waves begin to set up than another set of waves would come crashing in from the side, overlapping the other, doing so at angles that varied as much as 180 degrees. Durham was trying to hold the chopper at one hundred feet, but each time he'd see one of the rogue waves approaching, he was forced to pull up on his collective arm and let the thing pass. The writhing waters below had become a threshing machine, a sea of foam and spray, a bubbling pot of water, nothing short of amazing to behold.

As a result, the rescue at hand would be a fly-by-the-seat-of-your-pants kind of operation, one that called upon a pilot's ability to adapt. The plummeting readout on the altimeter, Durham soon learned, did not necessarily mean that his chopper was in a free fall. On this hellish night, it could well be implying that another seventy-footer was passing by in the darkness below. A soaring digital count, on the other hand, might mean the wave was pressing on, with the ensuing wave trough now occupying that space.

Durham knew the moment that Chris Windnagle slid his side door open. Over his own headphones, he could hear the huge white roar of blasting wind hurtling past. With the side door open, Windnagle, too, was confronted with the howling rush of the wind. Leaning forward, he carefully pushed his head outside until the jet stream began buffeting it. Yet even as his helmet vibrated in the wind, he was able both to send and receive messages. His cinched-up chin strap pinned the radio headphones built into his helmet tightly against his ears, screening out most of the external racket.

The moment Dave Durham turned downwind to deploy the flares, winds approaching ninety miles per hour, now swept his helicopter away. "Drop! Drop! Drop!" he ordered.

Windnagle moved fast to toss the only four flares that they possessed out the side door in a closely grouped sequence. "Flares away, sir," he announced.

As the helicopter sprinted downwind, Windnagle watched behind them, studying the darkness to see if any of the water-activated flares ignited. When he pressed ahead for a better look, the wind rocked him, and the drenching sea spray instantly coated the visor of his helmet. Then he took in a pleasing sight in the distance, as several of the flares exploded to life.

"Flares are in the water, sir!"

Dave Durham found himself blown so far back that it seemed like it took forever for the chopper to make the turn and fight its way back into the wind. Battling back under full power from far downwind was an unbelievably slow affair. The numbers on the digitized readout (which indicated the distance still remaining to the rescue scene) normally flashed by with the speed of those on a gasoline pump, but now they remained almost frozen in place, indicating that little real ground was being gained.

By the time they'd relocated them, the short duration flares were already beginning to burn out. Now in their dying throes, they began spitting small brightly colored fountains of lava and sparks a few unimpressive feet into the air. As the whitish orange cores suffocated and went out, the thin white streamers of steam and smoke trailing off of them went streaking across the face of the sea, swirling erratically as they went.

There was one further problem: The crewmen in the water were nowhere to be found. They were gone! Swept away, no doubt, by the wind, waves, and currents. Durham launched immediately into another downwind search. Then, in the distance, he spotted the minuscule white pulse of the EPIRB light flashing.

"Go ahead and conn me in," said Durham.

"Roger. Target in sight. Forward and right, uh, *one mile.*" Windnagle had never given conning directions to a pilot that involved anything like these logistics. Rarely did his guiding commands exceed one hundred feet. Such a conning order sounded ludicrous.

As they drew closer to the strobe light, the grateful voice of Lt. Russ Zullick leapt from the radio. "There are survivors at the strobe light. I see survivors at the strobe light. I count two survivors."

"I've got four survivors in the water," countered Windnagle. "I see four."

Durham's objective was to use the flare references to the best of his ability to aid him in placing the basket as near to the men as possible, moving the eighteen-thousand-pound aircraft about with an agile touch, flittering here and there like a hummingbird.

Now, as they manuevered into position, Windnagle started thinking about the people in the water, who were, no doubt, praying for deliverance, and his heart went out to them. Especially now, because they were flying low enough at times, he said, "to see what that crazy monster down there looked like."

Then Windnagle started thinking about their rescue swimmer, A. J. Thompson. He wondered if the pilots would use him to try to perform a direct deployment. He doubted it. He tried to picture A. J. dangling from the 7/16-inch stainless-steel cable as he was lowered into the apocalyptic scene below.

As it happened, Lt. Russ Zullick was contemplating the plight of A. J. Thompson, as well. A. J., he knew, was a pretty tough cookie. But they were 120 miles from their home base at Sitka and 60 miles out from the coast at Cape Fairweather, one of the most brutally rugged stretches of shoreline in the United States. No help would be possible should his cable break or one of the ten-story-high waves cripple him. Besides, he knew the Thompson family well and was more than a little fond of them. He'd seen A. J. with his wife and kids. How could he ever tell A. J.'s wife that he'd deployed him but then couldn't get him back? "Bringing him back alive again," says Zullick, "was one big, big concern." He needed to put the safety of his men first. It was one of the things that would later come back to haunt him. "Those people down there were still alive," he says today. "It wasn't like they were unconscious and alive. They were waving."

When Windnagle tried to lower the rescue basket, once again it was blown straight back. "Sir," he reported. "The basket's back underneath the stabilator." (The stabilator is the horizontal wing mounted on the tail of the H-60, some forty feet behind where the pilots sit.)

Though the hoist lift boasted a carrying capacity of more than two hundred feet of usable cable, there were times over the next hour and a half when the candy-cane warning stripes painted on the last twenty feet of the hoist cable came into view, warning Chris Windnagle that he was nearly out of line.

During a regular airlift, it is not uncommon for a helicopter crew to make a single approach to the victims, lowering the basket just once. But, just as Molthen and Adickes had been forced to do, Durham and his crew were compelled to make dozens of attempts. Once, Windnagle even managed to land the rescue basket in the water just thirty feet from the drifting crewmen.

But each time another gust of wind would hit them, and suddenly they'd go screaming backward. At such times, Durham would have to abandon the search and deal with the real and imminent danger of impaling the thirty-foot-long tail section of his plane on the slope of the wave behind them.

At one point, they went flying backward, tail down, at close to eighty miles per hour. Another time, the wind halted abruptly, and the chopper shot forward, leaving the survivors half a mile in its wake.

Durham had faced similar winds flying in another chopper in a hurricane off the coast of Puerto Rico. But it had been broad daylight at the time of that mission, and, had they been forced to ditch, they would have ended up in the Caribbean Sea, where the water temperature was eighty-five degrees.

Inside the helo, the crew was getting hammered. Relying solely on instruments in weather this barbaric, Zullick had always thought, was a little like playing a video game with one's own life. Never had it seemed so true as it was now. An experienced pilot has to believe in his instruments, but he also has to be able to call on something deeper within himself. Some call it intuition. Zullick referred to it as his "gut magnet."

"We've given it all we've got," said Zullick finally. "We're at bingo fuel. We're out. We gotta go. If we don't leave now, we're going to end up down there in the water right along with those people."

He knew, of course, that there was always the option of staying on-site longer and flying the helicopter, empty fuel tanks and all, to the lighthouse at Cape Spencer. But that would have meant getting the aircraft stuck someplace where no one else could utilize it, effectively taking one of only three functioning helicopters out of action. If either one of the two remaining choppers was to break down, as they often did, they would, in effect, be forcing a fellow Coast Guard crew into a rescue far offshore, with no one to fly backup and cover their tails in the worst winter storm in the history of Alaska.

F or the drifting members of the *La Conte* crew, the cruel drama playing out overhead seemed never-ending. There was no way they could know for sure whether the helo flying above them now was the one they had seen leave the scene or a different one. As always, each time the tottering chopper would try to maneuver into position over them, out would come the rescue basket, and back it would fly.

The ceaseless progression of hypothermia also continued to drain the minds and bodies of the frozen crew. Eventually, their ability to think would continue to grow more confused, and the blood pumping through their veins would slow and thicken to the viscosity of thirty-weight crude. When yet another seven-story wave dragged them under, released them, and passed anonymously into the night, no one bothered to complain.

Doyle could feel Mark Morley shaking violently, lying across his chest as he was. "I gotta make it to the basket," Morley told Doyle. "I gotta make this one. I really gotta make this one. I have to get there now, or I'm going to die."

"Oh no you're not," said Doyle. "We'll get you there. We'll get you to the basket."

Yet Doyle could see it was hopeless. The basket kept flying uselessly backward, dangerously close, once again, to the tail rotors, and the few times that it did find its way down to the water, it looked to be well in the distance. Doyle knew that patience was the key until the time was right, if it ever was going to be right. Eventually, he would have to free himself and cut Morley loose from the security of the lines now holding them. He was the only one who had a knife. But it remained sealed inside his survival suit. And since unzipping his suit would invite a prompt and surging flood of icy seawater, he would retrieve it only when he felt certain that the most opportune moment had arrived. Once the lines binding them were severed and they swam away, they would be leaving behind once and for all the comparative safety of the flashing EPIRB and the fellowship of their crewmates. The prospects were truly terrifying, the anticipation torturous. If they failed to reach the rescue basket and climb in before it was swept away, or if another wave caught them out in the open, there would be no way to swim back and relocate their buddies.

Often, when a wave would tumble them beneath the water, Gig Mork could feel the lines dragging across his legs. Sucked down into the cold black swirl of spinning darkness, he could feel people roll over the top of him and keep tumbling off into space. Unable to determine which way was up, he'd wait for the horrific currents to ease, so his suit could float him back to the surface once again.

Now the survivors decided to close ranks, drawing in close enough to interlock arms. Though the waves constantly separated them, one could always pull on the nearest rope line if the distance between members proved too great a reach.

The worst part, once the washing machine finally let them go, was keeping their feet under them. If the air in a person's suit got squeezed out of the area of the upper torso and forced down into the leg cavities, the individual's feet would float, capsizing him. "You really had to fight to pull your feet back down underneath you," says Mike DeCapua. "Because if you didn't, you were going to drown right then and there. God, that was horrible." Though it proved nearly impossible to master, they tried to remain in a seated position, their knees bent, their backs set at a forty-five-degree angle. They huddled together and prayed fervently that the storm would ease and the massive rogue waves would bypass them.

P repare to depart," came Russ Zullick's voice. "Bring the basket in. We've got to go. We've done all we can."

"Sir, those people are still down there," countered Windnagle.

Zullick could feel the pain in Windnagle's voice.

"Chris, are they still responsive?" he asked.

"Yes. They're still waving at us," replied Windnagle. "Sir, are we going to leave them?"

In nearly a decade of rescue attempts, Windnagle had never faced such an impossible predicament or failed in his efforts to hoist a survivor on board. Over the years, he'd almost routinely plucked the injured off of the bouncing decks of fishing boats. In gusting winds, he had lowered men dangling from the end of his hoist cable some one hundred feet below, setting the men down softly onto treacherous cliffside chunks of land no larger than a standard four-by-eight-foot slab of plywood.

What Chris Windnagle could not have known was that his friend Bob Doyle, the man he'd gone deer hunting with the season before, was one of the gaggle of dying fishermen waving up at him from the waters below.

After taking into account Zullick's repeated calculations, there was no doubt whatsoever in Dave Durham's mind that they didn't have enough fuel to remain on the scene a moment longer. At some point, Durham knew, he had a responsibility to his crew. We have to go out, but we don't necessarily have to come back, he thought, reciting to himself the old Coast Guard saying. Rescuing the men in the water was not more important than their own lives. The objective of every member of the Coast Guard who set out on a given mission was to do his or her very best, to practice service over self to the very edge of death, if necessary. Ultimately, however, their duty was to return alive. Durham knew that they had been flying out there on the extreme edge for as long as they dared. He was also certain that if he failed to look out for his own people, they too could easily be killed in the rescue attempt. It was time now to admit defeat and return to Sitka.

Finally, the order to abort sounded over Windnagle's headset: "Secure the cabin. Make ready for forward flight."

Obedient, but disheartened, Windnagle brought up the basket and stowed it away. Then he slid the side door shut. A few times during the scores of attempts he'd made to deliver the basket, Windnagle had seen several of the men wave up at him, and he, in turn, had waved back to them. To be so close, he thought. The disappointment left him feeling almost nauseous.

En route back to the base in Sitka, their slug-out with the unrelenting weather continued as Durham and Zullick fought eighty- and ninety-mile-per-hour head winds the entire way. Aside from one brief encounter with a third chopper racing to the scene, radio communications inside the helicopter soon ceased, followed by an inconsolable silence. All around them came the muffled whining of the transmission box and the lonely, monotonous sound of wind gusts plowing into them.

CHAPTER 14

When the second helicopter also rose into the sky and flew away, the collective disappointment of those adrift and watching from the sea below was almost too much. In spite of this, the men tried to encourage one another. "We can get through this," announced DeCapua. "We can ride this out. We can make it clear to daybreak if we have to. This isn't *that* bad. It'll be colder than hell, but I think we can hang on till they get here again."

Doyle, Mork, and Morley initially welcomed the notion. But their doubts returned as their struggle continued. The free-running waves broke down upon them with a merciless repetitiveness that approached the vindictive. They shivered uncontrollably as the icy seawater sloshed about inside their suits, suits that continued to fill bit by bit with each new dousing. Still, as they drifted, the crewmen found great comfort in facing their ordeal together, hearing the voices of fellow crewmates who had shared hard work and difficult times at sea and who had bellied up and sucked down the sweet, satisfying taste of liquor at Rose's Bar & Grill in the fishing port of Pelican, or at watering holes such as Ernie's Bar, the Bilge, and the Totem Bar down along the waterfront back in the postcard setting of Sitka. And so with loyalty and fondness, they locked elbows in a death grip. Having someone else with whom to share your misery somehow helped make the whole thing more tolerable.

"God," prayed Mike DeCapua aloud. "If you could part the Red Sea and let those Jews escape, then what have you got against me that you'd deliver me to this? I don't want to die like this."

"I'm not going to make it," said Mark Morley in a tired, flat voice.

But before Bob Doyle could respond, Morley collapsed in his arms, lapsing into unconsciousness. "Mark! Mark, what's up?" Doyle called into his ear. Morley remained motionless.

Doyle felt compelled to slap him a couple of times to try to bring him around. He struck him once, then again. The impact of his hand across Morley's face brought no response. His friend was clearly unconscious, or possibly even dead. But Doyle adamantly refused to let go of him, concentrating instead on the impossible task of keeping Mark Morley's face out of the water. Now, as each new wave rolled in over them, Doyle placed his gloved hand over Mark's mouth, holding his hand in this position until the impact of the wave wrenched Morley from his grasp.

Each time Doyle surfaced, he'd impatiently await the next flash from the EPIRB. Then he'd reconnoiter, looking around to see who was there. Even as he waited, he would begin searching the water around him, sweeping through it with long, forceful, straight-armed movements to try to locate the rope line leading to Mark Morley. Each time he was forced to choke back the unspoken fear that the skipper's rope loop might be empty and his friend gone. Doyle made it a point to determine the identity of those around him, asking their names as quickly as he bumped into them. The one who did not answer was always Mark.

Gradually, Bob Doyle's arms grew fatigued from the struggle to hold on to Morley. The worst of the waves drove them under and tore Morley from his grasp. And as one hour gave way to the next, Doyle fought the advance of fatigue and hypothermia by switching sides from time to time, long enough to allow his free arm to partially recuperate. Occasionally, a wave would catch them from the front, driving Morley's head back directly into Doyle's face. Eventually, Doyle couldn't tell whether his lips were swollen from the saltwater or from the head butting he'd received.

Though Doyle was physically wiped out, each time he detected the approach of another wave, he'd wrap his legs around Mark Morley and try to coax him into action. "Mark! Wake up! Wake up!" he pleaded.

Sometimes they'd crest over a wave, and it would turn into a kind of roller-coaster ride. Other times, the wave would drop on them like a wall of cinder blocks and they would end up tumbling across one another like rocks in a cement mixer. Some waves were so powerful that they'd force saltwater up each man's nose, or hold him under until he began to spasmodically inhale the sea itself.

During his twenty years serving in the Coast Guard, Bob Doyle had received a considerable amount of survival training. Now he tried to pass on anything that might improve his crewmates' chances. "Keep your eyes closed as much as possible," he warned. "If you don't, the saltwater will gradually swell your eyes open and you won't be able to shut them."

Mike DeCapua thought it a good thing to know, but he couldn't help but glance up once in awhile, especially when the choppers came roaring in over them. It was blowing so hard that he couldn't tell whether it was sea spray or particles of ice striking him. Either way, it felt like he was getting poked in the face with hundreds of pins.

Nearby, Bob Doyle experimented with a new way to carry Mark Morley. He tried carrying Morley higher on his chest, but he soon found that he was sinking down too much from the increased load. Unable to keep his own head above water, Doyle was forced to abandon the idea. Given the bellowing roar of the wind and the shell shock of the collapsing seas, Doyle found that there was no way to tell if Mark was still breathing. If he *was* still alive, Doyle was determined to do everything he could to see that he remained that way.

Sliding Morley back up onto his stomach, he drew him near and held on as they drifted through the coal black wilderness of unending storm waves, the crowning approach and punishing impact of which could be both heard and felt but not seen.

CHAPTER 15

When Capt. Ted Le Feuvre first arrived at the base on Japonski Island, he went directly to the Operations Center at the head of the stairs. Lt. Guy Pierce was standing watch at the time.

"Who was the last to speak to Bill Adickes's crew?" asked Le Feuvre.

"No one, sir," replied Pierce. "No one has spoken to the first helicopter in about forty minutes."

"Call Kodiak and tell them to launch the C-one-thirty," he said. "And I don't care what problems they're having; I want that flight on its way!" Captain Le Feuvre turned to Lieutenant Pierce. "We're going to have to launch that third helicopter," he said.

It was a rare event when all three helicopters were up and running. Thanks to Reggie Lavoie and Stu Merrill and their crews, however, on this night all three choppers had been serviced and were on-line and ready for flight.

Then Captain Le Feuvre said, "We're going to need to call in another crew."

"I already have the third crew picked out," shot back Pierce. "It's going to be Lt. Steve Torpey. And you, sir."

Several years before, Captain Le Feuvre had flown a rescue during Hurricane Juan down in the Gulf of Mexico. He knew how difficult it could be out there.

"You're the only one left, sir," added Pierce.

Originally from Southern California, Capt. Ted Le Feuvre joined the Coast Guard in 1975, holding California teacher's credentials and a bachelor's degree in psychology and Biblical literature. Working his way up through the various training schools, he was eventually sent to the largest Coast Guard base in the United States—that in Kodiak, Alaska. Several years later, he was reassigned as the commanding officer of the USCG Air Station in Sitka.

Over the years, Le Feuvre had paid his dues in Alaska. He'd become well seasoned, flying patrols over the fisheries in the vast, lonely expanses of the Bering Sea. He was one of six pilots who, working in revolving shifts of a month's duration, helped bring the H-65 cutter-based helicopter flight program on-line, flying off the highly exposed stern decks of one of the two 378-foot Coast Guard cutters that patrolled the westernmost reaches of the United States.

He spent the next two years working in revolving shifts, swapping out every two or three weeks, depending upon the weather. Such a regimen proved hard on his married life. During the first year alone, Le Feuvre was gone from home approximately two hundred days.

Now, as acting commander of the base in Sitka, Captain Le Feuvre listened as Guy Pierce continued to bring him up to speed. The chopper flown by Dan Molthen and Bill Adickes had been on the scene now for more than an hour. They had spotted between two and five people in the water, but the wind and waves were horrendous. So far, they hadn't been able to rescue anyone.

Earlier, Guy Pierce had struck on an idea and had called the Anchorage Airport and requested that they attempt a radio intercept of any Alaska Airlines flight that might be passing over the area. They were in luck. Soon, the high-flying pilot of a Boeing 737 radioed down from 33,000 feet on his HF set and was able to open up communications with the helicopter flown by Dan Molthen and Bill Adickes.

Now, Captain Le Feuvre and a growing crowd of Coast Guard support personnel were listening over a live mike, hanging on every word of the somewhat broken transmissions. The radio relays proved sketchy at best. But one portion of a message overheard sounded like "Understand. You are in the water."

Hearts stopped and blood pressures soared as the fantastic information struck home. "And you're in seventy-foot seas?" came the follow-up to the indecipherable reply.

"What a minute," someone in Ops Center said. "They can't be in the water. They wouldn't be able to transmit if they were in the water. The HF radio they're broadcasting over is an AC-powered system. The helicopter's rotor blades would have to be turning in order for them to transmit." The boys were out there, caught in a tight place for sure, but they were still in the air. It was only a communications glitch. Intellect over emotions—essential in thinking a given situation through.

When Lt. Steve Torpey drove up and parked in front of the base hangar, he knew immediately that something vitally important was under way. The station was all lit up like a little city. Flight mechanics and communications personnel were running to their posts or headed off in pursuit of some essential information.

Last-minute checkups of the two gleaming orange, black, and white H-60 helicopters sitting inside the hangar were already under way, with qualified personnel hovering around them, attending to every detail.

Torpey hustled up the flight of stairs, rushed down the hallway, and stepped into the Operations Center. He could feel the tension in the room as he entered. However, it was not until Lt. Guy Pierce began giving his preflight briefing that Torpey felt his adrenaline start to flow. He learned then that he was going to leave the air station and fly out to who knew where.

Steve Torpey was fully aware that his last days as a pilot in Alaska were coming to a close. His tour would end soon, and they would ship him out for warmer climes. He had only one regret, a nagging sense of somehow having missed out. Only recently, he'd been complaining in private that although there'd been several dramatic high-seas helicopter rescues launched out of Sitka during his two-year tenure there, the chance to play a direct role in one of them had somehow eluded him.

Every red-blooded American pilot hopes for a mission that he can hang his hat on, a mission in which he can put it all on the line, risking all in a bid to save the lives of others. Now, as he listened to the briefing, Torpey was suddenly struck by the fact that the mission at hand might just be such a case. Then, uncharacteristically, his hands started shaking, and he thought to himself, This is it! As the plan to save the drifting men took shape around him, he felt a strange and yet growing certainty that this flight would be one of those missions where he'd be required to call upon everything he knew if he was going to pull off the rescue and bring everyone back alive.

At the present moment, Lieutenant Pierce explained, the first chopper was returning, and the second chopper was on-scene, trying once again to hoist the people from the water. Communications were sporadic at best.

When Pierce finished his briefing, Captain Le Feuvre and Lieutenant Torpey headed for the stairway leading to the maintenance center to prepare for the flight. As Steve Torpey went out the door, he turned to Pierce and said, "Don't worry, we'll get them."

At that moment, it occurred to him that he might have just put his foot in his mouth. Which got him to thinking, Uh-oh, I've really done it now. I've kind of committed myself to doing something here. Torpey wondered what could have made him say such a thing. He would look back on it as a kind of premonition.

With eight-month-old Connor at home and his wife, Kari, four months pregnant at the time, Torpey would need to fight against the distraction of hearth and home. Being a pilot, he knew full well that he had to separate his flying life from his private life.

With flight mechanic Fred Kalt running the hoist, Mike Fish as rescue swimmer, and Lee Honnald as a flight mech backup, it seemed to Torpey that he and Ted Le Feuvre had lucked into a superb team of experienced men.

The crew gathered in the maintenance control area to discuss their game plan.

"All right," said Torpey, "what can we do to improve our odds here?"

One of the maintenance men suggested that they take along extra flares. "Yah, that's a great idea," shot back Torpey. "Mike, hustle on up to the pilot locker and grab every smoke flare that you can get your hands on!"

Mike Fish returned with a caravan of men carrying cases of flares. The standard number of flares issued to a given helicopter was generally just five; Torpey and Le Feuvre would take twenty-six.

Then, a first-class petty officer came up with an effective way to illuminate the rescue basket for all to see. While they waited for the first helo crew to return with the last of the NVGs, Fish, Kalt, and Honnald taped dozens of fluorescent green Chem-Light sticks onto the rescue basket's steel frame.

They knew that during the previous rescue attempts that night the wind had blown the rescue basket so sharply aft that it had been in danger of wrapping around the tail section of the chopper like fishing line around the end of a trout pole. Somehow they would have to control the basket better. Flight mechanic Fred Kalt decided to take along two fifty-pound weight bags to use as ballast.

Steve Torpey found himself in the unusual position of launching out on a major mission with his own base commander. As the two pilots hustled across the tarmac to the H-60 helicopter waiting there, Torpey realized that he and his commanding officer had not discussed who was going to sit in the pilot's seat and actually do the flying.

In the past, Le Feuvre had spent years flying out on rescue missions in some of the most remote areas of this wilderness state in the smaller, more maneuverable H-65 helicopter. He was as capable as even the most experienced of military pilots at flying it. But since the H-60 had come on-line, Le Feuvre's energy had been primarily focused on overseeing the running of the entire air base there at Sitka, not swapping out each day as a duty pilot. As base commander, Captain Le Feuvre was required to fly just forty-eight hours every six months, while a pilot flying every day might log in three hundred hours in the same period.

When the captain climbed up into the right seat and started strapping on, Torpey looked up at him. "Captain," he said, "how do you feel about that right seat there?"

In any other branch of the U.S. military, this would have been an audacious thing to say. But rather than being offended, Captain Le Feuvre looked over at Torpey and calmly replied, "Steve, I understand exactly where you're coming from. I'd probably be doing the same thing if I were in your shoes."

Without further argument, Captain Le Feuvre unbuckled, jumped down out of his seat, hiked around to the other side of the helo, and climbed up into the copilot's chair. Not another word was said. Torpey felt deeply appreciative of, even honored by, the captain's actions.

With the chopper loaded and fueled, the crew sat anxiously awaiting the return of Dan Molthen and Bill Adickes and their crew. As they were waiting, an ambulance rolled up and stopped on the runway next to the hangar.

The moment the first chopper touched down, Mike Fish and Lee Honnald ran over to help lift Sean Witherspoon into the ambulance. Then they hurriedly gathered up the NVGs and ran back to their own chopper. At the same time, Molthen and Adickes rushed to brief Le Feuvre and Torpey over their radio.

Taking an extra crewman was a great idea, they emphatically agreed. The conditions out there were next to impossible. Their own flight mech had gone into something akin to shock. The ambulance now carting him away served to confirm as much.

With the engines switched on and the rotor turning, Torpey and Le Feuvre put on their goggles, raced through their mandatory checklist, and lifted off. As Torpey roared into the blustery heavens, he pointed the chopper's nose on a westerly course, rising to an altitude of six hundred feet as he sailed into the inhospitable black skies ahead.

With their radar indicating Mount Edgecumbe on the right, they flew past Cape Edgecumbe and then turned almost due north. Then, quickly entering the "fly-to point" on the computer, they aligned themselves with the most direct route possible to the last known position of the drifting crewmen. It was not until they made their turn that the storm imposed itself fully upon them. The weather was bad in Sitka. But just past the turn, it got downright mean. Torpey had known it would be windy and rainy, but he had expected to have some degree of visibility. Once they went airborne, however, he found that he could see absolutely nothing.

Fred Kalt, thirty-eight, grew up in Tampa, Florida, and joined the Coast Guard in 1987. Over the next decade, he won the respect of those with whom he flew. Pilots he's worked with say that he earned a reputation as a gifted flight mechanic largely for the calm, clear way he was able to communicate visual images over the radio during even the most stressful of in-flight maneuvers. He had served in places such as Reedsport, Oregon; Clearwater, Florida; and Cape Cod, Massachusetts, before being assigned to Sitka. Happily married, he had every intention of pulling off what some now considered to be an impossible rescue and return home to his wife, Barbara, and their two young daughters.

Originally from Modesto, California, strong-armed Harold "Lee" Honnald, twenty-nine, husband to wife Bernice, and father to daughters Hillary and Marissa, would ride along as a fifth crewmember and backup flight mechanic to Fred Kalt. Honnald's 225-pound body, athletic six-foot two-inch frame, and years of experience in the air would be welcome assets on such a formidable mission.

Mike Fish, age thirty, was the only Alaskan-born crewman on board. Born and raised in Wasilla, outside of Anchorage, he attended Wasilla High School, where he played hockey; then, after graduating, he went on to the Coast Guard Academy in New London, Connecticut. After that, he attended the grueling six-month course at the USCG swimmer boot camp in Elizabeth City, North Carolina.

Fish had been in the Coast Guard for eight years when Lt. Guy Pierce chose him for this rescue mission. "You're going as backup," Pierce told him. "But just as a precaution. You probably won't even be used." Later, Fish learned that the first helicopter crew had discovered survivors in the water but had experienced serious difficulty in getting anywhere near them.

Now, en route to the last known position of the drifting survivors, Fish worked intently to establish radio communication with Kodiak, which would serve as his primary radio-support contact. He was supposed to check in every fifteen minutes. If Kodiak didn't hear from him within that time period, they'd launch a helo or airplane and begin a search.

"Comsat Kodiak. Comsat Kodiak," he called. "This is six-oh-three-six. This is six-oh-three-six."

"Six-oh-three-six, this is Comsat Kodiak. Go ahead," responded an operator at the base in Kodiak.

"Six-oh-three-six is airborne from Sitka, en route to the Fairweather Ground," replied Fish. "I have five people on board. Request that you accept my radio guard at this time."

"Rescue six-oh-three-six, this is Comsat Kodiak. Roger, have your guard. Primary five megs [which is channel 5696], with secondary [channel] eight-nine-eight-three. Standard on flight ops positions every fifteen minutes. Next call at oh-one-twenty-seven-hundred hours."

"Roger," replied Fish.

Immediately, he called his home base back in Sitka. "Sitka Air. Sitka Air. Six-oh-three-six. I have established radio comms guard with Comsat Kodiak. Six-oh-three-six is en route to the Fairweather Ground with five people on board."

Sitka acknowledged. In the poor atmospheric conditions, it would prove to be the last radio contact he would have with their home base for the duration of the flight.

Lt. Steve Torpey never expected to fly so fast. For now, as they sprinted through the pitch-dark sky toward the waiting survivors, he looked down and took in the 225 knots recorded on the ground speed (247 miles per hour) instrument. Like their predecessors, Torpey and Le Feuvre were being pushed along by an additional tailwind of 70 knots.

Ten minutes from the scene, they "got comms," acquiring the second helo (flown by Dave Durham and Russ Zullick) on the TCAS (traffic collision avoidance system). Torpey found it a little unsettling that while flying over such a huge expanse of ocean, they could come so close in passing each other en route. In Alaska, pilots generally fly around with the "big sky, little airplane" theory. Sometimes this just doesn't hold up. These aircraft, however, avoided each other with little effort.

"Hey, Dave. I got you on TCAS," said Torpey.

As the two helicopters did a "handshake in the air," Cmdr. Dave Durham began briefing Torpey and Le Feuvre on what they were about to face. Things were bad out there, he said. They had departed the scene with no survivors and were returning to Sitka. The seas on-scene were 70 feet or better, explained Durham. He passed along the coordinates of the survivors' last-known position, then strongly suggested that they remain above 150 feet. "You're really going to need to use your flares," said Durham. "You will need them as a reference. Do not, under any conditions, try to hoist the survivors without first deploying your flares."

Durham gave Torpey and Le Feuvre a number of suggestions on how to approach the sea. He said that he'd allowed only plus or minus ten degrees on his attitude (the degree the helo and blades tilt during a given maneuver). Torpey felt that was playing it a little conservatively. He'd allow himself more leeway. He would later be forced to admit that this was a calculation that would soon plunge him into the kind of wild-assed trouble from which helicopter pilots do not often escape.

Torpey could tell that Commander Durham was really shaken up. Durham, he knew, was a fine pilot and a great guy who freely gave of himself. Torpey knew how hard it must have been for both Dave Durham and Russ Zullick to use the discretion they had, to bring their crew back alive even though it had meant leaving the drifting survivors behind.

Unbeknownst to Lt. Steve Torpey, he was now one step closer to being granted his wish. He would soon find himself at the epicenter of the most challenging open-sea helicopter rescue in the annals of the U.S. Coast Guard. Immediately upon passing, the two helicopters began pulling away from each other, distancing themselves at the combined speed of approximately three hundred miles per hour.

Commander Durham called back once more. "Hey," he said, "make sure and allow plenty of fuel, because you've got head winds all the way back." Then all radio contact was lost.

En route to the scene, rescue swimmer Lee Honnald could see the faint white strip of the wave crests peeling off the waves. Even from an altitude of three hundred feet, he could make out the faint glow of fluorescent algae in the crashing surf. The waves were so tall, it looked like their copter was flying at an altitude of just fifty feet. "How close *are* we to the water?" Honnald asked Fish. "It looks way too close."

As they neared the rescue scene, Mike Fish again contacted his radio guard in Kodiak. "Comsat Kodiak! This is Coast Guard Rescue six-oh-three-six. Over." But he heard nothing. "Comsat Kodiak! Comsat Kodiak! This is Coast Guard Rescue six-oh-three-six. Over."

Again and again, Fish tried to reach Kodiak, but he received no reply. He punched in different sets of frequency numbers on his computer screen—FM, VHF, and 156.8. Then he tried to reach Juneau. "Comsat Juneau! Comsat Juneau! This is Coast Guard Rescue six-oh-three-six. Do you read me?" But again, no response.

With each new silence came the realization that no one knew exactly where they were or how they were doing. A hollow feeling of isolation fell upon Fish. Now we're out here all by ourselves, with all the people still in the water, he thought.

Torpey passed over the fly-to point without glimpsing anything of the survivors. Also confusing was the location of the DND locator beacon signal. Dropped by one of the preceding helicopters, it was now more than three miles from what their computers referred to as ground zero. Wherever the 406 EPIRB is, there the crewmen will be also, reasoned Torpey, choosing to key on the EPRIB signal instead.

No one will probably ever know exactly how fast the strongest winds were blowing that night. A pilot who was in the process of being blown out of the sky would hardly be checking his wind-meter gauge to determine its precise speed as he plummeted toward the sea. As the wind roared around them, individual gusts drove into the H-60's body with the thump of a chunk of firewood tossed against the side of a house, while a mixture of rain, snow, and sea spray hissed against their windshield, abrading it like particles of sand.

All the noise inside made it difficult for the pilots to concentrate on flying. At one point, each one of the pilots' radios began simultaneously blaring the *Pew! Pew! Pew!* DNB signal, that unnerving alert frequency that sounded like a cross between a European police siren and an automobile alarm. Torpey knew he was on the verge of becoming "task-saturated." He switched off the audio portion of both alarms and glanced at the DF needle homing in on the EPIRB's pulse. They were flying downwind at a height of just three hundred feet when they whipped right over the top of the men.

In calm weather, an experienced pilot flying an H-60 helo can turn around in a few hundred feet, but on this night, by the time Torpey was able to complete his 180-degree clockwise turn back into the wind, his fly-to point readout told him that he had been blown 6,000 feet downwind of the drifting crewmen.

Man, did I ever overfly that, thought Torpey. He accelerated to an air speed of one hundred miles per hour, moving ahead against the eighty-mile-per-hour winds, and even stronger gusts, at a ground speed of between ten and twenty miles per hour. Such a cautious pace proved to be a wise choice. They were creeping warily forward when they chanced to spot the strobe light about one hundred yards away.

"There's the strobe light!" said Ted Le Feuvre.

"I've got the strobe light at one o'clock," Torpey radioed the crew.

When they first spotted the embattled survivors, the weather was so rough, they flew around for close to ten minutes, trying to calculate how to even *approach* the water. Torpey and Le Feuvre could see the forlorn huddle of what he assumed to be fishermen, who were getting severely flogged. The wind shrieking down the waves seemed to tear at the indistinct figures, driving a miserable chop against them, and launching geysers that disintegrated into a searing white mist.

Fish was busy monitoring three different channels at once when a friendly voice cut in. "Coast Guard six-oh-three-six, this is Coast Guard one-seven-oh-one. We're on scene and right above you at this time," came the voice of the C-130 pilot circling overhead. "We can take your radio guard at this time."

From that moment on, every fifteen minutes, Fish would report to the C-130 circling overhead. Its pilot would, in turn, pass on all information to those standing by in Kodiak, who, in turn, would relay it to Juneau, who would ultimately relay the same message to Sitka. There was no easy way to communicate out on the Cape Fairweather Ground.

Mike Fish radioed the pilots up front. "Pilot. Swimmer. Sir, do you want me to change into my swimmer gear now?" The gear Fish referred to was a one-piece dry suit pulled snuggly over a jumpsuit made of fleece. "I'm willing to go in if you need me to."

"Go ahead and get dressed," replied Torpey. "But, Mike, we're not going to use you for this, because we might not be able to get you back."

Fish felt more than a little disheartened by this news. With legs braced wide, he rose up from his tiny desk compartment and small computer screen. He leaned hard against his gunner's belt, staggered toward the door opening, and took another long, hard look at the survivors and conditions below. The waves were immense, craggy monstrosities. As he watched, strips of whitewater raced randomly down their broad, sweeping slopes, and plowed mercilessly into the tiny struggling figures below. In such a historic Gulf of Alaska storm, Fish knew that once he was lowered into the water, all the youth, training, determination, and natural athletic ability that he possessed would be almost useless against such hellish forces. He was torn between the desire of every rescue swimmer to do his job and the reality of his superior's final veto. It wasn't his place to argue with the pilot's decision, but he wanted them to know that if they wanted to deploy him, he was ready and willing.

CHAPTER 16

To Mike DeCapua, it somehow all seemed ridiculous, the chopper being so close for so long, while he and his buddies were slowly dying.

Now a wave fell upon them, driving them close to twenty feet below the surface of the sea. It tossed them end over end through its spiraling tide. Mike DeCapua bobbed to the surface, having nearly drowned, to find everyone gone. In his hypothermic stupor, he couldn't quite figure out how or why.

Then, in the blink of the strobe light, Bob Doyle spotted him. DeCapua was twenty feet from Doyle and the others and was being blown steadily away. The last wave had apparently washed him out of his rope loop, but his mind was too sluggish to comprehend this. Equally disturbing, DeCapua was inadvertently dragging the EPIRB along with him.

Doyle screamed at him. "Mike! You've gotta come back! None of us can leave! You don't have your rope on! And, damn it, you *have* to make it back! They'll find you all right! They'll find your dead body, because you've got the EPIRB! But how is anyone going to find the rest of us? They won't be able to find us at all!"

DeCapua turned then and clumsily made his way back to the group. He slipped the rope loop back over his shoulders, securing it around his waist as best he could, and once again joined his shipmates.

S teve Torpey fought to hold the chopper at an altitude somewhere near 150 feet. He could make out an undefined number of figures clustered together around an orange buoy, with the blinking flash of the EPIRB going off in their midst every ten seconds or so.

As he flew closer, Torpey was finally able to observe the storm waves firsthand. They were "absolutely gigantic," he said, the largest he or Captain Le Feuvre had ever seen in thirty-two years of combined Coast Guard experience. Worse yet, rogue waves approached in nebulous patterns from different directions, erupting into giant spouts of spewing foam as they collided.

Torpey had never seen such seas. Flying in Hurricane Juan down in the Gulf of Mexico several years before, he'd encountered forty-foot seas and seventy-mile-per-hour winds while attempting to hoist men off a sailing boat sporting a mast sixty feet high. But a number of the waves now stacking up on one another directly underfoot were easily twice that size.

The first order of business was, of course, the deployment of flares. Eventually, they would drop dozens of them. Torpey's plan was to move upwind and drop them as the aircraft slid back over the survivors.

As the crew in back rushed to prepare, he started forward, and as he did, both the survivors and the EPIRB they clung to disappeared from view. Now, as the powerful windshield wipers pounded back and forth in front of him, he found himself squinting to see through the spray-washed windshield for a possible reference point. With no visual correlations left, Torpey felt an old but familiar feeling rise in the pit of his stomach. He'd experienced the same thing while flying as a rookie pilot out of San Francisco. At the time, he'd been practicing training hoists off of a forty-one-foot sailboat. When he lost the reference part of the boat, he ended up pulling the basket through the rigging. Just moments before it had happened, he had felt it—that feeling in the pit of his stomach—which told him that something was not quite right, that he was in over his head.

Now, as Torpey moved ahead of the EPIRB, everything went black, and he said to myself, This is bad. "Drop the flares," he ordered. "*Drop the flares!* Just throw them out. Just get 'em out. All I need is a reference. Drop! Drop! Drop!"

"Smoke's away. Smoke's in the water, sir," replied Fred Kalt. "We've placed three Mark-fifty-eights and two Mark-twenty-fives in the water."

The flares emitted a kind of yellowish orange glow, while their smoking cores burned a brilliant white. They crawled up and over the waves like strings of Christmas tree lights moving along in centipede motion.

"Okay, good," replied Torpey. "But I'd like to light up the area better, to give us a better reference. So let's drop some more in the water."

Torpey glanced down at the artificial horizon on his attitude indicator and thought to himself, I'm just going to apply a little back-cyclic here.

Before he could counter it, the impact of the cold, blasting air pitched the nose of the helicopter thirty degrees up. Then came what Torpey described as "this huge rushing feeling" of being swept away, "of screaming backward." Torpey fought to bring the nose back down so that it would slant toward the water in front of them. To accomplish this, both Captain Le Feuvre and Steve Torpey pulled as much power as they dared, without overtorquing the engine. If the transmission gave out, they knew, the chopper would fall from the sky like a shotgunned goose with both wings crumpled, and they would crash and die.

As the overpowering gust of wind flung the men and their chopper back, Torpey fought helplessly to level out his rearing aircraft and bring it under control. "And the vision that will never, ever leave me," he would later recall, "is that of the ocean waves, several thousand feet of them, rushing out from under us." The world scrolled by at breakneck speed, sweeping forward, out from under the transparent chin bubble at his feet, as the helo screamed backward through space. Both Torpey and Le Feuvre wrenched up on the collective arm as much as they dared, but the chopper continued to plummet.

In the rear cabin, Fish, Honnald, and Kalt yelled almost in unison, "Altitude! Altitude! Up! Up! Up!"

As they continued to speed backward, the departing wave below rose to meet them. Honnald and Fish were quick to notice the swells rising toward the bottom edge of the cabin door. They knew their threshold had been reached. The helicopter had now exceeded the furthest extent of its capabilities.

Rescue swimmer Mike Fish's heart was pounding like a jackhammer, and he thought, This helo could go down so easy! If called upon to do so, he could, with the single tap of a finger, send out a Mayday and their position, as well—before they struck the water and their communications were lost altogether.

Only by pulling full-collective and applying maximum power were Ted Le Feuvre and Steve Torpey able to halt their descent. Torpey climbed to the comparative safety at the three-hundred-foot level, only to discover that they'd been blown downwind some three thousand feet from the survivors. It would take another twenty minutes to fight their way upwind and reacquire the target.

F or Mike DeCapua and his crewmates, it "seemed like an eternity" before the third helicopter arrived, and when it did, the intense beam of its searchlight found them, lost them, then located them again, occasionally illuminating their beleaguered members with a shifting blast of spray-filled light.

Then Bob Doyle spotted flight mech Fred Kalt crouched in the side door of the helo. Doyle couldn't tell for certain who, exactly, it was. But, as a fellow member of the Coast Guard, he probably knew him. He tried to stand as high as he could out of the waves and began, he said, "waving for all of us, waving like crazy."

Bob Doyle drifted on his back, clutching Mark Morley's motionless body. Overhead, he could see the third spray-slickened Jayhawk helicopter fighting to stay with them. The eight-ton aircraft was being tossed back and forth across the sky "like a gnat in a wind tunnel." And, once again, he watched as it was carried away.

Now, as he waited, Doyle felt a bout of melancholy and despondency sweep over him. He decided to try to talk telepathically to his daughter. Feeling somewhat confused from the effects of hypothermia, Doyle asked her, "Please tell Mommy that Daddy's in a lot of trouble and have her get ahold of the Coast Guard." Then Bob Doyle grabbed Mark Morley's chin and lifted it from the sea. "Hang in there, Mark," he said, offering encouragement to Morley's silent, bloodless face.

Holding tightly to his skipper now, Doyle could feel him shaking violently. He was relieved to know that the skipper was still alive. But Morley was almost beyond hypothermic now. Doyle knew that Morley's body temperature had to be in the low eighties and that even if the Coast Guard somehow instantaneously rescued them, the man might very well still be lost. Over the past hour, Morley had shivered through the final stages of hypothermia. And then he wasn't shivering anymore.

Doyle, too, was in worse shape than he had realized. The muscles in his arms ached so much that he could barely hold on to Mark Morley. Then he began to hallucinate. Doyle found himself in California with his former wife, driving along on a warm afternoon through a sun-kissed scene of free-rolling hills. Just as abruptly, it became night again, and the flares in the distance looked exactly like automobile headlights. Doyle thought, How strange. Then he began to cross back over again from that visionary state. No, Bob, he told himself forcefully. Those hills are waves, and those headlights are flares. But even then, he began seeing what appeared to be "friendly waves," and he found himself observing, in the pale yellow light, what he described as the "grandeur" of the ocean writhing around him.

Now, in his mind, the flares became a gathering of fireflies dancing. Their swirling paths left behind tracer trails, and as they skittered across the waves, they illuminated the tumultuous world around them in a yellowish haze, while turning the water in the immediate area to a pea soup green. Doyle could see the sulfur smoke being whipped at a furious rate by the wind, sometimes in eddies and other times stream-

222 \ *Spike Walker*

ing up the waves with the wind, occasionally filling his nostrils with the acrid smell of sulfur.

Then Doyle experienced a surge of hope, followed by a moment of clarity. People are trying to help us, he realized. And most of us are still alive. "We're going to do it!" he said aloud. "It's going to happen."

"Hey, I gotta take a leak!" announced DeCapua, unimpressed by Doyle's sudden revelation.

"Well, go in your suit," shot back Gig Mork.

To DeCapua, it seemed a little like peeing in his own bed. However, the relief he felt upon so doing was short-lived. Then the stifling cold of the water sloshing about inside his suit returned, and he wished that he hadn't urinated.

A ware of the fact that both he and Torpey were fast becoming task saturated, and shaken to the core by the fact that the next downdraft could well carry their chopper, nose-first, into the next towering wave, Captain Le Feuvre was suddenly struck by a possible solution. He and Lieutenant Torpey would divide the controls! He would be responsible for working the collective and keeping them at a safe altitude, while Torpey would work the joystick, the main controls, and actually fly the helicopter.

Theoretically, it was a radical move. Such a concept ran contrary to everything a pilot was trained to do. In time, it would be looked upon by flight school understudies as that rare type of instantaneous innovation that is, on occasion, manifested by exceptional people caught in insurmountable predicaments.

One longtime Coast Guard SAR pilot would later describe it as "a moment of pure genius." Hitting upon the concept of dividing the controls while caught flying in perhaps the worst difficult challenge any Coast Guard helicopter pilot has ever faced was something that could never be taught.

Torpey grasped the clarity of the notion almost instantly. "Yes!" he agreed. "You run the collective and keep us at a constant altitude. And I'll just fly the plane."

Left now with fewer responsibilities, Lt. Steve Torpey once again went to work with Fred Kalt to try and drop the basket as close to the survivors as possible, laboring all the while to produce a stable hover above the tiny human forms drifting over the Texas-size waves. Some of the waves looked big enough to reach up and swat them from the sky. He fought to maintain visual contact with the survivors and tried once again to get the basket lowered and pluck the small shivering huddle of fishermen out of the sea. But in the wind and seas they were encountering, it still seemed highly unlikely that they'd be able to land the basket anywhere near the men.

Kalt's conning commands began at around two hundred feet. "Forward and right two hundred," he said. "Forward and right fifty."

Torpey felt the wind slacken and the chopper leap ahead. "Back and left one-fifty," came Kalt's calm, undeterred voice.

Neither Torpey nor Le Feuvre were able to see the basket trailing behind them. Once, Kalt managed to drop it to within sixty-feet or so of the survivors. There was no way to determine whether or not those adrift far below could even see the basket. But if they did, they seemed extremely reluctant to free themselves from the lines binding them and make a swim for it. At liberty now to concentrate completely on his flying, Torpey came to understand that it would be necessary to bank as sharply as thirty degrees, or even as much as an unheard-of forty or forty-five degrees, in order to accomplish the task. The crewmen were being swept along by the currents and wind so fast that if Kalt asked him to go forward and right forty degrees and he failed to carry out that command immediately, everything would shift, the distances would change, and the effort would be wasted.

With growing confidence in his flight mech, Torpey began jockeying about the sky with quick, exaggerated movements, snapping the aircraft in and out of rolls as fast as Kalt requested them. Pushing the limits of aggressiveness, he caught sight of the rotor blades sweeping down in front of him several times, far below where he'd ever seen them dip before. Yet he could never really see the waves clearly. Most of the time, he could make out only the white, wind-whipped streaks of sea foam stretched across the face of the approaching wave. He could see the phenomenal waves themselves only when they closed to within a hundred yards or so of the chopper.

Occasionally, as Torpey watched the flares floating off in the black space, he'd see them rise overhead, and then he knew he had to begin climbing.

"Okay, Captain, we've got another big one coming," Torpey would say.

At such times, his altitude readout would often maintain that they were remaining at just forty feet, when in reality, they'd actually been climbing steadily up the slope of the gigantic wave at about the same rate as it had been approaching.

Sometimes, during the hundreds of attempts Kalt made, the basket would clip a wave and then, along with the movement of the helo and wind, it would launch into a violent, oscillating swing. Then flight mech Fred Kalt would haul the basket all the way up to the door and start from scratch. Another hour of continuous effort left Kalt feeling more than a little weary, and he began to entertain the possibility that he was doing something wrong. Perhaps his strategy had been flawed all along, his tactics ill conceived, and in spite of his best efforts, he was making it all more difficult than it really needed to be.

Torpey, too, was having his doubts. In spite of his masterful, even artful, maneuvering, things were shifting around him way too fast. For a long time, he didn't think that they had much of a chance.

"Hey, Lee," Kalt said, finally turning to Lee Honnald. "Would you like to try to do some hoisting?"

"No, you're doing a good job," shot back Honnald.

Torpey also vetoed the idea. "Fred, you're doing good," he told him. "We're getting closer."

Kalt felt encouraged. He knew the officers flying the plane were performing superbly under near-impossible conditions.

Logic might dictate that the basket be lowered far downwind from those in the water and then just dragged forward up the line until it reached them. In seventy-foot waves, however, such an effort would be met with such force, Kalt knew, that it would either break the hoist cable or send the rescue basket skipping across the sea.

When possible, Kalt began each hoisting cycle with the survivors in the two o'clock position. Then, as he lowered the basket, he'd conn Torpey back over the top of them. Ideally, he'd drop it down approximately twenty yards in front of them, allowing the force of the waves to wash it toward them, all the while playing out slack in an effort to keep the wildly gyrating chopper from jerking the basket out of position.

"Back and left fifty," said Fred Kalt. "Forward and right thirty."

As the distances to target diminished once again, Steve Torpey's hopes rose. Kalt was performing his job with a level of candor and efficiency that allowed a pilot to place his trust in him. Kalt was a flight mech who always seemed able to communicate information to the pilots in such a way as to provide them with a clear mental picture. Torpey didn't *need* to know everything. He just needed to do what Kalt told him to do.

"Forward and right twenty. Forward and right ten. Hold!"

Torpey thought that under the present circumstance, *Hold* was an extremely relative term. Flight mechs used it when they wanted you to stay put. Torpey knew the situation now was probably too dynamic to hope to remain over the same spot for more than a few seconds, but he would try.

In the black void ahead, he watched a line of flares trailing up and across, then down and over the waves. Traveling along in irregular columns, they looked like transient rows of airport runway lights.

Then, strangely, everything seemed to come together. The basket landed surprisingly close, and as Torpey slid back over the area, Kalt thought he spied some sticklike lengths of retrotape moving in all the blackness below. They seemed to break away from the pack, move sluggishly forward, and align themselves inside the basket. He couldn't see the whole image, just the blackness and the retrotape.

"I think we have someone in the basket," announced Kalt.

Holy cow, we've got someone! Torpey thought gratefully.

Fred Kalt played out slack at full speed. He hoped to allow the blurry stick figures below time to climb into the rescue basket. But at that moment, a giant wave plowed into the basket, sweeping it back and under the helicopter, as far as its cable could reach. With a snap, the hoist cable came bow-tight and began grinding into the side and underbelly of the chopper. Kalt leapt to ease the tension and wear on the cable. "Lee! Push! Push against the cable!" he yelled.

Lee Honnald hit the deck. He'd always found better leverage for pushing while lying on his stomach on the floor. Both men soon broke out into a saunalike sweat. But although they pushed mightily, the cable refused to budge. More than a year later, Lee Honnald's neck would still smart from the strain.

Kalt paused from the effort, stuck his head out into the buffeting winds, and peered underneath the helo's belly. He could see only a silver blur of retrotape far below. But it appeared to be shining back at him from inside the basket.

"Ready for pickup!" he radioed Torpey.

"Conn me in," shot back Torpey.

"Back and left fifty," began Kalt, pausing between each command. "Forward and right twenty. . . . Forward and right ten. . . . Now over top. Hold position. Preparing to take the load. Taking the load." Kalt then said, "Basket is clear of the waves. Clear to move back and left thirty, sir."

As the basket rose, Kalt strained to see through the horizontal deluge of snow, sleet, and blowing spray. The visibility was so poor that he still wasn't able to tell *what* he had.

CHAPTER 17

L istening to his fellow crewmates, Bob Doyle was certain that he was in the best shape of any of them. Gig Mork was "as tough as shoe leather," enduring without a word of complaint. Mark Morley was grievously cold. And Mike DeCapua was also sliding toward serious trouble.

Then the moment for which Doyle had so fervently hoped and so patiently waited during close to seven hours of freezing hell came to pass when the rescue basket plopped down in the water just thirty feet away.

Seeing his chance, Doyle wrapped his legs around Mark Morley, unzipped his own suit, reached inside, located the knife he had dangling from a loop of halibut ganion he wore around his neck, and slid it carefully from its sheath. Then he painstakingly zipped his suit all the way back up, sliding the sealing mechanism up over his chest and up along the underside of his chin, securing it just below his mouth. Though some seawater did spill in, Doyle was relieved, even delighted, that he'd managed to retrieve his knife without flooding his survival suit altogether.

"Bob, you take Mark," yelled Gig Mork. "You're probably a better swimmer than I am. Take him to the basket! Mike and I'll wait and catch the next ride."

With those words, Mark Morley suddenly jolted awake. His revival startled Doyle. It was as if Morley had been hibernating the entire time, lingering in a physical state somewhere near death, lost in the numbed semiconsciousness of the extreme stages of hypothermia.

"We're going to do it, Mark!" shouted Doyle, astonished at his lost friend's sudden recovery.

"You damn right we're going to do it!" agreed Morley.

Doyle was thrilled to have him back. He drew Morley in close then and yelled into his face. "This is it, Mark!" he announced, his voice building. "We gotta go now, man! We gotta catch this one! This is our chance! We're going to make it! We're going to do it! This is it! Do you hear me? I need everything you've got!"

With his adrenaline pumping, Doyle cut the ropes that bound them. Doyle was amazed at Morley's determination to live. Yet in spite of it, Doyle soon discovered that his skipper could barely move. Without his glasses, he was nearly blind now, as well. But he was still fighting. Morley, he realized, was "one hell of a fighter." And with that, Doyle began dragging Morley through the water toward the waiting basket.

"Let's go, Mark! Let's go!" repeated Doyle again and again.

"I'm trying! I'm trying!" Morley assured him.

They slid down the face of the approaching swell and managed to reach the basket, which was almost completely submerged in the body of the wave. Doyle immediately set out to help Morley into it, but he quickly discovered that his friend was so stiff, and his survival suit was so filled with seawater, that there was no way to accomplish the task. Instead, he worked his way around to the opposite side of the basket and crawled inside. Quickly positioning himself on his knees, Doyle reached out between the corner posts and cable rigging, grabbed Morley under the arms, and tried to pull him into the basket. He managed to get Morley's arms and elbows inside, but then, as he tried to yank the rest of the skipper's body aboard, the wave dropped out from under them, leaving them suspended in air.

As the water fell away, Mark Morley was left dangling in space, clutching the side of the basket and struggling mightily to bear up under, in addition to his own weight, the sizable burden of seawater in his suit, all of which was now threatening to break his grip and strip him away.

Blind to the details of the drama unfolding below, Fred Kalt began hoisting them toward the waiting helicopter at top speed.

"Hang on!" yelled Doyle to his friend as they rose.

Dangling beneath the helo on the end of the 150-foot length of cable, they began swinging back and forth through the sleet-filled space, spinning slowly as they rose, in long pendulum-like arcs.

"Don't drop me, Bob!" begged Mark Morley, his pasty white face and pleading eyes peering up at Doyle. "Please don't drop me!"

"I'm not going to drop you, Mark!" screamed Doyle. "Just hang on!"

Doyle was on his hands and knees inside the basket, pushing frantically down on Morley's arms. But as the chopper dipped and rolled, the basket responded in kind, leaping and falling and heaving about in ever-tightening circles as it ascended toward the helo's cabin door.

"Hang on to me, Bob! Hang on!" yelled Mark Morley.

Except for the sticklike patches of retrotape occasionally reflecting back, those riding the basket remained invisible to the men in the chopper. The basket swung back and forth under the aircraft's belly, emerging only briefly. When it did, the grinding force of the cable rubbing against the helo eased, allowing Fred Kalt a better angle on the basket.

"Hang on, Bob!" yelled Morley, still clinging to the side of the rising basket.

"He was looking at me," Bob Doyle recalls, "and he said, 'Don't drop me!' And I said, 'I'm not!' I tried to grab onto the hood material on the top of his head, biting at it with my teeth, but I couldn't."

"I yelled at him, 'We're there! We're almost there! Hang on, Mark! Hang on!' "

"We got up to the helicopter, and Mark yelled, 'Hang on!' But I couldn't hang on to him any longer, because we were just hanging and hanging and hanging. He was still hanging, and he was looking me in the face, and I could feel him slipping."

When Doyle looked again into Mark Morley's blanched face, he saw a poignant expression of disbelief lingering there.

"He was freezing," recalls Doyle. "I was looking into Mark's eyes when he fell. Then I just saw him floating through space."

Those inside the helicopter had a somewhat different perspective. The moment the basket outside rose even with the side door, Fred Kalt proclaimed flatly, "Survivor is at the cabin door."

Then, just as he'd done ten thousand times before, he swung the rectangular-shaped basket into a lengthwise position and reefed back on it.

"Bringing in the basket, sir," he added.

But the basket refused to budge. Kalt couldn't figure it out. He'd raised the basket up to the door and stopped it in exactly the place he always had. Perhaps he'd failed to lift it high enough. Kalt hoisted it a few inches higher and attempted once again to pull it aboard, but the basket still refused to swing in. Some part of it seemed to be bumping into the ledge of the doorway.

"The basket won't come in!" he radioed Lee Honnald finally. "Pull, Lee! Pull the basket! It's not coming in!"

Kalt sat down on the floor, propped one foot on either side of the door opening, and pulled forcefully on the nearest end of the basket. "Pull!" yelled Kalt, giving it his all.

"I'm pulling as hard as I can!" said Lee Honnald, joining in the effort.

Normally, pulling in the basket was a perfunctory part of the exercise. Mike Fish couldn't grasp why the basket wouldn't slide right in as it always did. As he peered down near his crewmate's feet, he spotted the hooded head and drenched white face of a man clinging to the outside of the rescue basket. His hands and arms were actually draped inside the far side of the litter. He was straining desperately to hold on, while the man crouched inside the small basket was fighting frantically to pin the man's arms there and keep him from slipping.

Two healthy young Coast Guard men, their systems charged with adrenaline, could easily exert the combined pulling force of five hundred pounds or more in such a situation. Each time they yanked on the rescue basket, however, the clinging figure was slammed against the side of the helicopter.

Then the battered survivor looked up at Fish, and, just for a moment, their eyes met.

"Fred! There's someone hanging on the basket!" yelled Mike Fish, pointing.

In just the time it took Mike Fish to point with his arm and speak those seven words, the man (Mark Morley) vanished. Fish was astonished. One second the man was there, and in the next, he was gone.

The instant Morley fell, the basket came sailing in, carrying Bob Doyle inside. Kalt glanced at Fish. He was soaked with sweat, his face red and dripping from the slap of the wind and spray blasting him. "A guy just fell," reiterated Mike Fish.

Hoping for the best, Fish glanced back at his computer screen to see how far the man had fallen. He was sickened by what he saw. The fluorescent green numbers on the face of the altitude gauge read 103 feet.

A heavy silence followed. The watery impact after falling from such a height would essentially be like striking concrete.

"What's going on?" Torpey demanded. "What's happening?"

"I think someone fell," replied Kalt.

"Who fell?" asked Torpey. "How'd a guy who was *in* the basket fall *out*?"

"I think there was someone hanging on the outside of the basket," replied Kalt.

Mike Fish helped lift the survivor from the basket. The fisherman was almost inert with cold. In the dim indigo light of the rear cabin, he could see the man's face pressing through the circular hole cut in the hood of his survival suit. There was something faintly familiar about it.

As Kalt shoved the rescue basket back out the side door, Fish dragged the survivor off to the side and strapped him into a seat against the far wall. Then the man pulled back the hood of his survival suit.

No one on board could believe it. It was Bob Doyle! He was one of them. He'd retired as a Coast Guard warrant officer the year before, saying that he was going to follow his dream of becoming a commercial fisherman.

"Good God, it's Bob Doyle!" Fish radioed for all to hear. "Hey, we've got Bob Doyle aboard here with us!"

"*Our* Bob Doyle?" replied Steve Torpey. He glanced back, but could barely recognize the man. Doyle now had a thick red beard, something he had never had while serving at the USCG Air Station back in Sitka.

"Who fell?" Kalt asked Doyle.

"The skipper, Mark Morley," he replied. "I think he's probably dead."

Now Mike Fish began plying Doyle with a rapid-fire series of questions. "What boat are you guys off of? What happened? Where are the other people? How many people were on the boat? And how many are in the water now?"

"There were four of us in the water," said Doyle. "There were five people on the boat, but we lost Dave Hanlon. He got swept away early on. I think that he, too, is probably dead." He paused, then said, "I had ahold of Mark, but I was losing my grip. And I was starting to get pulled out of the basket myself. I did everything I could to hold on to him, but I just couldn't hold on to him any longer. That's when he slipped and fell off."

When Bob Doyle and Mark Morley first untied themselves and ventured out toward the rescue basket, those left behind feared for them.

What's going to happen if they don't make it? thought Mike DeCapua. If they don't make the basket and another wave catches them out there, we're not going to be able to get together again.

"Yes! Yes!" yelled DeCapua as the hazy, dripping forms of the basket and bodies rose from the sea.

One man was inside the basket, while the other appeared to be hanging from the side. Once airborne, however, the chopper carrying them drifted steadily downwind, and the vision of both men and aircraft vanished into the storm.

"They're not going to come back, are they?" asked Mike DeCapua. "They aren't going to be able to get us, are they, Gig?"

"Oh, come on now," countered Gig Mork. "We're going to make it. But whatever you do, just don't let go of the EPIRB. If you *do* let go of that baby, I'll drown you myself!"

"Okay, Gig. Okay."

As Fish looked after their first survivor, Steve Torpey let the helicopter slide back and spotted the body of Mark Morley. He was floating facedown in the water. Torpey saw him drift up and over the crest of a wave, then slide down the other side. He was spread-eagled and, if not dead, clearly unconscious. At that point, Torpey was faced with a momentous decision. For a time, he studied the body for any sign of life or movement. He was finally forced to conclude that, without help from either their rescue swimmer or Morley himself, there would be no way of getting him into the basket. In such a violent sea, however, there was no way that either he or Ted Le Feuvre could, in good conscience, deploy their rescue swimmer.

"Sir, who do you want to go for next?" asked Fred Kalt.

"Let's go for the two guys next to the EPIRB," replied Torpey regretfully.

Despite the emotional roller coaster of gaining one survivor, then losing another, Torpey and Kalt had acquired, in their flight maneuvers, an almost telepathic communication. Snatching the one fisherman from the sea and bringing him safely on board had served to solidify that connection and boost their confidence.

"Fred, begin the hoist again," said Torpey.

Kalt played out approximately 125 feet of cable and started conning his friend into position. "Forward and right three hundred feet," he said.

Twenty minutes of trial and error later, of losing ground and position, and then regaining it, Kalt radioed Torpey. "Basket's in the water, sir. Hold position."

This time, as Kalt watched, he saw the hazy figures of what appeared to be the last two fishermen abandon the EPIRB, free themselves from the security of their rope loops, and begin making their sluggish way toward the fluorescent form of the rescue basket. Once again, as the helicopter teetered in its tenuous hover, Kalt patiently tried to allow the almost indecipherable figures all the time he could before taking up the slack.

M ike DeCapua and Gig Mork had been waiting for the right moment to make their move. To DeCapua, the idea of leaving the security of the EPIRB and lines behind was "scary as hell." Then they saw the basket drop down on the side of a wave well off and away from them. They would have to swim a ways, but they decided to go for it.

But when Gig Mork loosened the grip he had on Mike DeCapua, he discovered that his friend could barely move. "Come on, man!" encouraged Gig Mork, tugging on him as they went. "You can do it! Hell, we're almost there!"

S ir, I think we have the survivors in the basket," Kalt said, radioing his pilot. "Preparing to take the load." There was nothing more to be done except hoist them, and Kalt made haste now to accomplish that task.

When the wind-battered basket and its exhausted cargo broke free of the sea, Gig Mork and Mike DeCapua were caught still climbing aboard, clinging tenaciously to the outside of it, they had risen perhaps forty feet toward the comfort and security of the chopper hovering above, when a wave six stories high drove into them.

Crouched in the chopper's doorway, Fred Kalt hit the lift switch, flipping it to its maximum up setting. But he knew it was hopeless. There was no way to alter the potentially disastrous encounter unfolding before his eyes. The head-on collision between the basket and the towering breaker that reached nearly up to the chopper itself was unavoidable.

Mork and DeCapua braced themselves as the oncoming wave exploded over the basket, burying it under several fathoms of moving sea. They could hear the helicopter engines revving high under the strain.

They surfaced, choking. As the basket rose, Mike DeCapua was nearly stripped away. He fumbled for a handhold, caught himself, then slipped again, tumbling awkwardly backward. I'm dead, he thought as he plunged into the sea.

"Somebody else fell," radioed Lee Honnald in the helicopter. "A wave hit him."

"He's all right, isn't he?" shot back the captain.

"Yah, he's still swimming."

While the impact of the wave knocked Mike DeCapua off the basket, Gig Mork continued his ascent. His wiry, labor-hardened body was wrapped around the frame of the basket as tenaciously as a monkey to a cage. Stunned by the collision, Mork nevertheless held fast. The second he felt himself break free of the water, he inhaled deeply of the cold January air. Though his survival suit was heavy with seepage, he maintained a death grip on the wire corner cable of the rescue litter, and as he rose on his spray-soaked journey, he could feel himself being pressed down by the G-forces and encountered the cold buffeting of the storm winds as he climbed toward the clacking chopper overhead. There's no way I'm going to let go of this! he thought.

He'd been hoisted nearly to the chopper by the time he realized that Mike DeCapua was missing. He's gone! Mike's gone! thought Gig Mork. I'm going up. I can't help Mike now. If I let go now and fall back down there and go after him, I'm not going to make it, either.

"The tension," recalls Gig Mork, "got worse and worse as I drew closer to that chopper. You're so tense the whole time, seven hours of fighting that stuff, of getting so close and wanting to get there. You're going and you're going and you're going, and all the while, it's a real adrenaline rush. And then you get there and—*boom*—you feel like butter on the skillet—you just melt.

"Inside the helicopter, one of the Coast Guard guys pulled me down between his legs and left me lying there. I just lay there for a while. I couldn't move at all."

As he looked around, Mork expected to see Mark Morley already on board. "Hey, Bob!" he called to Doyle from his prone position on the floor. "Where's Mark?"

"He didn't make it," replied Doyle.

"What do you mean, he didn't make it? Where the hell's he at?"

"He fell from the basket."

Gig Mork received the news in silent disbelief.

"Where's Mike?" asked Bob Doyle finally.

"He fell, too," said Mork dejectedly.

CHAPTER 18

With Bob Doyle and Gig Mork safely on board, and Mark Morley and Mike DeCapua still waiting to be rescued, Torpey and Le Feuvre came to an undeniable crossroad, their "bingo" point. They knew that they had to depart immediately if they were going to make the fuel-consuming, into-the-wind journey back to Sitka.

But with two shipwrecked sailors still in the water, Le Feuvre paused to calculate the distance to Yakutat. Normally, it would have taken him about a minute on the computer to accomplish such a task. But on this night, in the gyrating space of the helicopter's forward cabin, it took him fifteen. Finally, he called the C-130 circling overhead, their only link with the outside world, to double-check his work and make sure that he had it right.

"Hey, help me out," he began. "We've still got people in the water here, but we're running low on fuel. We'd like to remain here on-scene and see if we can't get these guys, but if we don't leave real soon, we're not going to have enough fuel to get back to Sitka. The way I figure it, if we go to Yakutat instead, we can remain on-scene here another half hour or more. So I need you to help me out here. I need you to confirm that the distance, heading, and projected fuel consumption figures that I've come up with are accurate. I need to know if you get the same thing."

Moments later, they called Captain Le Feuvre back and corroborated the fact that his calculations involving fuel, wind, speed, and distance were correct. Having received confirmation, Ted Le Feuvre turned to his pilot and explained the situation.

Torpey received the news with mixed feelings. With people still in the water, they had to stay as long as possible. But if they failed to save everyone, going to Yakutat would mean that in effect they were taking that particular helicopter out of the game. Taking one of only three choppers out of the action could pose a problem. Also, hanging it so far out over the edge for so long made Torpey think twice.

Captain Le Feuvre was sure he could read Torpey's mind. He had been so deeply concentrating on plucking the hapless fishermen from the sea that he hadn't really had time to think about fuel or Yakutat at all. Torpey's first thought would be, The captain is new to the H-60. Do I trust him to figure this out? Are those figures accurate? Does he really know what he's talking about here? In fact, this was exactly what Torpey was thinking, something he admitted to Le Feuvre later that evening.

"Look," Le Feuvre told Torpey, trying to assure him. "I've checked these calculations with the C-one-thirty guys, and they've confirmed that my figures are correct. If we go to Yakutat, which is much closer, we'll have a good tailwind and we can stay out here a little longer."

"How do you feel, Fred?" Torpey asked his flight mech. "We're thinking about extending our time out here by going to Yakutat when it's all over. Do you feel like you can do some more out here?"

"I feel all right," said Kalt. "Let's continue."

"Okay, then let's get some more flares down in the area. I want to drop them just forward of the guy who fell."

Then Kalt noticed where a section of hoist cable had been rubbing up against the metal sides of the helicopter through scores of failed rescue attempts and was now beginning to unravel. "Sir, our hoist cable is starting to fray," Kalt radioed.

The news brought Steve Torpey up short. If the line were to billow out, or "birdcage," it would compound the problem immensely. However, with the fuel running low, and with at least one of the two remaining people in the water still apparently alive, Torpey felt the possible gain outweighed the inherent risk of the line parting.

"Sir?" said Fred Kalt.

"I think at this point we need to continue," said Torpey.

"Roger, sir. Cable going down."

"Begin conning me in."

M ike DeCapua surfaced to find everyone gone. I'm through. I quit, he thought. They're never going to find me again out here. Besides, I don't have anything more to give.

Mike DeCapua hadn't seen Mark Morley's fall. He was sure that both Doyle and Morley had made it safely aboard the helicopter. Never in his life had DeCapua felt so discouraged and alone. Drifting now through the darkness, certain that the rest of his shipwrecked buddies were safe, if not warm and dry, DeCapua felt at once abandoned and forsaken.

God, what have you got against me to put me through this? he thought. Why couldn't I have just had a heart attack, or have gotten run over by a truck, or shot dead in a bar fight, something simple like that?

Stripped of the rope lines, buoys, EPIRB, and the support and companionship of his fellow crewmates, with several gallons of heart-stopping seawater sloshing about in his suit, DeCapua felt like one dispossessed. It was then that he finally and completely gave himself up for dead. The hell with it, he reasoned. That's it. I'm going to sleep. I quit.

He could feel the next waves lifting him, the hissing spray scouring his face, and the icy rush of seawater washing in through the neck area of his suit. The water was flushing right down over his heart now and cooling the very core of him. I'm going to freeze to death, he concluded. "I can't stand it any longer!" he cried aloud.

He had just finished surrendering when the rescue basket touched down gently in the water just twenty-five feet away. DeCapua could see the fluorescent green of the Chem-Light sticks, which were tied to the bottom of the semisubmerged basket, glowing under the water.

"What got me to the basket the first time was gone," he would later recall. "My arms wouldn't work anymore. My legs didn't work. I didn't even know how I was swimming. I wasn't really swimming. I was just trying. Maybe it was a breaststroke. I don't know. I had no feeling in my arms and legs. None. But somehow, I was making headway. I honestly don't know how I got there. But the next thing I knew, I was inside the basket, and I was airborne.

"When I got into the basket, I fell onto my back, and it started lifting me up. And I knew at that moment that there was and is a God. I knew it. There is an intelligent force that knows what it's doing and manipulates the planet."

DeCapua lay sprawled on his back on the steel-mesh floor, his feet sticking out through the wire rigging and seawater draining from the neck opening of his suit. As he rose into the heavens, he could hear the growing roar of the jet engines and feel the chopper jerking spasmodically under the load. The blasting beam of the floodlight washed repeatedly over him, and as he neared the helicopter, he felt the greeting blast of the 120-mile-per-hour downdraft of the rotor-blade wash. And he yelled aloud, "Thank you, God! Oh, thank you, God! Thank you for getting me into this basket alive!"

It was close to 3:00 A.M. when Fred Kalt hoisted Mike DeCapua from the water. DeCapua had risen almost to the helicopter when Kalt noticed a twenty-foot length of line dangling from DeCapua's waistline. A large beach-ball-sized buoy was attached to the lower end and was thrashing about in the wind. Kalt was left with few options. He couldn't very well lower the man back down into the water. Instead, he brought the basket up slowly. DeCapua was almost level with the side door when the line somehow slipped free of him. Instantly, it flew back and wrapped itself around the HF radio stanchion, a small but important transmitting tube sticking out from the side of the helicopter's tail. Then the large orange buoy tied on one end of the line began beating out a frantic rhythm against the tail section of the chopper. Kalt decided against informing his pilots. There was nothing anyone could do.

They were pulling Mike DeCapua inside when the buoy and line broke free, tearing off the HF long-wire antenna as it departed. Kalt and Honnald exchanged a look that seemed to say, Can you believe it?

When they pulled DeCapua aboard, they found that he was in bad shape, the coldest of any of the men they had recovered. Fish stripped his suit off of him and placed him in a TRC (thermal recovery capsule) to try to warm him up.

Once inside the chopper, Mike DeCapua's foggy mind struggled to interpret what he saw around him. Then DeCapua noticed that, apart from the chopper crew, he could count only Gig Mork, Bob Doyle, and himself. They had stripped him of his clothing and were putting him in another one of the bunny bags when he yelled to the closest crew member, "Hey! Where's the skipper?"

"He didn't make it," the man said.

"How the hell is he *not* here?" protested DeCapua. "Who are you guys? A bunch of postal workers? And now you're going to tell me you lost the damned letter? Come on, where the hell is Mark?"

With three survivors on board, and the glow from their flares dying out in the water all around them, Torpey and Le Feuvre were, in fact, angling back upwind and across the water to try to relocate Mark Morley. With no strobe light to direct them, and numerous canyonlike troughs to search, it proved to be a formidable task. When they finally came upon him, they moved forward and dropped several more flares.

"He doesn't appear to be moving," said Fred Kalt.

"Let's try to see if we can get the basket down to him," said Torpey. Eventually, Kalt was able to actually nudge Mark Morley's body with the rescue basket. "I've touched him with the basket, sir, but he isn't even moving," said Kalt, who then attempted to use the basket to scoop up the man's lifeless body.

To Ted Le Feuvre, Kalt sounded desperate. He knew the young flight mechanic felt at least partly responsible for losing the *La Conte*'s skipper, who was now floating facedown in the battering seas. Captain Le Feuvre had been listening to what was going on, and he continued to evaluate his crew's mental and emotional state. He was certain now that his men had become so task-oriented that they were now willing to risk all to make the rescue happen. They were determined to recover Mark Morley's body, no matter what. They'd been trying for nearly thirty minutes, when Le Feuvre decided to intervene. "We've got three people," he said finally. "It's time for us to go now."

Torpey agreed.

"But we could keep going," put in Kalt. Fish agreed.

With increasing fatigue taking its toll on all of his crew, Le Feuvre felt that their ability to concentrate was beginning to wear thin. He'd already noted that after close to two hours of focused intensity, the control imputs Lieutenant Torpey was now making weren't quite as crisp as they had been.

It was a difficult decision. Le Feuvre and Torpey wanted to give Mark Morley every possible chance to survive. "And what did I actually know?" Torpey would say later. "I knew he wasn't moving and that he was probably dead, and that, either way, there was no way to recover him. There was no way to get Mark Morley aboard our helicopter."

"Crew, we've given it a good try here," said Captain Le Feuvre finally. "We've recovered three people, but Mr. Morley here doesn't appear to be responsive. We've been doing this for over two hours now, and we're wearing out. We've done all we can here. We're also getting low on fuel. We need to head back. It's time for us to retire to Yakutat."

"But before we leave," cut in Torpey, "we need to toss out another four smokes to mark the position here."

As the helo powered forward into the battering winds, the crew in back tossed out four more flares in one quick flurry.

"Drop. Drop. Drop. Drop," called out Torpey.

"Flares are away, sir," replied Kalt.

"Complete Rescue checklist part three," shot back the captain. "Secure for forward flight," which meant to bring in the hook, store the basket, shut the side door, and button up the cabin.

Kalt closed the door. "Ready for forward flight," he said. "Single engine–capable."

"Single engine," confirmed Torpey.

"All right, we're out of here," said Captain Le Feuvre, taking over the controls and sprinting toward the base in Yakutat.

As they rose into the night, Steve Torpey would forever remember passing over Mark Morley and seeing his relatively tiny open-armed body along, indifferent now to the endless barrage of savage seas.

With the loss of Mark Morley, theirs would be a bittersweet victory. Up front, Steve Torpey turned off his floodlight, flipped down his night-vision goggles, and sighed deeply. Now, with the rescue portion of the mission behind him, he felt a wall of fatigue pressing in on him. He was so wrung out, he found it difficult even to talk.

As the chopper pounded its way toward Yakutat, passing easily now over even the tallest of the seas, a subdued atmosphere descended on the crew. In the back, rescuers and the rescued alike rode along in stupefied silence, staring at the rescue basket on the cabin floor, its bony frame glowing a neon green in the dark. Mike DeCapua could see the tops of the heads of both pilots. They were looking straight ahead, their heads bouncing in a staccato of sharp jerks as their chopper beat its way toward shore.

CHAPTER 19

Tamara Morley was home alone with Kyla in their waterfront abode when the storm winds had first awakened her. For a time, she lay in bed listening to the windows rattle and the whole house shake. She knew that it was the season for severe winter storms. Tamara was also painfully aware that an unusually intense one had moved in over the area from off the Gulf of Alaska, and that Mark and his crew might well be catching the brunt of it in a leaking seventy-seven-foot wooden boat, without a life raft.

But Mark, she knew, was considered a hard-core fisherman by any standard. He'd spent several seasons wrestling a living from the primitive and tempestuous waters of the Bering Sea, to the very edge of the polar ice cap. Once, while long-lining for codfish there, he'd broken his arm. The skipper had refused for three weeks to take him back into port to get it treated.

Mark was fishing on a catcher-processor in those same waters when Tamara learned that she was pregnant. When, with the help of the marine operator, she called him with the news, Mark was ecstatic. He made it clear to Tamara that he wanted to get married. "But he wanted to do it right," recalls Tamara. "He wanted to get me a really nice diamond. He told me, 'When you walk into a room, I want every man in there to know how much I love you.' "

Recently, however, Mark had felt a growing sense of his own mortality. He asked Tamara to look into taking out a life-insurance policy for him. "It was really strange," she recalls. "He even talked about how he wanted to be buried."

"When I go, I don't want anybody crying over me," he told her the week before his final trip on the *La Conte*. "I want them to party and laugh and remember the good things. And I don't want a bunch of money wasted on me. I just want to be buried in an old cedar box."

Then he told Tamara something that he'd never mentioned before. He said that sometimes in heavy seas, the *La Conte* scooped seawater like a submarine, and it truly scared him. Her bow would dive down, but then it wouldn't bounce back like it should. "I don't want to go out," he told Tamara. "I really don't want to do this. But I've got that gear out there. I want to have a clean slate when I get off the boat. I'm ready for a shore job, but I don't want to abandon these guys yet. They've been working their butts off for me."

At the journey's end, Morley planned to take the *La Conte* to Juneau and tie her up. Tamara would meet him there, and together they'd share a romantic ferry ride back to Sitka, where he'd try to find work onshore for a time. Finding a job was a safe bet for Morley. On the boat, they called him "Toolbox," because of all the tools he carried around with him. "He could fix anything," she adds.

When the H-60 helicopter carrying the *La Conte* survivors touched down in Yakutat, communicating proved to be a most uncomfortable thing. The aircraft's two flight mechanics were especially shaken.

"They were just devastated about losing the skipper," recalls Ted Le Feuvre. "There's a tendency to focus on the one you lost, kind of like the parable of Jesus as the shepherd. You've got the ninety-nine, but you search for the one who's missing. I think it's part of the way God created us, to have compassion for the one who's missing. But sometimes that can be misguided when applied in a negative way. My crew was really focusing on the one they lost.

"And I told them almost exactly what I'd told another crew about a year before. They had dropped somebody. They couldn't get him in because his survival suit was filled with water. And he weighed about probably four hundred and fifty pounds, they estimated, with the body and the seawater in the suit.

"Kalt and Honnald and Fish were just crushed that they'd lost this guy. And I said, kind of scolding them, 'You cannot focus on that. We just accomplished something that two other helicopters weren't able to do. You've got to realize that you have delivered three people back to their families who would *not* have survived otherwise. You have given them the best Christmas present anyone could ever give. We have saved three people; three people who would have perished. You are going to return these men back to their children. Those children will have a father now. And you've given those children back their fathers. You cannot do any greater thing than that. You can focus on the negative. Or you can focus on the positive. It's your choice.' "

In Yakutat, they found the storm in full vigor, thrashing the area with intimidating gusts of wind and rain. Honnald, Kalt, and Fish worked to transfer Bob Doyle, Gig Mork, and Mike DeCapua over to the waiting ambulance and the Yakutat Emergency Medical Staff. Ironically, the ambulance driver was none other than Eli Hanlon, David Hanlon's brother.

"I want to thank you for trying to help out my brother," he said.

"Hey, we all did what we could," Gig Mork assured him.

I nside the hospital emergency room, Gig Mork called his mother and told her that they were in Yakutat.

"Really? What are you doing up there?" she shot back.

"Mom, we had a big catastrophe here. The boat sank, and we lost two guys. Now we're up here in the hospital."

"Are you all right?"

"Yah, I'm doing fine."

Bob Doyle, Mike DeCapua, and Gig Mork were sitting in the ER, waiting to be released, when they learned that a U.S. Coast Guard helicopter had airlifted another survivor out of the water. "He has signs of life," declared a nurse.

All thoughts turned to Dave Hanlon. Or perhaps the courageous Mark Morley had come fully alive once again. A sense of cheerful anticipation filled the room. A small crowd was standing near the emergency room entrance when the ambulance pulled up. They soon discovered it was the body of Mark Morley that lay inside, still clad in his survival suit. The driver told them that he was dead.

Later, a nurse asked Doyle, DeCapua, and Mork if any of them wanted to go in and view Mark Morley's body.

"They asked us if we wanted to go in and view the body," Bob Doyle would later recall. "And I said, 'Yes, I do.' And I got to have some closure with him. I had to. I stood beside him and said, 'You know, Mark, I couldn't hold on any longer. I'm sorry.' And I leaned forward and kissed him on the forehead.

"The community of Yakutat was wonderful," says Doyle. "The nurses were great. They fed us and brought us some clothes. We left for Juneau at approximately two-thirty P.M. the following afternoon. But all I could think of at the time was that Mark was really gone."

Tamara Morley's phone rang at 3:00 A.M. She recognized the voice as that of Scott Eckles, the ship's owner. "I hate to be telling you this," she heard him say, "but I have the worst possible news. The *La Conte* went down. They pulled three of the guys out of the water. I don't know who they are yet, but Mark is strong. I'm sure he was one of them."

For the few hours, Tamara called the Coast Guard base in Sitka every half hour. When she learned that they were in Yakutat, she called the hospital there. A male nurse came to the phone.

"Is Mark Morley okay?" she asked. "Is he alive?"

"Yes," the man replied. "I do believe that he is alive. I heard him cough a little while ago. Yes, I believe he is."

Tamara wanted to speak to Mark "Now! Immediately!" But then she thought better of it. I'll let them work on him, she calculated. I'll let them get him stabilized; he's probably not out of the woods yet.

Then she called the Morley family in Michigan and told them the great news. But when she called Yakutat again, they wouldn't give her any information, nor would they allow any of the survivors from the crew of the *La Conte* to speak with her. "Finally," Tamara recalls, "the lady at the clinic broke down crying."

"He didn't make it," she said, sobbing.

"I couldn't hold the phone anymore," recalls Tamara. The thought of calling Mark's mother and family again back in Michigan was too much for her. "I just couldn't." She would not be able to sleep for several days.

CHAPTER 20

Mark Morley was buried at the Riverside Cemetery in Westland, Michigan. During his funeral, the eulogist said, "In just the time he had, Mark Morley did twice the living most of us will do living out our entire lives."

There is a lighthouse etched into the face of Morley's horizontal headstone. It stands as a kind of sentinel over the engraved words:

Mark Roger Morley, Feb. 10, 1962–Jan. 31, 1998.

We started missing you long before you were gone. We will keep loving you long after the memories bring you back.

On August 12, 1998, Tamara Morley gave birth to Mark Morley, Jr. Gregarious, cheerful, full of energy and grinning mischief, little Mark is the walking image of his father. He and his half sister, Kyla, enjoy robust health and lavish portions of love.

Approximately a year after the *La Conte* sank, Tamara Morley found herself unable to remain near the fishing industry that dominates the culture of coastal communities such as Sitka in southeast Alaska. "I thought some time away would help," she says.

She knew she could always find work in Alaska. In the past, she'd worked in canneries, processing king and tanner crab, in Pelican, in fresh-pack lines in Sitka, and as a production foreman in Petersburg. A tireless worker, she'd even been presented with several Employee of the Month awards.

"But in Sitka," she says, "I heard those helicopters taking off and landing every day from the U.S. Coast Guard base, and it was torturous. I needed to get out of Alaska for a while and get a grip."

She moved to a bedroom community outside of Detroit, Michigan, with Mark Junior and Kyla, to make a fresh start close to Mark Morley's family, and his grave. "I wanted to be close to him," she says. "If Mark had survived," adds Tamara Morley, "and Dave Hanlon had been lost, that would have broken his spirit; he would not have been able to go on.

"They say it gets better with time," she says. "But I don't know; the pain never seems to ease. Some days are better than others. But I'm learning how to live with it.

"I get angry that Mark didn't make it. But the USCG didn't have to go out in that. It was such incredible weather. They could have said, 'Hey, this is *not* possible.' And no one would have blamed them. Then they send *three* helicopters out there?"

Tamara will always be indebted not only to the men of the U.S. Coast Guard who risked their lives during the many harrowing attempts made to save the crewmen of the *La Conte* but also to the crew of the helicopter that deployed out of Kodiak the next day, and the rescue swimmer who actually entered the water and retrieved Mark Morley's body.

"I am so grateful to the Coast Guard for doing that," she said recently. "Because if they hadn't found him, I think that I'd always believe that he was still out there."

She especially wants to express her appreciation to Bob Doyle, she says, "for trying so hard to hold on to Mark. I can't believe he was able to hold on to him at all! Think of the physical condition he must have been in. I think that *he* is a hero. I think he was wonderful out there. I want him to know that. And I want him to forgive himself for not being Superman."

In February 1998, two weeks after the *La Conte* sank, Bob Doyle hired on as a deckhand on a crab boat working out of Sitka and shoved off on yet another adventure. In retrospect, he knows that if he'd leapt out of the basket after Mark Morley when he fell, he, too, would have died. Doyle dismisses the argument that a life raft might have saved their lives. "To be honest," he says, "I'd heard about rafts, and I wouldn't have wanted to be in one. I think we would have gotten killed in a raft. I just can't imagine being inside one and having waves that size crash on you like they did that night."

Records also seem to support this conclusion. Throughout history, it seems, life rafts have been torn apart by storm waves nowhere near the size the crew of the *La Conte* faced. One might further reasonably speculate that had Mark Morley and his crew somehow managed to inflate a raft, launch it, climb inside, and float safely away, and had they been able to accomplish this as their wooden ship rolled from under their feet, such a storm would have eventually torn it to shreds, dumping the untethered crewmen into the sea and dispersing them to the currents like so many pieces of flotsam.

Mike DeCapua, too, continued to fish, though it proved to be a different experience for him now. "January 31, 1998, is my new birthday," he told me recently. "That's when I was reborn. The year since then was the best year that I've ever had. I have a new chance. Prior to the sinking, I was bitter. I walked around ticked off about life all the time, and my lot in it. All the little things, impatience, psychological disorders, compulsiveness—you name it.

"Now, I'm just trying to navigate alone through my own harbor. If I can do that, I'll be a happy guy. That night taught me what's important in life. When we were bobbing around out there in the black like that, *petty* turned out to be everything *not* in that survival suit."

He says, "Looking back, I don't blame the skipper at all. It was all of our faults, everybody who was there. It wasn't just Morley's fault. I don't place any blame on him whatsoever. We are alive today because Mark Morley maintained authority and direction. What he said made sense, and our crew reacted accordingly. Had the skipper relinquished that authority even for a moment, had he wavered, we would not have responded the way we did, and there would have been chaos."

For months, nothing more was known about David Hanlon. Then, approximately six months after the *La Conte* sank, two young deer hunters found a body that had mysteriously washed up on a remote beach on bear-infested Shuyak Island, off the northern tip of Kodiak Island. Using fingerprints and dental records, police investigators soon identified the body as that of David Hanlon. He'd apparently drifted the six hundred miles from the Cape Fairweather Ground before washing ashore there.

Loved by his family, and respected by his peers, David Hanlon was buried by his relatives in a Native American ceremony, according to their ancestral tradition, in the Tlingit village of Hoonah. Vaughn Westcott, Tamara Morley's mother, attended the funeral.

Mike DeCapua would always remember Hanlon as someone who fought hard and went down fighting. "Dave Hanlon didn't come unglued," recalls DeCapua. "He didn't freak. He didn't panic. He didn't tax anybody to take care of him. He was a good worker, a hard worker. He'd been fishing all his life. He'd fished *with* some of the best, *on* some of the best. I respected the man."

Yet even today, DeCapua continues to struggle with the notion that perhaps he left too much slack in the rope loop he tied around David Hanlon's midsection.

"I carry his ghost because I tied his knot," he says. "And I'll never know whether or not I tied the knot right. But when Dave turned up gone, all we had was a loop on the end of Gig's suit. Yet I know, in my heart of hearts, that I tied that knot right. I've got to sleep with that for the rest of my life."

The U.S. Coast Guard rescue of the perishing seafarers off the foundering fishing vessel *La Conte* had forced the H-60 pilots and their crews to hang it out on the ragged edge of disaster farther and longer than any helicopter rescue mission in Coast Guard history. Never before had pilots and crews been tested so thoroughly or flown for so long through such deadly extremes as Ted Le Feuvre and Steve Torpey and their brothers did that wild January night off the coast of Alaska.

They had successfully battled world-class seas, fought eighty- and ninety-mile-per-hour winds, and were sucker punched by invisible williwaws that exploded out of the canyonlike wave troughs and nearly destroyed them. Plunging into a meteorological nightmare, they'd carried out the rescue without radio communications, all the while maneuvering in a tar black void as they dodged the unpredictable and the bizarre.

In the spring of 1998, a U.S. Coast Guard admiral presented Capt. Ted Le Feuvre, Lt. Cmdr. Steven Torpey, Fred Kalt, Mike Fish, and Lee Honnald with the Distinguished Flying Cross.

Over the next few months, they would fly to San Diego to receive the Naval Helicopter Association's award; to Washington, D.C., to receive an award from the Association of Naval Aviators, as well as the *Rotor Wing Magazine*'s Heroism Award; to Jacksonville, Florida, for a second NHA award; and, finally, back to Washington, D.C., where, in a ceremony held at the Smithsonian Institution, they received the Aviation Week and Space Technology's Laureate Award, presented along with other honors bestowed on such distinguished guests as Sen. John Glenn and famed X-15 test pilot Scott Crossfield.

Wherever they went, Ted Le Feuvre, Steve Torpey, Fred Kalt, Lee Honnald, and Mike Fish managed to keep their heads and maintain the same kind of steadfast esprit de corps loyalty to one another that had seen them through the impossible.

Yet through it all, there remained this lingering sense of disbelief, that the whole thing just "couldn't possibly be true," says Capt. Ted Le Feuvre today. "It was beyond anything that any of us had ever experienced. It's that one data point that was so far out of the norm that it caused us to question ourselves: Did it really happen that way?"

But in the months following the rescue, the feeling they most often shared during the awards ceremonies and the VIP balls, says Le Feuvre, "was this grateful, almost dazed state of appreciation and incredulity that we'd been through something so dangerous, it was an absolute miracle that we had survived. We shouldn't have survived. We were going down. And yet, we were able to pull this off. I am absolutely convinced that it was by God's grace that we didn't crash. And it was by God's grace that we were able to save those men. There is no other explanation."

CHAPTER 21

I n 1990, Skip Holden, the skipper and owner of the F/V *Marlene,* and his wife quit the fishing business, sold their boat, and moved away from Cordova. Eventually, they bought a 250-acre ranch in northern California. Skip works as a musician now. He writes songs and, when not playing gigs in some local dig, creates music that is both imaginative and pleasing. Inspired by the hellish circumstances of his ordeal that night up in Prince William Sound, he named one song "Mayday."

Part of the song goes as follows:

> Now, I don't mind being wet and cold. And I don't mind being hungry. But when I turn my radio on, *can anybody hear me?*
>
> My wife, she thinks I drowned today. I know for sure she's worried. Well, I'm trying real hard not to scream. But *can anybody hear me?*

"It was kind of like being in a war," says Skip Holden, looking back on the experience from his ranch. "I still feel guilty because I lived and they died. They wouldn't even have been out there if it wasn't for me, if I hadn't been in trouble."

Phil Thum, the skipper and owner of the fishing vessel *Keeper,* was the one who called in the Mayday and relayed the messages to the crew of the C-130 circling overhead. He works as an electrician today in a town near Ogden, Utah.

Jim Hatfield, the C-130 pilot who was circling Pat Rivas and his crew when the crash occurred, eventually retired from the Coast Guard and moved to Palm Desert, California. These days, he flies Boeing 747s for Northwest Airlines, carrying passengers to the Orient via the Circle Route. His first stop, more than a thousand miles north of Seattle, is the international airport in Anchorage, Alaska. The final approach into Anchorage takes him directly over Prince William Sound.

"I fly over the area a couple of times a week," Jim Hatfield recently told me. "And I can't help but think of those guys, and their wives and kids, and about how they're doing. It was an absolute tragedy. Four of my brothers died. I think about it every time. And I ask myself, What could I have done differently?"

"What *could* you have done differently?" I asked him.

"I don't know," he says flatly. He paused and breathed deeply, per-haps recalling how he and Dale Harrington had immediately brought the C-130 down and, in the hope of spotting their fallen comrades, flew along the deck just fifty feet above the turbulent waters. "If you weren't there," he adds, "or if you have never been in something like that, it's hard to explain. But it was just absolute, sheer terror."

Following the sinking of the fishing vessel *Bluebird,* Jim and Jill Blades brought two more children, both girls, into the world. They named them Annie and Lindy.

Then, a few years ago, as Alaskan residents, they entered and won an Alaskan land lottery and were granted the deed to a section of prime waterfront land on a pristine island not far from Sitka. Jim soon built a sawmill there. With the lumber he cut, he constructed a large surfside home, complete with a spacious living room, beam ceilings, and a huge rock fireplace, all of which he created with his own hands. He designed the fireplace with a knee-high hearth, where family and visitors alike can step out of Sitka's cold, blustery weather and warm their rain-dampened backs.

In addition to the main house, Jim, with the help of his family, has also built several very comfortable guest cabins, which they rent to tourists throughout the summer. The cabins come complete with queen-size beds, hand-hewn wooden bed frames, and wood-burning stoves. The cabins are located directly behind their home. It is a beautiful, secluded setting, one that includes a tall stand of hemlock trees and fish-flush waters running right past the picture windows.

The Blades appreciate the additional income during the summer months, and they enjoy their privacy the rest of the year. They have a sauna, too. But in spite of such modern conveniences, the Alaskan wilderness refuses to be tamed. Jill and her two daughters were soaking in the sauna not long ago, when two brown bears, which had apparently swum out to their island undetected, rose up on their hind legs and stood staring at them from only a few yards away.

Clint Blades was just six years old when the *Bluebird* sank from under his father and him and rescue swimmer Jeff Tunks towed both of them to the waiting basket. Clint was still in high school when he went to Germany and volunteered his time to work as a Christian missionary. Now in his twenties, Clint remains close to his church and holds fast to his biblical ideals, while making his living as a foreman at a local lumberyard.

John Whiddon, the pilot who flew the HH-3F helicopter that terrible night back in 1986, retired from the Coast Guard years ago, but he chose to remain in Alaska. He and his wife currently live in Kodiak, where they own and operate several businesses, including Mail Boxes, Etc., and a small fish-packing firm.

I caught up with John on a cold December day at his mailing business in Kodiak. "What a tremendous relief it was," he said. "When you're responsible for those people, not just the people you're trying to rescue but also the guys you work with every day, it's a big concern. And though I was able to bring those guys back safely, I really do have to give the credit to God."

A few days later, John Whiddon stopped me on a street in Kodiak to tell me about the surprise phone call that he'd just received. After fourteen years, Clint Blades had called to thank Whiddon for saving his life.

All five men of Whiddon's crew were decorated with the Distinguished Flying Cross. Rescue swimmer Jeff Tunks was also presented with Alaska's Medal of Heroism, as well as the Coast Guard Foundation's Admiral Chester R. Bender Award for displaying exceptional courage in the face of extreme danger.

When I finally caught up with Tunks, he was stationed at the U.S. Coast Guard base in New Orleans. I asked him if he would share with me what had happened that night out on Sitka Sound, how he felt about it, and, specifically, what it was like to save the lives of two people he'd never met.

"It was a great team effort," said Tunks succinctly. "How fortunate I was to help in such a noble cause."

CHAPTER 22

The relationship between fishermen and the sea, and the airborne alliance of those sworn to watch over them, continues today all across the vast ocean reaches and tidelands of Alaska. Win or lose, the nature of the lives lived and the spirit of the adventures undertaken linger on in the psyche of most Alaskans. Whether captured in some history book or passed on orally, as is the Native tradition, these chronicles connect the people to the land as firmly as a three-inch bowline stetching between a Dutch Harbor crab boat and its cannery dock.

Throughout the winter of 1999, a year after the *La Conte* sank, several horrific cold fronts hammered the state of Alaska, creating chill factors of one hundred degrees below zero in some areas.

During the January tanner crab season off the Pribilof Islands in the Bering Sea, over two hundred crab boats found themselves caught in the icy grip of that winter's record cold. Some of the vessels became encased in the destabilizing tonnage of spray-ice three feet thick, ultimately looking more like floating ice-sculptures than Alaskan crab boats.

Anticipating this very possibility, the Coast Guard insightfully placed a covey of H-60 helicopters and a team of pilots and mechanics adjacent to the fishing grounds on nearby St. Paul Island. Over the next few weeks, dozens of pilots launched out on scores of missions, plucking no less than thirty-eight injured or endangered fishermen from the rolling decks of some twenty-eight crab boats.

One blustery night, when the weighted end of a rope line was being lowered (as a precursor to the rescue basket itself) from an H-60 chopper to the lightless, foundering hulk of the 135-foot F/V *Nowitna*, it became entangled in her fifty-five-foot-high mast. Skipper Thorne Tasker took it upon himself to try and remedy the matter. As the powerless vessel drifted in substantial twenty-five-to-thirty-foot seas, and with her mast arching back and forth through the black, spray-filled space in 100-degree swaths, Tasker climbed high into his vessel's rigging, wedged his feet and ankles around one end of a catwalk, and, as disbelieving Coast Guard chopper pilot Lt. Cmdr. Paul Ratté hovered overhead, hung upside down and pulled the rope free, thereby releasing those above to complete the rescue and save both himself and his crew.

Working under severe icing conditions, engaged in the world's most dangerous occupation, the crab fishermen encountered nature's worst. They spent long, drawn-out weeks laboring in the long arctic darkness, chipping away at the buildup of ice on the railings, decks, and wheelhouses of their vessels, wielding baseball bats, crowbars, and sledgehammers to achieve this task.

As the season continued, crewmen worked for twenty, thirty, even fifty hours without sleep. Though not always incapacitating, the on-deck injury rates during the season reached 100 percent among many of the crews. These tenacious young workers were struck by 750-pound crab pots, bruised by pot launchers, and nipped by frostbite, and had their fingers crushed between block and line. On several occasions, rogue waves flattened entire crews and swept them across their icy decks, scattering their bodies like bowling pins. Two crewmen, one on the F/V *Sea Fisher*, and another on the F/V *West Point*, were washed overboard and lost forever.

When Siberian-born storms pushed the polar ice pack south into prime fishing grounds, skippers were forced to weave through the flat white pads of floating ice as they searched that cold wasteland for their bright orange crab pot buoys. In some instances, the ice floes snagged their buoys and lines and dragged the pots as far as twenty-five miles from where they had originally been placed.

In the end, however, these tough, determined fishermen persevered long enough to catch several hundred million pounds of opelio crab (sold as snow crab at local Sizzler steak houses), and deliver them alive to waiting processors. On some boats, shares topped $50,000 per deckhand.

In all, during the 1999 season, two boats sank and seven fishermen lost their lives—in a season lasting just sixty-six days.

CHAPTER 23

Be it the beauty of the land, the love of flying, or the spell of the sea, those who have experienced Alaska often leave a bit of their hearts behind. In time, most will return, either in person or as mental travelers. It was as I neared the end of my second year of research and writing that I began to understand this.

The Coast Guard pilots and crews whom I interviewed, many of whom I befriended, are now scattered to the military winds: Bill and Carin Adickes to Sacramento, California; Russ and Debra Zullick to Kodiak, Alaska; David and Trish Durham to Clearwater, Florida; Steve and Karl Torpey to Mobile, Alabama; and Dan and Theresa Molthen to Elizabeth City, North Carolina.

Recently, Dan Molthen, now Commmander Molthen, piloted a high-seas SAR mission out of "E-City" and set a record for the number of people airlifted by an H-60 in a single flight. He and his crew hoisted twenty-six crewmen, two at a time, off a tanker that soon sank far out in the Atlantic.

As for Capt. Ted Le Feuvre, today, from in his office in Miami, Florida, he can look out on a far less demanding terrain than the ones he faced daily flying out of Sitka. In Florida (or Mobile, or

E-City, for that matter), a helicopter pilot can climb to three hundred feet, point his (or her) aircraft in virtually any direction, and fly ahead without fear of plowing into a nearby mountainside, though .30-caliber machine-gun bursts from angry South American drug runners can also be quite hazardous.

These days, Le Feuvre can look back with a certain satisfaction on what he accomplished in Alaska, and he recalls with awe the natural splendor he saw there. In his mind's eye, he can still remember with perfect clarity the most spectacular sight he ever encountered during the years he served there. It happened while flying on a brilliant, sun-kissed day across the broad, high face of the Hubbard Glacier up in Disenchantment Bay.

At the time, he and his copilot were flying along, paralleling the massive face of the ice field at an altitude of two hundred feet, when, as if choreographed just for them, an enormous iceberg calved off from the field. In a spectacular display of power and ultimate authority, the frosty blue chunk, perhaps three hundred feet long and twenty feet deep, broke away and plummeted into the bay.

At that moment, it seemed to Le Feuvre as if God himself had said, "Hey, I'll grant you this. So enjoy." It didn't just break off and tumble forward, crashing to earth like a toppling tree. The monstrous slab parted suddenly from the body of the ice field. Then, as if in slow motion, it began to accelerate in its descent through the cool, pristine air. And it did so with a kind of dignity, remaining upright as it fell, frozen in the same thirty-degree angle as when it had first broken free.

The calm blue water swallowed the iceberg whole, then exploded into a brilliant white geyser of foam and sea spray as the deep, fjordlike waters reacted violently to the massive displacement. As Le Feuvre watched, the bulge of a wave rolled smoothly across the bay, advancing in the form of a round blue wrinkle. The departing wave lifted and lowered everything in its path. And as it moved, countless gleaming white fragments of drifting ice rubble scrolled up and over its creamy blue face.

There are other memorable scenes that Captain Le Feuvre and his fellow pilots have witnessed in Alaska. Like the wintry vision of "ice fog" (created whenever arctic winds contact the relatively warm thirty-eight-degree sea). Tossed by the prevailing winds, the fog sometimes tumbles across inlet waters, creating fascinating apparitions that have been known to leap hundreds of feet into the air while dusting passing helicopters in thin sheaths of ice.

Or the stunning beauty one pilot found in a box canyon near Haines when he came upon the spectacle of dozens of waterfalls standing hundreds of feet high, frozen solidly in place by the Yukon cold drafting down out of Skagway. The tall ice structures clinging to the sheer rock cliffs on either side of him looked as if they had frozen over all at once, their waterfalls halted in a single, cascading moment. As he hovered near and observed, the spectacular columns of gleaming ice began to sparkle and glow in resplendent hues of roseate red and dazzling orange as the rays from the brief winter sunset fell fully upon them.

Then there's the sight of mountain goats rolling in the perennial snow fields high among the peaks of Baranof Island, where they go in summer to escape the pestilent mosquitoes that seek their blood. Or the sight of kayakers paddling, the bright colors and toylike plasticity of their slow, minuscule vehicles visible for miles in the distance as they pick their way along some tiny portion of the thirteen thousand miles of shoreline in southeast Alaska. Or the spectacle of humpback whales in nearby Frederick Sound, often scores of them, leaping free of the sea in a raucous celebration of life.

Or the surreal vision of an ice-cream-white, one-thousand-foot-long cruise liner, swimming pool and all, sitting as if frozen onto the mirror-calm face of a bay, her cabin lights glittering in the cool blue-black dusk of another long summer's evening. She's been caught lounging in front of the Johns Hopkins Glacier, a broad, jagged field of slow-moving ice that winds its way up into the mountains for tens of miles, the face of which dwarfs even the liner.

363.123   Walker, Spike.
WAL
            Coming back alive.

$24.95